D1594365

Scandinavia in the Age of Vikings

Scandinavia in the Age of Vikings

Jón Viðar Sigurðsson

Translated by Thea Kveiland

Cornell University Press

Ithaca and London

First published 2021 by Cornell University Press

Printed in the United States of America

Library of Congress Cataloging-in-Publication Data

Names: Jón Viðar Sigurðsson, 1958– author.
Title: Scandinavia in the age of Vikings / Jón Viðar Sigurðsson ;
    translated by Thea Kveiland.
Other titles: Skandinavia i vikingtiden. English
Description: Ithaca [New York] : Cornell University Press, 2021. |
    "Originally published 2017 in Norwegian by Pax Forlag A/S under
    the title Skandinavia i vikingtiden"—Title page verso. |
    Includes bibliographical references and index.
Identifiers: LCCN 2021007636 (print) | LCCN 2021007637 (ebook) |
    ISBN 9781501760471 (hardcover) | ISBN 9781501760488 (epub) |
    ISBN 9781501760495 (pdf)
Subjects: LCSH: Vikings—Scandinavia. | Civilization, Viking—
    Scandinavia. | Vikings—Scandinavia—Social conditions. |
    Scandinavia—History—To 1397.
Classification: LCC DL65 .J5913 2021 (print) | LCC DL65 (ebook) |
    DDC 948/.022—dc23
LC record available at https://lccn.loc.gov/2021007636
LC ebook record available at https://lccn.loc.gov/2021007637

To my children and granddaughter

Contents

Illustrations

Figures

Maps

Author's Note

This book is, to a large extent, a translation of a book I published in 2017, *Skandinavia i vikingtiden*. In preparing the present volume, I have had the opportunity to make some changes and to expand the discussion about the roles women and slaves played in Viking Age society.

While working on this book, I received valuable comments and contributions from several people: S. C. Kaplan, Kate Gilbert, Eira Kathleen Ebbs, and members of the research group of premodern history at the Institute for Archaeology, Conservation, and History, University of Oslo. I would also like to thank the two reviewers who read the manuscript for their very constructive comments. Thank you all very much!

Timeline

Within Scandinavia	Abroad
726 Kanhave Canal built	
737 Nordvollen in Danevirke built	
	c. 753 Swedes established Staraya Ladoga (nr. present-day Volkhov, Russia)
	c. 789 Vikings attack Isle of Portland, Wessex
	793 Vikings plunder Lindisfarne
	799 Vikings raid Aquitaine
808 Reric destroyed and merchants moved to Hedeby	800 Charlemagne organizes defenses against Vikings
813 Danish kings in "Vestfold"	814 Death of Charlemagne
822–823 Archbishop Ebo's mission to Denmark	
c. 825 Danish coinage minting in Hedeby begins	
829 Ansgar's first mission to Birka	

(continued)

Within Scandinavia	Abroad
834 Oseberg burial mound built	834 Dorestad (in present-day Netherlands) raided
	839 Swedes reach Constantinople (Istanbul)
	839–840 Vikings winter in Ireland for the first time and found Dublin
	842 Vikings winter in Francia for first time
	843 Carolingian Empire divided
850 Ansgar builds churches at Ribe and Hedeby	850 Vikings winter in England for first time
852–854 Ansgar's second mission to Birka	
854 Horik, king of Denmark, killed	859 Vikings raid the Mediterranean
	860 Vikings attack Constantinople (Istanbul)
	862 Vikings found Novgorod
	865 The Great Army invades England
c. 870 Vikings colonize Iceland	878 Danish colonization of England starts
	879 Rurik makes Kiev center of the Kievan Rus'
c. 880 Battle in Hafrsfjord	886 Alfred the Great allows the Vikings to control the north of Britain under Danelaw
	899 Alfred the Great dies
	907 Swedish Vikings in Constantinople (Istanbul)
	911 Viking chief Rollo is granted land in Normandy by the Franks
	924–939 Athelstan's reign as king of Wessex and Mercia (924–927) and England (927–939)
930–934 Erik Bloodaxe king over Vestlandet	
c. 935 Gorm king in Denmark	936–973 Otto the Great reigns over the Holy German Empire
946–961 Hakon Adalsteinfostre king over Vestlandet and part of Trøndelag	941 Rus' Vikings attack Constantinople (Istanbul)
948 Bishops appointed to Ribe, Hedeby, and Aarhus	

Within Scandinavia	Abroad
c. 958 Harald Bluetooth king in Denmark	954 Eric Bloodaxe thrown out of York
958 Death of Gorm the Old, buried at Jelling	959 Danelaw established in England
c. 965 Christianity becomes the official religion in the realm of the Danish kings	
965–970 Hakon Earl of Lade rules over Norway	
968 Danevirke strengthened	
c. 970 Sigtuna founded	
c. 985 Svein Forkbeard king in Denmark	980–1015 Vladimir rules over Kiev
991 Olaf Tryggvason defeats English at Maldon	c. 990 Vikings settle Greenland
995 Olaf Tryggvason king over Vestlandet and Trøndelag	
1000 Battle at Svolder	
1000–1015 Erik and Svein rule over Norway	
1014 Svein Forkbeard dies; his son, Harald, becomes king of Denmark	1013 Svein Forkbeard conquers England
	1014 English reject Cnut the Great as king
1015 Olaf Haraldsson king in Trøndelag, Vestlandet, and Viken	1016 Treaty between Cnut the Great and Edmund Ironside
	1016 Cnut the Great becomes king of all England
1019 Cnut the Great takes Denmark	
1030 Olaf Haraldsson killed in the Battle of Stiklestad	
1035 Cnut the Great dies	
1035 Agreement between Magnus Olafsson the Good and Harthacnut	
1042 Magnus Olafsson also king in Denmark	1042 End of Danish rule in England
1043 Magnus the Good defeats Wends at Lyrskoghede	
1047–1064 Conflict between Harald Hardruler and Svein Estridsson	
	1066 Harald Hardruler killed in the battle of Stamford Bridge
	1066 Battle of Hastings
	1075 Last Danish invasion of England

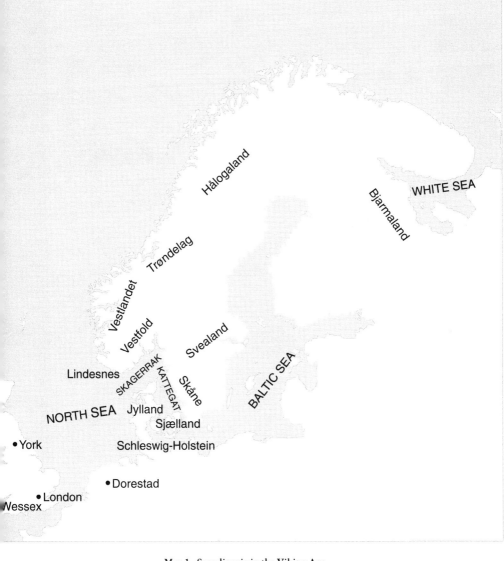

Map 1. Scandinavia in the Viking Age

Scandinavia in the Age of Vikings

Introduction

Characteristics of the Viking Age in Scandinavia

Vikings are arguably as popular as they have ever been. There are endless television series, documentaries, and books about them; however, these focus mainly on the Viking activities *outside* Scandinavia—the plundering of England and Ireland, the discovery of Iceland and Greenland, the establishment of trading routes into Russia and Constantinople (Istanbul), and so on. In this book, we will focus instead on what was happening *inside* Scandinavia and on some key aspects in Scandinavia's formation during the Viking Age: politics, social networks, conspicuous consumption, warrior mentality, social stratification, religion, farms, and power centers. Our main attention will be on the power games that shaped Scandinavian society—though perhaps not in the way you might usually expect when you think about the Vikings. At home, they were not particularly bloodthirsty. In most cases, local power games were acted out peacefully, as the players competed to display their wealth in the form of great feasts and gifts. Consumption was a Viking's most important virtue. The brutality we usually associate with the Vikings was displayed abroad.

The **Danish kings** dominated politics in Scandinavia during the Viking Age (c. 800–1050). This was no coincidence but rather a consequence of aggressive neighbors in the south. To the west of Scandinavia, there was no threat. The Sami people in the north, an indigenous Finno-Ugric people, were not dangerous either—on the contrary, they were a source of tax revenue. Neither did the people on the other side of the Baltic Sea nor those across the North Sea pose a threat. The only risk of attack came from the south, where persistent pressure from the Slavic and Germanic peoples had long required the Danes to produce kings who could both defend and attack. During the Viking Age, the Danish kings controlled most of the central areas of Scandinavia (maps 1 and 2). Their realm stretched from Schleswig-Holstein in northern Germany to Jylland (Jutland) and Sjælland (Zealand), across Skåne (Scania) in Sweden, and on to Lindesnes (the Naze) in Agder county, Norway. These areas were not only the most central geographically, they were also the most densely populated. In 1042, the Norwegian king Magnus Olafsson became king of Denmark as well, based on an agreement made with the Danish king Harthacnut in 1036. This deal, and the subsequent wars between the Danish and Norwegian kings, not only turned the political situation in Scandinavia upside down, it also marked the end of the Viking Age.[1]

In Scandinavia, if we exclude the Sami language, a single vernacular language was spoken during the Viking Age: the so-called *dönsk tunga*, or **Danish tongue**. Scholars are not by any means in agreement about the origin of this term, but it was probably created by foreigners to describe the language spoken in the kingdom of the Danish kings, *lingua Danorum*, and was later used to refer to the language spoken in all of Scandinavia.[2] That only one language was spoken in Scandinavia made all communication easier, helping to create a common Scandinavian identity and aiding the Danish kings in expanding and solidifying their power base.

Viking Age society was a **network society**. All of Scandinavia was tightly connected by social networks created by friendship and family ties. Friendship was arguably the most important social bond. However, the type of friendship we refer to here cannot be compared with modern friendship. It must be understood as a political concept. Viking Age friendship was a kind of contract between two individuals, with clear reciprocal duties established through support, gifts, and feasts. We can distinguish between two types of friendships: the vertical relationship between chieftains and householders, and the horizontal connections between chieftains and between chieftains and kings. One main difference between these two types of relationships is loyalty. In vertical relationships, loyalty and trust were strong: the householders supported the chieftains in return for protection. In horizontal relationships, loyalty and trust were weak: chieftains and kings changed their friends in accordance with their changing political goals. All friendships had to be renewed on a regular basis, mainly through hospitality and gift giving. Generosity was the key to power, and it was based on wealth: revenue from agriculture, property, trade, and looting. Because these incomes were unstable, loss of income meant a loss of power, as the chieftains and kings could no longer fulfill their obligations to their friends. For this reason, the political situation in Scandinavia was **unstable**. Inheritance laws also contributed to political instability. The prevailing rule of inheritance was that power and wealth should be divided equally between legitimate and illegitimate sons, and in some cases this led to conflict between brothers.

Scandinavia was also connected through kinship. Families in Scandinavia were bilateral, meaning that each individual belonged to both their mother's and their father's families. Only children of the exact same parents had identical families. The overlap between families was therefore extensive, and conflicts of loyalty could easily arise if kinsmen began to fight among themselves. In such disagreements—as in disputes between one's friends—the ones who ended up in the middle had to mediate. They could not support one kinsman over another. Because of this pressure to mediate, Scandinavia was primarily a **peaceful region**.

Scandinavian Viking Age society was also a showy society, characterized by **conspicuous consumption**. The nonviolent rivalry between the Scandinavian rulers took the form of symbolic displays of power. Who could hold the greatest feasts, give the most valuable gifts, build the largest halls, ships, and burial mounds? Despite this competition, the social elite also cooperated extensively. It was essential for them to work together to carry out successful raids abroad and organize profitable trading excursions. The increase in trading that began in northwestern Europe at the end of the 600s laid the foundation for Viking expeditions. Numerous marketplaces were established, such as Dorestad along the Rhine, and old cities, such as London, became important trading centers. One reason Scandinavia was drawn into this trading network was an increasing demand for fur, the best of which came from the northernmost regions of Europe.

The **warrior mentality** of the North is most clearly reflected in the representations of Valhalla and Folkvangr, the legendary destinations of all those who died in battle. Scandinavian Viking Age society can be characterized as a warrior society. This means that there was no clear distinction between householders and warriors, and that the rulers, chieftains, and kings were also military leaders. All free men had the right to bear arms, but the main responsibility of warfare fell on the social elite and the *hirð* (a group of warriors that served as a retinue to chieftains and kings). A *hirð* could help preserve peace within the chiefdom or kingdom. Nevertheless, the mutual friendship between the householders and chieftains meant that there was little risk of these warriors being used to put economic pressure on the householders. Chieftains and kings depended on support from the householders in their quest for power and on raiding expeditions. The coexistence of a warrior mentality and presumed peacefulness within Scandinavia did not create a contradiction. It simply means that the majority of **violence took place outside Scandinavia**. Violence was the Vikings' most important export.

There was **clear social stratification** in Viking Age Scandinavia. At the top of the social hierarchy sat the king and chieftains—this group held significant power. The majority of Scandinavian people were householders, but within this group there were important social and economic differences: while some owned large estates, others lived in shacks with a couple of goats. At the bottom of the social hierarchy were the thralls (singular *þræll*, the Old Norse term for a slave), a group with next to no rights.

At the beginning of the Viking Age, there were only two royal families, those of Sweden and Denmark, and many hundreds, if not thousands of chieftains. By around the year 1000, the number of royal families had grown to four. The two "new" families originated in Vestlandet and Trøndelag, both in Norway. Despite their titles of earl rather than king, the earls of Lade in Trøndelag were on the same level as the other royal families. However, by the end of the Viking Age, they had disappeared from the political scene. This leaves us with three kingdoms, all of which still exist today, albeit with very different borders.

A key feature of political development in the Viking Age is that the power of the king increased at the expense of the chieftains, whose numbers were sharply reduced. Some of the chieftains were extremely powerful, and it seems that in many cases the kings assisted them in achieving their positions. This demonstrates that there was not necessarily conflict between powerful chieftains and powerful kings. On the contrary, it was beneficial for the kings to have mighty chieftains within their kingdoms, as long as those chieftains supported their king. In the written sources, the difference between kings and chieftains is often unclear. In this book, the term "king" will be used exclusively for heads of the aforementioned four families, and "chieftain" in place of the various other names (for example, *hauld* and *hersir*) given to leaders at the level below the kings.

The Norse religion was an **elite religion**, meaning that the chieftains were the ones who made offerings to the gods. In this role, they acted as a link between the gods on the one hand and their friends on the other. This helped strengthen and justify their powerful position: the chieftains were friends of the gods. Except in Svealand, the role of the kings within the Norse religion is somewhat unclear. This is why the kings actively participated in the introduction of Christianity in the mid-900s. In the new religion, they became the highest authority in the church. Over the course of the next century, all of the Scandinavian kingdoms officially became Christian, a process that radically changed the ideology underlying leadership and society. Harald Bluetooth (c. 958–986) is honored for Christianizing the Danes around the year 960. In Norway, the introduction of Christianity is connected to the three kings Hakon Adalsteinfostre (c. 933–960), Olaf Tryggvason (995–1000), and Olaf Haraldsson (1015–1028), the last of whom succeeded in having Christianity adopted as the country's official religion around 1020. The rather delayed formation of Sweden meant that their adoption of Christianity happened somewhat later than in most of Scandinavia. The Christianization of Scandinavia was in no way unproblematic, not least because of the tension it created in the relationships between the kings and chieftains.

Farms were the basic building block of Scandinavian society during the Viking Age, both socially and economically—they created the framework for daily life. In Norway, the single farm was the most prevalent type of settlement, while in Denmark and Sweden, the farming village predominated. In both cases, the household was the basic unit running the farm. There was a significant difference between the size of a chieftain's household—some of which comprised tens, if not hundreds of people—and that of the poorest householders, who worked their farms without the help of any other adult laborers. The regional differences within Scandinavia were also substantial; naturally, this had consequences for the farms and what they produced. However, life and work on the farm, whether it was large or small, and whether it lay in the north or south, followed a set yearly cycle. The **production of food** was the focus of the entire society. Viking Age society lived hand to mouth, and there was no form of food storage that could be relied on in the event of a crisis.

Kings' and chieftains' farms were the **power centers** of society, with administrative, ceremonial, economic, military, religious, and ideological functions. This is where many of the most important decisions were made, and where the grandest feasts were organized, including religious gatherings. Some of these power centers maintained their significance for hundreds of years, while others were in use for only short periods of time. The stability of power centers cannot necessarily be explained by the enduring power of a single family. The general pattern found across medieval Europe is that the average aristocratic family did not manage to survive for more than three generations. There is no reason to believe that the situation was any different in Scandinavia. We must therefore distinguish between the continuity of power centers and the continuity of ruling families. The power centers were centrally located. It was important for kings and chieftains to have access to good information regarding the political situation, in order for them to react to it appropriately. The main channels of communication in the Viking Age lay along the coast, up the large rivers, and around the greater lakes. The waterways bound Scandinavia together. Today, these waterways have changed. Isostatic uplift since the Viking Age has altered the coastline, meaning that many places that once were located along the coast now lie further inland.

For purposes of raiding, exploring, and trading, a good **seagoing ship** with a sail was a necessity. There were two main types of Viking ships: the longship (*langskip*), a warship, and the *knarr*, a merchant vessel. Both types of ships were improved on during the Viking Age, when they were made larger and more seaworthy. The Gokstad ship, which was built around 890 and found in 1880 in a Norwegian burial mound, is a good example of a sophisticated longship. Like all Viking ships, it was clinker-built with overlapping planks and had the rudder on the starboard (right-hand) side. The boards of this ship were not nailed to the ribs, but fixed to them with clamps set on the boards. This meant that the ship was flexible, strong, and prepared to withstand rough weather, which was proven in 1893 when a replica of the Gokstad ship was sailed across the Atlantic to the World's Columbian Exposition in Chicago. A prerequisite for crafting and developing both ships and weapons was good access to **iron**. The extraction of iron in Norway and Sweden increased during the 700s and 800s. Within the contemporary borders of Denmark, however, there was no iron production during the Viking Age.

There are many different types of **sources** that provide information about the Viking Age in Scandinavia, the most important being archaeological and written sources. The principal written sources are skaldic verses, Eddic poetry, chronicles, and sagas—for example, Adam of Bremen's *Gesta Hammaburgensis ecclesiae pontificum* (*The Deeds of Bishops of the Hamburg Church*), Saxo's *Gesta Danorum* (*Deeds of the Danes*), and the kings' sagas, such as those found in the collection called *Heimskringla*. These sources have serious issues that diminish their reliability as historical witnesses, not least of which is the lengthy period between the occurrence of events and their documentation—a lag that often exceeded three hundred years. Furthermore, the written sources' focus is on the social elite and their struggles for power. Over the last decades, fewer and fewer scholars have been willing to use these sources, especially the sagas, to study the Viking Age. There can be no doubt that the saga authors were influenced by the time they were working in, and that many details of their portrayals of the past are distorted. It is important to stress the difference between the society the saga authors describe and the one they actually lived in, for example regarding the position of women. However, the discussion about the value of the sagas as a source has only touched on this problem to a small degree. In this book, we will use the abovementioned written sources not as factual records, but as presenting an *idea* of how Viking society functioned. The fact is, we cannot properly understand the societal power games without the help of the sagas. Another reason for reintroducing the sagas is to stimulate debate about them—as sources they are simply too important to be ignored when discussing the Viking Age. A further problem regarding the written sources is the uneven balance between the Scandinavian countries. Most of the chronicles are about events involving the Norwegian and Danish kings. That affects the balance of this book.[3]

Archaeological materials are the most important source of our knowledge of Scandinavian society during this period, and new excavations continue to broaden our horizons.[4] However, using archaeological material as a source also has its problems. In what social context should we interpret these materials? Moreover, archaeology has clear limitations. For instance, it cannot tell us anything in particular about social networks or power games. We must therefore use both types of sources to attain the clearest possible picture of society during the Viking Age.

This book is written for the reader taking their first steps into the fascinating history of the Vikings in Scandinavia. It contains eight main chapters; the first two focus on the political developments in Scandinavia in the Viking Age, while the remaining six discuss different aspects of the culture, from networks and power games to the economical foundations and how the enormous wealth the Vikings brought back to Scandinavia affected the region's social fabric and structure.

Further Reading

Ashby, Steven P. "What Really Caused the Viking Age? The Social Content of Raiding and Exploration." *Archaeological Dialogues* 22 (2015): 89–106.

Barrett, James H. "What Caused the Viking Age?" *Antiquity* 82 (2008): 671–85.

Baug, Irene, Dagfinn Skre, Tom Heldal, and Øystein J. Jansen. "The Beginning of the Viking Age in the West." *Journal of Maritime Archaeology* 13 (2018): 1–38.

Ghosh, Shami. *Kings' Sagas and Norwegian History: Problems and Perspectives*. Leiden: Brill, 2011.

Griffiths, David. "Rethinking the Early Viking Age in the West." *Antiquity* 93 (2019): 468–77.

Heen-Pettersen, Aina Margrethe. "The Earliest Wave of Viking Activity? The Norwegian Evidence Revisited." *European Journal of Archaeology* 22 (2019): 523–41.

Myhre, Bjørn. "The Beginning of the Viking Age." In *Viking Revaluations*, edited by Anthony Faulkes and Richard Perkins, 182–204. London: Viking Society for Northern Research, University College London, 1993.

Sawyer, Peter H. "The Causes of the Viking Age." In *The Vikings*, edited by R. T. Farrell, 1–7. London: Phillimore, 1982.

——. "The Viking Expansion." In *The Cambridge History of Scandinavia*, vol. 1, *Prehistory to 1520*, edited by Knut Helle, 105–20. Cambridge: Cambridge University Press, 2003.

Chapter 1

THE POWERFUL DANISH KINGS

In the village of Jelling in central Jylland, Denmark—the site of a royal farmstead during the tenth century—there are two rune stones known as the Jelling stones. The smaller Jelling stone weighs approximately three tons and was erected around 950 by King Gorm (d. c. 958), the alleged son of the legendary king Harthacnut, to commemorate Gorm's wife, Queen Thyra. Fifteen years later, the larger Jelling stone, which weighs about twelve tons, was erected. One side of the larger stone features a carving of the crucified Christ, the earliest such image found in Scandinavia. The other side bears an inscription that reads: "King Harald ordered this monument to be made in memory of Gorm, his father, and in memory of Thyra, his mother; that Harald who won for himself all of Denmark and Norway and made the Danes Christian." King Harald (d. c. 986) had this rune stone placed between the two large (seventy-five yards in diameter and up to twelve yards high) burial mounds he also had built in memory of his parents, to mark his country's conversion to Christianity and his political and military domination of Scandinavia.

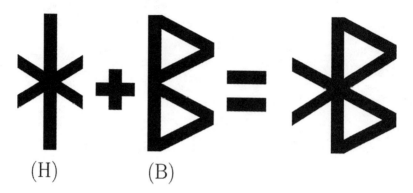

(H)   (B)

Figure 1. Bluetooth logo: ᚼ [Hagall] and ᛒ [Bjarkan].

More than one thousand years later, Harald's nickname, Bluetooth, was borrowed by Intel developers for the name of its new wireless technology: just as Harald had united Scandinavia, so the Intel engineers saw their innovation as one that could unite digital devices. The company's logo is a composite of the runes for H[arald] and B[luetooth].

King Gorm and his descendants dominated Scandinavian politics throughout the 900s and into the 1000s.[1] Their realm stretched across Schleswig-Holstein in northern Germany and also included Jylland (Jutland), the islands of Fyn (Funen), Sjælland (Zealand), Lolland, Falster, and Møn in Denmark; Blekinge, Skåne (Scania), Halland, and Bohuslän in Sweden;[2] and the area around Oslofjorden (Oslofjord) from Østfold to Lindesnes in Norway (map 3). We do not know when the Danish kings secured control over these areas, but it is likely that the region around Lindesnes became the northwestern border of their realm around the year 800. The Danish kings thus controlled most of central Scandinavia and therefore all the trading and traffic in and out of the Baltic Sea, as well as the majority of trade and sea traffic north of Lindesnes. These areas were also the most densely populated in Scandinavia. The other parts of Scandinavia (map 2), which we will address in the next chapter, were divided between the kings of Vestlandet, the earls of Lade, the kings of the Swedes, and local chieftains in Götaland.

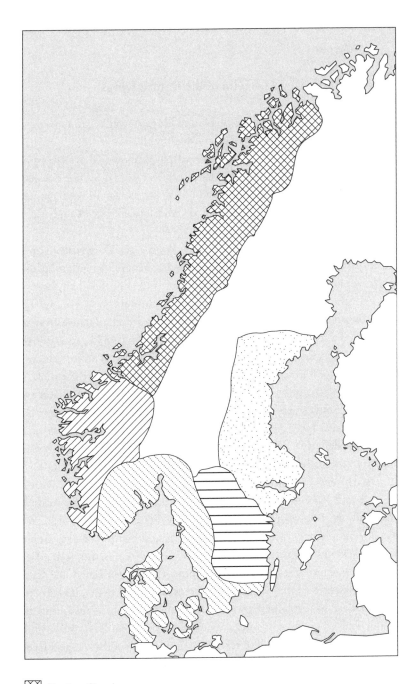

Earls of Lade
The kingdom of Vestlandet
The realm of the Danish kings
Götaland
Kingdom of the Swedes

Map 2. The main political division of Scandinavia

South Scandinavia: The Realm of the Danish Kings

Although it is unclear just when the Danish kings' power began to increase, we do know that they were well established by the early 700s.[3] The main arguments in favor of a strong centralized power circa 700 are two great engineering projects: the Kanhave Canal and the Danevirke. The Kanhave Canal, which nearly bisected the island of Samsø (Samso) in Kattegat, was around 550 yards long, twelve yards wide, and four feet deep, and was in use from circa 726 to 780.

An even earlier expression of the kings' power is the Danevirke (map 4), a defensive fortification spanning the narrowest point of the Jutland peninsula, from the end of the Slien fjord in the east to Hollingstedt on the river Treene in the west, in present-day Schleswig-Holstein in Germany. The Danevirke consists of several ramparts built to protect the Danish from attacks from the south by the Slavic and northern Saxon peoples, and later, the Carolingian Empire. Construction of the Danevirke began around the year 500 and expanded in several phases until the end of the twelfth century. In 737, the so-called Nordvollen (North Wall) was built. It measured over two yards high, about eleven yards wide, and over eleven miles long. Altogether, the Danevirke is forty-eight miles long, making it the largest prehistoric or Viking Age defensive installation in northern Europe.

Archaeologists have claimed that a Danish kingdom probably appeared in the sixth century, perhaps through a process of amalgamation, with its core in South Jylland, Fyn, and Sjælland.[4] We can see a similar process of consolidation of power in Iceland in the Free State period (930–1262/64), where the number of chieftains was reduced from about fifty or sixty around the year 1000 to six or seven around the year 1200. As an island, Iceland did not face any external military threats, unlike the Danish kingdom; nevertheless, there was a rapid decline in the number of chieftains. This reduction can best be explained by the chieftains' difficulties regarding the "production" of capable sons to take over their positions. This was a problem the Danish chieftains, like chieftains and lords worldwide, also faced. Kingdoms to the south also exerted significant pressure on the Danish kingdom. As a result, one family took over the role of war leaders; that is, they took upon themselves the task of defending the region and attacking the enemy.[5] This must have intensified the process of amalgamation of power.

Although the Danish kings were powerful, the kingdom was unstable, as were the Norwegian and Swedish kingdoms. This was due in part to the manner of succession (the factors that decided who should rule after a deceased king).[6] Succession was decided both by inheritance and by choice, since the right of succession was connected with specific families, but the kings also had to be elected at an assembly known as the *þing* (the plural is also *þing*). As with inheritance more generally, succession practices involved the division of the kingdom and the title among all sons, both legitimate and illegitimate. Maintaining the integrity of the kingdom was not a concern. This sometimes resulted in the kings' sons ruling together, but at other times it led to bitter conflicts between them and their supporters.

When discussing the Danevirke and the development of the Danish kingdom, it is important to note that the Danevirke protected not only Jylland, but also other parts of southern Scandinavia—an important factor for the expansion of the Danish realm. After the kingdom was established, it began to expand around Kattegat and Skagerrak and to incorporate new chiefdoms. Most of these chiefdoms were small and unable to mount any real resistance to Danish expansion. Furthermore, many of these chieftains must have found it beneficial to enter into an alliance with a more powerful neighbor. The Danish kings were able to protect them not only from southern threats, but also eventually from troublesome neighboring chieftains; because royal power was built on these alliances, kings would have had a strong interest in discouraging conflict between chieftains.

There are few written sources that refer to the size of the Danish realm in the Viking Age. The most important ones are the *Royal Frankish Annals*, the story of Ohthere of Hålogaland, and the kings' sagas, which we will discuss in chapter 2. The *Royal Frankish Annals*, our main source for Danish history at the end of the 700s and beginning of the 800s, were composed in Latin between 741 and 829. They provide an annual account of events in Francia, the kingdom of the Franks, as well as information on neighboring kingdoms.

In 813, the *Royal Frankish Annals* tell us, the "princes and people" of Westarfoldam refused to submit to the Danish kings Harald and Reginfrid. These princes and people were probably the local chieftains and their supporters. What is more difficult to understand is why they would not submit. Were the chieftains trying to free themselves from Danish rule, or to prevent an expansion of the Danish kingdom? Unfortunately, the *Royal*

Map 3. Regions in Scandinavia

Frankish Annals do not explain why. However, they do tell us that after the death of the Danish king Hemming in 812, two candidates, Gudfred and Anulo, fought to succeed him. This conflict led to both their deaths, but since Anulo was considered to be the victor, his brothers Harald (d. c. 852) and Reginfrid (d. 814) were made co-kings. What is especially interesting is that as soon as they ascended to the throne, the brothers brought an army to Westarfoldam, an area situated "on the northwestern outskirts of their realm, facing the northern tip of Britannia [Scotland]" (my translation).[7] This clearly emphasizes how important this area was for the power of the Danish kings. The *Royal Frankish Annals* do not reveal the result of Harald's and Reginfrid's warpath in 813, but we can assume that the Danish kings were victorious. It is unlikely that the Danish kings used military force to secure their control over Viken (the area that stretched from the Göta River to Lindesnes), or that they kept a standing army there. The economic cost of such an effort would have been too high, and, in the long run, would not have provided the desired result of securing their power base. The best way to establish and protect their power was to use marriage and gift giving to establish friendships with the local chieftains, something we will return to later.

Almost all researchers agree that Westarfoldam refers to modern-day Vestfold.[8] However, this interpretation is debatable, especially since Vestfold does not face Scotland. Another, more believable interpretation is that it refers to Agder.[9] There is nothing in the Norse sources to suggest that Vestfold was ever called anything other than "Vestfold." For instance, in the saga of Olaf Tryggvason, Harald Bluetooth gives Harald Grenske (c. 960–995) the title of king and dominion over "Vingulmark [on the east side of the Oslofjorden], Vestfold, and Agder to Lindesnes" on the same terms his kinsman had enjoyed.[10] The confusion surrounding Westarfoldam is probably best explained by the suggestion that the *Royal Frankish Annals*, and possibly also contemporary Scandinavians, assigned the name Vestfold to a larger region than we do today. If we accept the proposition that Westarfoldam refers to Agder and the area around Lindesnes, which is the most believable interpretation, it will signify that the area was already part of the Danish kingdom by 813.

This is partly confirmed by the story of Ohthere of Hålogaland. Ohthere was a powerful, wealthy merchant who lived "the furthest north of all Norwegians," somewhere in Hålogaland. Sometime between 871 and 900,

Ohthere traveled to the court of Alfred the Great, king of Wessex. Alfred, who was extremely interested in geography, had the details of Ohthere's travels recorded. Ohthere wrote of his journey across Bjarmaland, in the north, and of his route from Hålogaland to Kaupang in Vestfold and on to Hedeby, located just inside the Danevirke. He did not specify where he sailed into the Danish kingdom, but he most likely did so when he passed Lindesnes, since Denmark (*Denemearce*) was to his left side when he sailed from Kaupang to Hedeby, from Vestfold across Oslofjorden, and along the coast of Østfold and Bohuslän.[11]

Both the *Royal Frankish Annals* and story of Ohthere of Hålogaland thus indicate that the Danish kings had dominion over the coastline on the northern side of Skagerrak as far as Lindesnes, as discussed below. It is uncertain exactly how far into Norway their realm extended, but it probably went all the way up to Romerike and Hedmark (map 3). Supporting this theory are the so-called knights' graves (*ryttergraver*) found in Romerike and Hedmark, which date to somewhere between the second half of the 800s and the early 1000s. A complete knight's grave contained weapons (swords and spears) as well as shields, bulls, riding equipment, horses, personal items, vessels containing food and drink, board games, and perhaps a currycomb. These warriors are believed to have been individuals associated with the Danish kings.

Power and Iron

Hegemony over Viken afforded the Danish kings control over the trade routes to and from northern Norway, along the coast, up the main waterways, and inland. This was extremely important as it secured access to crucial products and resources—especially iron, which was essential to Denmark's military operations.[12] There is no indication that iron ore was mined inside the borders of contemporary Denmark between the 600s/700s and the 1100s/1200s, but there was some minor iron production in Blekinge, Skåne, and Halland. This means that the greatest war machine in Europe during the Viking Age was completely dependent on the importation of iron.

Almost nine thousand iron production sites are known today in Sweden and Norway from the period approximately 200 BCE to 1800 CE, but it is still unknown how many of those were operating in the Viking Age.[13] In Norway, it seems that iron production greatly increased in the 700s and 800s, as for example at Møsvatn in upper Telemark. The extraction of iron was already underway in the early 500s, with a yearly production of perhaps 440 pounds. Iron production increased to two to three tons per year by the beginning of the Viking Age, around 800 CE. One ton of iron was required to produce two thousand axes or one thousand swords. Production levels remained unchanged until around 950 CE, when they increased again; we know of more than two hundred iron production sites around Møsvatn. The same development occurred in other parts of Norway as well, for example in Numedal, Hallingdal, and Valdres in Oppland. At the same time, more marginal areas were able to participate in iron production as the result of greater access to raw material and easier and more effective production processes, and that iron production was being organized under the control and direction of local chieftains.[14] The Norwegian chieftains thus controlled a resource that was essential to the Danish kings, and this is probably a major reason why the Danes expanded into Viken as systemically as they did. For the warlike chieftains and kings of Scandinavia, having access to iron and weapons was just as necessary as having power over people. Moreover, we should not forget that householders, not only in Denmark but also in the whole of Scandinavia, needed iron to make tools and work their farms.

The importance of iron can also be seen in Gästrikland in Norrland, Sweden. There are indications that local chieftains with connections to the king in the Mälar region controlled iron production there. Production was probably divided among several farms, a system also found in Hälsingland. The fact that the area known today as Dalarna was referred to during the Viking Age as Járnberaland—the area where people carry iron—shows that extensive mining of iron occurred in the Swedish realm. Weapons were also acquired from abroad—not least among them Frankish weapons, particularly swords and spears, which were highly treasured.[15] We see this most clearly in the poem *Rígsþula* (*The List of Rig*), which tells the story of an earl who fought with Frankish spears.[16]

The use of weapons and other tools made of iron required whetstones to sharpen them. Geological analyses of whetstones from eighth to early ninth century Ribe, a town in Jylland (map 8), show that the majority were quarried close to Lade in Trøndelag, Norway.[17] This was the residence of the earls of Lade, and there can be little doubt that they controlled this export and probably the production of the whetstones as well. It was therefore important for the Danish kings to be on good terms with the earls of Lade, who controlled not only whetstones but the trading route to Hålogaland, a source of furs, down, walrus ivory, and ship ropes made of whale hide. These trade goods may partly explain the longevity of the alliances between the Danish kings and earls of Lade, although another equally important factor was the earls' power.

All Roads Lead to Jelling

The Danish kings moved regularly between their various royal farms, where their incomes were collected. When sufficient supplies had been gathered, the king and his *hirð* would travel to a farm and stay there until the food ran out, before traveling to the next one. It was easier to move people than to move food. In addition, such an arrangement helped make the kings and their power more visible and kept their kingdoms united. This formed the basis of the so-called itinerant court system, which we also find in Sweden and Norway. Itinerant courts were a common feature of the Germanic kingdoms of the Early Iron Age and Early Middle Ages.[18]

During the period from the first half of the 900s to 986 (the death of Harald Bluetooth), the Danish kings developed Jelling, which lies in southern Jylland, into both their personal residence and the center of the kingdom. The only settlement of comparable size in Scandinavia was the religious and political center of Uppsala, in Sweden. The king's residence at Jelling was surrounded by a palisade and had a spectacular great hall at its heart. This great hall was surrounded by several smaller longhouses with different functions. The otherwise symmetrical construction of Jelling made it an entirely unique building complex. It was not only a political and military center for the Danish kings, but also an unmistakable symbol of their power.[19]

One possible reason why the kings chose Jelling as their seat of authority was that they wanted to build a temple for the god Odin. It is likely that the royal Danish family had made Odin their main god early in their rise to power.[20] The dynasty needed to legitimize their superior position, and it was therefore imperative that the world of the gods reflect the earthly political order—meaning that Odin, the preferred god of the Danish royal family, needed to be the most powerful among the Norse gods.[21]

Another reason for the Danish kings' devotion to Jelling was its centralized location. Although the Danish kingdom covered a vast area, it did not take long to travel from one end to the other. It took Ohthere five days to sail from Kaupang in Vestfold to Hedeby (map 8). We do not know how long it took him to sail from Lindesnes to Kaupang, but it was probably somewhere around one or two days. This implies that a person could travel from Lindesnes to Hedeby—from one end of the kingdom to the other—in about seven days (weather permitting). No other kingdom in Europe enjoyed such favorable travel conditions. It was even possible to travel from Aalborg to Norway in a single day, and it only took two days to travel inland from Aalborg to Viborg, and one week from Viborg to Hedeby.[22] Based on this small amount of information about travel times in the Danish realm, we can presume that it would have taken no more than three to five days to travel by boat or on foot from Jelling to anywhere in the kingdom. In other words, the Danish kings were able to deploy large forces to and from the king's seat at very short notice. However, it should be added that with the geography of the Danish realm facilitating such good communication, the Danish kings would have been able to gather a large force not only in Jelling, but anywhere in the realm, in a relatively short amount of time. This easy mobility contributed to the Danish kings being among the most powerful people in Europe.

Harald, Svein, and Cnut

The inscription on the large Jelling stone reads: "King Harald ordered this monument made in memory of Gorm, his father, and in memory of Thyra, his mother; that Harald who won for himself all of Denmark (*Danmǫrk*) and Norway (*Norvegr*) and made the Danes Christian."[23] The interpretation of this short inscription has led to serious debate. For instance, there is discussion surrounding which geographical areas the names Denmark and Norway refer to. When Ohthere sailed from Kaupang to Hedeby, he said that Denmark was on the port (left) side of the ship for three days. In other words, Denmark stretched across Vestfold, the Oslofjorden area, Østfold, and Bohuslän. It is therefore likely that the parts of the Danish realm that lay between Vestfold and Lindesnes would have been included in the name Denmark. This would mean that the term referred to the entire area ruled by the Danish kings at the end of the 800s, and it therefore seems likely that the Danes whom Harald Bluetooth Christianized included people living in

Viken.²⁴ One of Harald's priorities must have been to see that Christianity spread throughout his entire kingdom, not just parts of it.

The name *Norvegr* on the Jelling stone probably refers to the kingdom of Vestlandet. According to the kings' sagas, Harald Bluetooth secured his position there with the support of his kinsmen, the sons of Erik Bloodaxe (son of Harald Fairhair). With their help, Harald Bluetooth was able to defeat their uncle Hakon Adalsteinfostre around 960. Norway of the 900s can therefore be divided into three areas of political power: Viken, under the rule of the Danish kings; middle and northern Norway, the domain of the earls of Lade; and Norvegr, the Vestlandet kingdom, in which the Fairhair family and the Danish kings fought for control.²⁵

There is no doubt that Harald Bluetooth was a powerful king. Most of the ring forts, or *trelleborgs* (the name *might* be connected to "thralls"), were built around 980, the end of his reign, and like the Jelling complex, they were a symbol of the king's power. Today we know of six ring forts: Fyrkat and Aggersborg in Jylland, Nonnebakken at Fyn, Trelleborg at Sjælland, Borgeby in Skåne, and the newly discovered fort west of Køge at Sjælland (map 4). Of these, Aggersborg is the largest, at 262 yards in diameter and containing forty-eight longhouses. It has been suggested that a ring fort also existed in Oslo around the same period. The strongest argument to support this idea is the place-name Þrælabo(e)rg, found in Magnus the Lawmender's municipal law from 1276 and mentioned in sagas from the end of the 1100s and the first half of the 1200s. It seems certain that Oslo was a strategically important location. Snorri Sturluson in his *Heimskringla* (a king's saga from around 1230) tells us that Harald Hardruler (d. 1066) stayed in Oslo because the location made it easy both to attack and to defend against the Danes.²⁶ For a long time, scholars thought that there were military reasons behind the constructions of the ring forts. Today, the common view is that these forts were primarily used as royal administrative centers, places where the kings' income was collected. However, the ring forts and Jelling were only in use for a very short time, due to the struggle with England in the late 900s.²⁷

Harald Bluetooth was seemingly forced to abandon his throne by his son, Svein Forkbeard. Svein was a very powerful king, although he was briefly driven out of Denmark by the Swedish king Erik the Victorious. In 1013, Svein Forkbeard was made king of both Denmark and England, but he died only a few months later. After intense conflicts, Svein's son, Cnut, who would

Map 4. *Trelleborger* (ring forts)

later acquire the suffix "the Great," managed to lay claim to his father's position in both England and Denmark.

Part of a king's power lay in the number of people he commanded. We do not know exactly what the population of Scandinavia was during the Viking Age. However, it is likely that around three million people lived in the three Scandinavian kingdoms around the year 1300. There were about five hundred thousand people in Sweden (not including the Finns, although the Swedish realm did include Finland at this time). In Norway, which stretched across the Swedish areas of Bohuslän, Jämtland, and Härjedalen, the number of inhabitants was around five hundred thousand as well. Denmark, which included Skåne, had around two million residents.[28] It looks as though the population in Western Europe doubled during the period circa 650 to 1000 and then tripled in the years from 1000 to 1340.[29] If we use these numbers to calculate the population of Scandinavia, it would have been approximately 650,000 around the year 800, and one million around 1050. Probably more than half of the population of Scandinavia lived in areas controlled by the Danish kings. These calculations are not particularly dependable, but they do give us an indication of the powerful position the Danish kings held in Scandinavian politics.

Let us now turn to the other Scandinavian kings and chieftains who lived in their shadow.

Further Reading

Benedictow, Ole Jørgen. "Demographic Conditions." In *The Cambridge History of Scandinavia*, vol. 1, *Prehistory to 1520*, edited by Knut Helle, 237–49. Cambridge: Cambridge University Press, 2003.

Dobat, Andres Siegfried. "A Contested Heritage: The Dannevirke as a Mirror and Object of Military and Political History." In *Schleswig Holstein: Contested Region(s) through History*, edited by Michael Bregnsbo and Kurt Villads Jensen, 193–217. Odense: University Press of Southern Denmark, 2016.

——. "Danevirke Revisited: An Investigation into Military and Socio-political Organisation in South Scandinavia (c AD 700 to 1100)." *Medieval Archaeology* 52 (2008): 27–67.

——. "Viking Stranger-Kings: The Foreign as a Source of Power in Viking Age Scandinavia or, Why There Was a Peacock in the Gokstad Ship Burial?" *Early Medieval Europe* 23 (2015): 161–201.

Holst, Mads Kähler, Mads Dengsø Jessen, Steen Wulff Andersen, and Anne Pedersen. "The Late Viking-Age Royal Constructions at Jelling, Central Jutland, Denmark." *Praehistorische Zeitschrift* 87, no. 2 (2012): 474–504.

Jessen, Mads Dengsø, Mads Kähler Holst, Charlotta Lindblom, Niels Bonde, and Anne Pedersen. "A Palisade Fit for a King: Ideal Architecture in King Harald Bluetooth's Jelling." *Norwegian Archaeological Review* 47 (2014): 42–64.

Loftsgarden, Kjetil. "The Prime Movers of Iron Production in the Norwegian Viking and Middle Ages." *Fornvännen* 114 (2019): 75–87.

Pedersen, Anne. "Monumental Expression and Fortification in Denmark in the Time of King Harald Bluetooth." In *Fortified Settlements in Early Medieval Europe: Defended Communities of the 8th–10th Centuries*, edited by Christie Neil and Herold Hajnalka, 68–83. Oxford: Oxbow Books, 2016.

Randsborg, Klavs. *The Viking Age in Denmark: The Formation of a State*. London: Duckworth, 1980.

Rundberget, Bernt. *Tales of the Iron Bloomery: Ironmaking in Southeastern Norway— Foundation of Statehood, c. AD 700–1300*. Leiden: Brill, 2017.

Skovgaard-Petersen, Inge. "The Making of the Danish Kingdom." In *The Cambridge History of Scandinavia*, vol. 1, *Prehistory to 1520*, edited by Knut Helle, 168–83. Cambridge: Cambridge University Press, 2003.

Skre, Dagfinn. "Towns and Markets, Kings and Central Places in South-Western Scandinavia c. AD 800–950." In *Kaupang in Skiringssal: Norske oldfunn*, edited by Dagfinn Skre, 445–69. Aarhus: Aarhus University Press, Kaupang Excavation Project, University of Oslo, 2007.

Tveitan, Ole, and Kjetil Loftsgarden. "The Extensive Iron Production in Norway in the Tenth to Thirteenth Century: A Regional Perspective." In *Viking-Age Transformations: Trade, Craft and Resources in Western Scandinavia*, edited by Ann Zanette Tsigaridas Glørstad and Kjetil Loftsgarden, 111–23. London: Routledge, 2017.

Chapter 2

Kings and Chieftains in the Shadow of the Danish Kings

In this chapter we shall discuss political development in the other parts of Scandinavia, and how it was affected by the Danish kings. We will start with the rather uncertain situation in Sweden, before moving on to Trøndelag and Vestlandet. Finally, we will look at the most important event in Scandinavian politics in the Viking Age—the 1036 agreement between the Norwegian king Magnus Olafsson and the Danish king Harthacnut, which led to Magnus Olafsson becoming king of Denmark in 1042. One consequence of this power shift was that Viken became part of the Norwegian realm, greatly reducing the military power of the Danish kings and conversely increasing that of the Norwegians.

Geats and Swedes

Large parts of the geographical area that now is known as Sweden was divided between the territory of the Swedes—with the area around Mälaren

(Lake Malar) at its core—and that of the Geats—with Götaland (Gothia or Gothland) as the central region.[1] Between these two districts was a large forested area that made all overland communication difficult. The terms Swedes and Geats are somewhat problematic, not least because they are not ethnic terms. In the sources, the term Swedes is often used for both groups. When Ohthere from Hålogaland described Norway to King Alfred, he said, "Beyond the mountains Svealand (Sweoland) borders the southern part of the land as far as the north, and the country of the *Cwenas* borders the land in the north."[2] Around the same time, another story was being documented for Alfred as well. This was the story of the trade journey undertaken by Wulfstan, who described his travels on the Baltic Sea. Wulfstan said that Blekinge, Möre, Øland, and Götaland belonged to the Swedes (*sweon*).[3] However, these two records cannot be understood as proof of the existence of a Swedish country that stretched from the land of the *Cwenas* all the way south to Blekinge. It is likely that the terms Sweoland and sweon were used to refer to everyone who lived in Sweden, without indicating that the area comprised a single nation.

The political development of the Swedes and the Geats was not similar, as it does not seem as though any single royal family ruled the Geats. Archaeological investigations, not least those of the great barrows and longhouses, indicate that control of the Geatish region was divided between many chieftains.[4] There is reason to believe that the Danish kings formed alliances with these chieftains, and vice versa. It was beneficial for the chieftains to enter into this type of friendship, since they could make use of their connection in conflicts with other local chieftains. Such alliances were also important for the Danish kings, as they could call on the military forces of the local chieftains in times of war. Moreover, it reduced the risk of looting and plundering within their own kingdom.

However, among the Swedes, kingship was established early on and was already relatively well developed by the beginning of the Viking Age. Just like the chieftains in Götaland, these kings had connections to the Danish kings. One of the kings who reigned over the Swedes in the second half of the 800s was Björn, who was driven out by a rival. He went to Denmark to gather support—it is likely that he had friendship or kinship ties to the Danish kings. This is a good example of how the political game worked. When a king lost his power, he would seek support from his allies—in this case, the Danish king. And because the Danish kings were so influential, it was not difficult for them to affect political outcomes throughout Scandinavia. If the Swedish kings wanted to oppose the Danish kings, it was important for them to ally themselves with the Norwegians and rulers in Eastern Europe, especially the Polish or the Rus' (modern Russia, Ukraine, and Belarus).[5]

Erik the Victorious (c. 970–995) is the first Swedish king of whom we have reliable knowledge. He received his epithet after he defeated his nephews in a battle at Fyrisvellir near Uppsala. It is also said that he conquered the Danish realm for a short period around 992 to 993. Erik allied himself with the Polish ruler Boleslaw and married Boleslaw's sister Gunhild; their son was Olof Skötkonung. This alliance was formed in opposition to the Danish king Svein Forkbeard. When Erik died Gunhild remarried, this time to Svein.[6] This new alliance clearly shows how difficult long-term politics were. The death of one king could turn the political game upside down.

Olof Skötkonung succeeded his father Erik and went on to reign from around 995 to 1020. It is unclear what his epithet refers to, but one theory is that *sköt* is etymologically related to the word *skattr*, which means both treasure and taxes. If so, this would suggest that Olof paid taxes; if this was the case, he must have paid them to the Danish king Svein Forkbeard. Olof Skötkonung also fought together with Svein against the Norwegian king Olaf Tryggvason around the year 1000. This was despite the fact that Olaf himself had been allied with Svein just a few years earlier during a joint attack on London. Olof Skötkonung is the first king we know for certain to have ruled over the Mälar region as well as Götaland, and for this reason he is often referred to as the first king of Sweden. He was baptized and supported the Christian faith, and was probably the first king in Sweden to mint coins. Olof's son Anund Jacob (1022–1050) later formed an alliance with Olaf Haraldsson (1015–1028) against Cnut the Great (1018–1035).[7]

The Swedish king's decisions, both military and religious, were not made unilaterally. We see this in the hagiography *Vita Anskarii*, written by Archbishop Rimbert of Bremen-Hamburg between 865 and 876. It tells the story of St. Ansgar, who, among other things, had carried out two evangelizing missions in Sweden a few decades earlier. Ansgar is said to have asked the king of the Swedes' permission to begin his mission in 852. The king first took counsel with the chieftains and asked them if he should give Ansgar permission. They decided to "cast lots" to ask the Norse gods what they thought on the matter. The lots were positive. Thereafter, the case was brought up at the *þing* in the town of Birka, which also gave its assent. This account has been interpreted to mean that the king did not have much power.[8] However, as we shall see elsewhere, it appears that the most important principle for the Scandinavian kings was to ensure the greatest possible consensus surrounding their choices. This process helped them both to implement their decisions and to maintain peace within their realms.

In Sveariket, slightly north of modern Stockholm, lay Uppsala, a pagan sacrificial site. There was no comparable site to be found among the Geats, nor indeed in other places in Scandinavia. According to Adam of Bremen's chronicle (*The Deeds of Bishops of the Hamburg Church*) from circa 1075, there was a temple in Uppsala with statues of the gods Thor, Freyr, and Odin to which people gave offerings. In times of plague or famine, the people would make an offering to Thor; to celebrate a wedding, an offering was made to Freyr; and in times of warfare, the offering was given to Odin. Every ninth year, all the people of Uppsala had to participate or send gifts. Nine male animals were sacrificed and their bodies hung up in a holy grove near the temple. The accuracy of Adam's description of Uppsala has been an object of intense discussion, but we will not get into this debate here. In any case, there are three large barrows at Uppsala, as well as many smaller burial mounds. Archaeological excavations have also shown that there was a great hall in the area until around 800.[9] In other words, there is no reason to doubt that Uppsala was an important religious site. The kings' residence, Adelsö, was close by, as were the trading centers of Birka and Sigtuna (founded in the mid-eighth century and circa 980, respectively), both of which were situated along Lake Mälar.

The island of Gotland (not to be confused with Götaland) was relatively independent during the Viking Age and was not controlled by any foreign king. The island's central position made it a hub for trade in the Baltic Sea as well as for people and goods traveling in and out of it. There were dozens of trading places on the island, with Fröjel, and later Visby, the most central ones. Archaeological digs at Fröjel have shown that many visitors to the island had traveled from far away. This trade brought great wealth to Gotland, most clearly shown by the approximately seven hundred silver hoards discovered there. The largest of them, and the largest Viking Age treasure in all of Scandinavia, is the so-called Spilling Hoard, which weighs almost 150 pounds. One of the coins from the Spilling Hoard bears the inscription *Musa rasul Allah* (Moses is God's messenger) and appears to be a Khazar coin.

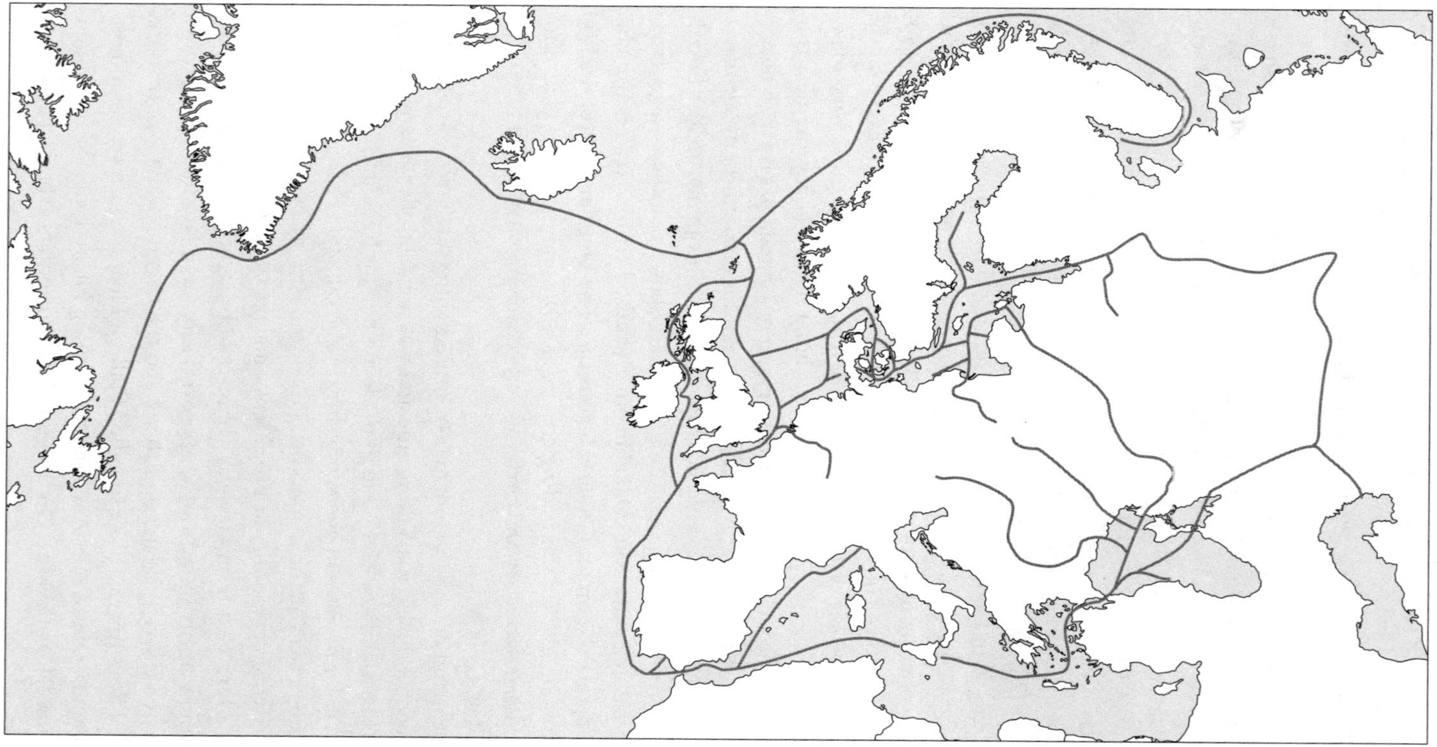

Map 5. Trading routes

The Khazars were a seminomadic people in Central Asia around 840. How this coin came to be in Gotland is uncertain, but it does demonstrate the scale of the Vikings' trading networks.[10]

Iron was imported from Sweden to Gotland, where it was processed and sold. It is not unlikely that a large portion of these exports went to Denmark, where as we have seen, there is no sign of iron production during the Viking Age. There is also every reason to believe that slaves from the Slavic regions as well as the British Isles and Ireland were bought and sold at the largest trading posts in Gotland, just as they were at other central trading posts in Scandinavia.

Finally, interestingly, Gotland did not have a king or any chieftains. The householders usually worked together, possibly in guilds. In Christian times, guilds were a social-religious community for householders and their households (family and workers) within a geographically delineated area. The guilds had their own leaders, but they were elected and there were no hereditary requirements for holding the position.[11]

The Kingdom of Vestlandet

The kings' sagas, in particular the ones collected in Snorri's *Heimskringla*, provide us with the basis for discussion of the unification of Norway in the period from the end of the 800s to the second half of the 1100s.[12] Snorri claimed that the process of unification began in Harald Fairhair's domain in Vestfold, where Harald was based when he conquered Oppland. Next, through an alliance with Hakon Grjotgardsson of Ørland, a man who was to become an earl of Lade, Harald was able to defeat the Trønder chieftains and secure control of Trøndelag. Finally, in about 880, he defeated the chieftains of the southern Vestlandet at the Battle of Hafrsfjord in Jæren in Rogaland. The unification of Norway was thus complete. However, we should be critical of Snorri's history: Harald Fairhair was primarily the king of the western counties. He ruled over Sogn and Fjordane, Hordaland, Rogaland, and parts of Agder, and the seat of his power was at Avaldsnes in Karmøy, outside Haugesund. This conclusion is supported by archaeological material from northern Jæren. There are fewer grave finds from after 900, which would suggest that farms were confiscated by the new royal family after the Battle of Hafrsfjord.[13]

The Battle of Hafrsfjord is particularly important to the politics and organization of Viking Age Scandinavia. It has been seen not only as the last battle in Harald Fairhair's unification of Norway, but also as the first attack on his kingdom, possibly by Danish leadership. In *Haraldskvæði*, a poem about Harald composed shortly after the battle, the skald Torbjorn Hornklofi (Horn-cleaver(?)) tells us how Harald the "great king" had won the battle, and comments that the *austkylfur* (men of the east) escaped to eastern Norway. One of Harald's opponents was known as Haklang, "the one with the long chin," a name we find again on a Danish rune stone from Lolland.[14] After the Battle of Hafrsfjord, it seems that Lindesnes became the border area between the kingdoms of Denmark and Norway.[15]

Several years after the decisive Battle of Hafrsfjord, Harald Fairhair married a Danish princess to reduce the threat posed by the Danish kings. Harald and his wife had a son named Erik Bloodaxe, who married Gunhild, the sister of the Danish king Harald Bluetooth, around 920. Harald Fairhair abdicated the throne circa 930 in favor of his favorite son; however, Erik's reign was quite short. Around 933, his half brother Hakon Adalsteinfostre (one fostered by Athelstan) returned to Norway from England, where he had been sent some years earlier.

Hakon had been fostered at the court of the West Saxon king Athelstan, one of the most important courts in Europe, where the sons of kings came to get an education in warfare and Christianity. This fostering arrangement was important for both Harald Fairhair and Athelstan. For Athelstan, it secured him an ally in the fight against Danish Vikings in Northumbria; for Harald, the relationship helped to keep his realm safe from attack.[16] But perhaps most important, at least from Harald's point of view, was that his young son was fostered in one of Europe's best organized kingdoms, so he could bring the knowledge he gained there home to Norway. Furthermore, Harald must have been aware that when Hakon returned from England he would be Christian and bring with him the Christian ideology that was gaining momentum throughout Europe. If Harald's kingdom was going to continue to develop its strength and survive the pressure from Denmark, it needed to imitate the best-organized kingdom known to the Vikings and establish centralized institutions. This theory is supported by the actions of Erik, Harald's favorite son and heir, who immediately abandoned the throne when Hakon returned to Norway. He never tried to overthrow his brother, and indeed accepted a new position as a follower of King Athelstan, becoming ruler of York in Northumbria.[17] Erik was killed in battle at Stainmore in northwest England in 954.[18]

Hakon Adalsteinfostre, also known as Hakon the Good, was undoubtedly one of Norway's most significant kings. He reigned for around twenty-seven years (c. 933–960), and it was he who laid the foundations for the Norwegian kingdom of the Middle Ages. Hakon's goal was simple: to introduce the English model to Norway. It seems likely that he had discussed this plan with his foster father, King Athelstan, and his most important supporter in Norway, Sigurd, Earl of Lade (c. 890–962).[19]

The Norwegian kingdom to which Hakon Adalsteinfostre succeeded can best be described as an overgrown chiefdom that stretched across Vestlandet. It had taken Hakon's father, Harald Fairhair, a long time to defeat the local chieftains and the Vikings who attacked the country, and Hakon's half brother, Erik, had not been in power long enough to leave any lasting marks on it. When Hakon took the throne, he also had a major challenge ahead of him: to protect his position as king.

The *Hirð*

The sagas tell us that Hakon used a very specific strategy to secure widespread support of the chieftains and householders; after he had secured their friendship, he was able to begin the task of increasing his power. The first step was to create a *hirð*. To Hakon, as to other kings, this was a prerequisite for exerting power. The *hirð* was not just a political tool, it was also a way for him to showcase his generosity and ambition, reinforcing his right to rule.

The institution of the *hirð* first developed in farm communities. In the north, *hirðmenn* were originally called housecarls (*húskarlar*), which emphasized the private service relationship between the householder and his warriors. The *hirð* entailed an extension of the mutually committed relationship of service between the householder and the housecarl, and the bond connecting the chieftain and the *hirðmaðr* (*hirð* man) was stronger than the original bond between householder and housecarl. The *hirðmaðr* and his lord were bound by both friendship and fidelity. The *hirðmaðr* was expected to fight for his chieftain, remain loyal to him, and if necessary, sacrifice his life for him. In exchange, the chieftain protected and supported his *hirðmaðr*. He was responsible for him and bore the responsibility for his wrongdoings. The chieftain rewarded fidelity and service with gifts: land, clothes, horses, weapons, rings, gold, and a share of spoils. The *hirðmenn* lived with their chieftain and ate at his table. The *hirð* constituted a fellowship with its own code of honor; besides the duty to their leader, *hirðmenn* were also responsible for their comrades—even seeking revenge on behalf of each other, for example. Because of this fellowship, the *hirð* could be used to establish and exert power, and it was fundamental to the king and his administration.[20]

Our sources most clearly document the *hirð*'s development in Scandinavia under the Norwegian kings. From the days of Harald Fairhair, we hear about the *merkismaðr* (mark's man), who was supposed to take care of the king's banner during war. In peacetime, he probably acted as an adviser. Another adviser was the *stallari* (stabler), who is found in sources written about the period dating to around the year 1000. The *stallari* had a higher position within the *hirð* than the *merkismaðr*. It was probably Olaf Haraldsson (1015–1028) who divided the *hirð* into *hirðmenn* and *gestir* (guests). The *hirðmenn* held a higher social position, while the *gestir* were recruited from the lower classes or were foreigners.

The details of recruitment to the *hirð* are not entirely clear, but probably the most common method among the chieftains was recruiting local men and giving them an education in weaponry at their farms. Such is the case

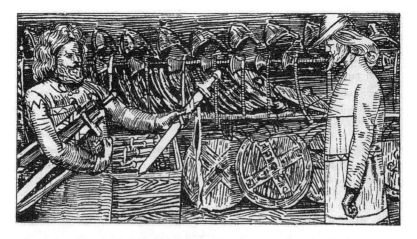

Figure 2. The *hirð*. The scald Sighvatr Thordarson receiving a sword from King Olaf Haraldsson. Source: *Snorre Sturlason kongesagaer*, trans. Gustav Storm (Christiania: J. M. Stenersen, 1899).

in *Egils saga Skalla-Grímssonar* (*The Saga of Egil Skalla-Grimsson*), which was written down in Iceland during the first decades of the thirteenth century and tells the story of a father and son, Kveldulf and Skalla-Grimr, who lived in Norway in the mid-800s. At Kveldulf's farm, many freed boys around the same age as Skalla-Grimr lived as Kvedulf's foster sons. Father and son hand-picked the boys according to strength, trained them, and shaped their character.[21] These foster sons were therefore bound to Kveldulf as if they were his own blood relations. *Egils saga Skalla-Grímssonar* is not a reliable source about Norwegian society of several centuries earlier. However, the picture drawn here of the recruitment to a chieftain's band of warriors exhibits clear parallels to the idea in Norse mythology of how Odin recruited his *hirð*. Half of those who died in battle made their way to Valhalla, where they became Odin's foster sons. During the daytime, the warriors (*einherjar*) trained in battle, and in the evenings, they ate and drank in Odin's hall. The warriors practiced every day to prepare for the great final battle, Ragnarok, in which they would fight on behalf of the gods against their enemies, the *jötnar*. The other half of those who died in battle went to Freyja, but there are no written accounts about the daily routine of the warriors at Freyja's farm, Folkvangr (field of the people, or field of the army).[22]

The kings, at least the most powerful ones, recruited their *hirð* not only from their own kingdoms, but also from outside them. This was certainly the case among the Danish kings in the 900s, whose *hirð* included warriors from other parts of Scandinavia and the Baltics.[23] Ambitious warriors approached the greatest kings, as it was more prestigious to serve a king than a local chieftain. The king's *hirð* was also used to establish and maintain friendships with powerful chieftains. This happened, for instance, through their sons becoming *hirðmenn* of the king.

The size of the *hirð* and the differences between the most powerful chieftains' *hirð*s and those of the kings is difficult to determine. The difference between the *hirð* of the most powerful local chieftains and the *hirð* of the weakest kings may not have been very great, but usually there would have been a large difference between the *hirð*s of local chieftains and those of strong kings. In addition, the size of the *hirð* varied according to whether the leaders were going into battle or not. In times of peace, they did not need a very large *hirð*. We can therefore presume that the number of *hirðmenn* varied from ten or twenty up to one to two hundred in peacetime, and up to several hundreds if not thousands during times of war.

As previously mentioned, the *hirðmenn* needed to be rewarded for their service, and they were usually given both gifts and a share of the spoils of war. An economic surplus was thus imperative to being able to keep a *hirð*, which could help kings and chieftains acquire even greater riches in the long run. At the same time, the *hirð* could be used to maintain peace in the kingdom or chiefdom. However, householders did not have to fear undeserved economic pressure from the *hirð*. Householders were, after all, the foundation on which the kings and chieftains built their strength, and if they were subjected to economic blackmail, they were free to terminate the friendship with their leader.

The leading men of the king's *hirð*, the so-called *lendir menn* (landed men), were usually local chieftains. Like other *hirðmenn*, the *lendir menn* had their private farms; however, as the kings' friends, they frequently were given the permission to run one or several royal farms. This strengthened their local position, making it easier for them to exercise their chieftaincies. The *lendir menn*'s private estates were usually not very large. They were therefore dependent on the income from raids and the royal farms to maintain their position in society, and since they were able to keep the royal farms only for the duration of the king's reign, they would always be reliant on his favor.

Serving the king administratively in another capacity were the *ármenn* (servants, stewards, sing. *ármaðr*, from *árr*; in Sweden, the *bryti*). They were usually of lower birth, and in some cases they were thralls. The *ármenn*'s responsibilities included administering the king's properties and collecting the land rent, the yearly fee from the king's tenants. The *ármenn* also collected fines paid to the king and managed confiscated property. On the whole, the number of *ármenn* was low. There is no reason to believe that they played a large role in local society. It has been claimed that the *ármenn* were the actual local royal administrators and that the *lendir menn* were called on only in more important cases. Even so, the supposed division of duties between the *ármenn* and the *lendir menn* must have created conflicts between them. It is unlikely that a chieftain of high birth would bow down to a royal *ármaðr* of low birth. Doing so would have been considered a loss of honor.

There is no reason to overestimate the effect of the royal administration on Viking Age Scandinavia. By all accounts, it was involved in only the most important conflicts, and even in these, there was little for it to do. We must therefore ask if the kings really could develop or were particularly interested in developing a large and effective administrative system. It looks as though local society, under the rulership of local chieftains, managed very well on its own, without much interference from the king.

At the death of the king, the *hirð* was dissolved. It was therefore imperative for a new king to assemble his *hirð* as quickly as possible. It is unclear to what extent the *hirð* of the previous king was included in the new one, but we must assume that there was at least some overlap. The new king needed a military retinue, and the warriors needed a new king for whom to fight.

Lawthings, the Naval Levy, and Christianity

Once his *hirð* was established, Hakon Adalsteinfostre could begin working on his plans to reform the Norwegian kingdom. One of his first actions was to change the organization of the regional lawthings (*lögþing*): the *Gulaþing* in Vestlandet and the *Frostaþing* in Trøndelag. The earl of Lade helped considerably with this reform. After this reorganization, rather than being *alþing* (all-things), in which all householders were to participate, each of the regional lawthings became a *þing* with a defined number of men from the different parts of the region. An organization such as this was favorable to the householders, since they were relieved of the costs connected with participating in the lawthings and could focus on working on their farms. Even so, there is reason to believe that rather more people than just the appointed men participated in the lawthings, especially when important matters were to be discussed. In addition, these *þing* were, as we will discuss in chapter 4, occasions for market days and social events. The reorganization of the lawthings probably also benefited the king, as Hakon could negotiate with the householders and establish new laws with more ease. Hakon seems to have been the one who laid the groundwork on which royal law in Norway was built. The honor has traditionally been given to Olaf Haraldsson, but according to both *Fagrskinna* and *Heimskringla*, most of his laws were continuations of Hakon's. In this respect, as in others, Hakon used the English model as inspiration.[24]

Also central to Hakon's reign was the establishment of the *leiðangr* (naval levy), an institution that was already fully developed in Wessex. Snorri Sturluson claims in *Heimskringla* that the threat from the Eriksons was the main reason for its establishment. He explains that after the death of their father, Erik Bloodaxe, and with support from Erik's maternal uncle, the

Danish king Harald Bluetooth, Erik's sons started attacking their paternal
uncle, Hakon, in order to gain control of his kingdom. In response, Hakon
created the *leiðangr*, a seaborne military organization led by the king, for
which householders provided ships, crew, weapons, and provisions. Its formation was probably high on the list of Hakon's priorities, because he was
familiar with the Viking attacks that both his father and foster father had
endured. It could be used for both defense and attacks, at home or overseas.
In contrast with the English *leiðangr*, which was primarily organized around
infantry, the Norwegian one was first and foremost a maritime institution.

All evidence points to the local chieftains being responsible for the *leiðangr*'s administration in the beginning. With time, the royal office acquired
more and more control, but it was not until the twelfth and thirteenth centuries that a unified *leiðangr* organization emerged in Norway. After the
leiðangr was introduced in Vestlandet, Trøndelag was next. A *leiðangr* probably already existed in Denmark and Sweden, which might also have inspired Hakon. If the Danish kings could mobilize large masses of people to
build the Danevirke, as we have seen, it is probable that they could call on
corresponding forces to defend their country as well.[25]

Hakon returned from his stay in Wessex a Christian. When he arrived
in Norway, he immediately started his Christianization of the realm, first in
Vestlandet, and then in Trøndelag. In Norway, we can find about sixty stone
crosses: twenty-four in Rogaland, nine in Hordaland, and eighteen in Sogn
and Fjordane, all in the core areas of Hakon's realm. Dating these crosses is
problematic, but most of them were probably made during Hakon's rule. He
was highly successful in Vestlandet, but in Trøndelag he was met with monumental resistance and had to abandon his plans—primarily because of the
crucial role the Norse religion played in the power base of the earls of Lade.
Nevertheless, Hakon's efforts at Christianization are not to be made light of.
He was, by all accounts, the one who built the first churches and sent for English clerics to preach the new faith.[26] He did not attempt to establish the
new religion by force of arms, however—another strategy he brought with
him from England.

Hakon came a long way toward elevating the Norwegian Vestlandet kingdom to the level of other contemporary European kingdoms. He established
important institutions and started processes that would become crucial to the
future of the Norwegian kingdom. He managed to Christianize the core area
of Vestlandet, as well as to introduce a new *þing* organization, new laws, and

an efficient defense system against outside enemies. His success was the result of his ability to secure the friendships of the chieftains and householders, his skill as a collaborator, and his willingness to listen to wise counselors. Another reason for Hakon's good fortune on the throne was the longevity of his reign. Of the saga kings, only his father, Harald Fairhair, ruled for a longer period of time. It was also of great importance for the development of the Vestlandet kingdom that Harald had eliminated the most powerful chieftains and confiscated their lands, since these properties formed the economic base for the royal family.

The Earls of Lade

Erik Bloodaxe did not attack his half brother Hakon after Hakon became king. However, as we have seen, Erik's sons did. After Erik's death in 954, they started fighting Hakon for power, supported by their mother and her brother, Harald Bluetooth. Many battles were fought, and after the battle of Fitjar near Bergen, circa 961, Hakon died. Two years later, the Eriksons killed Sigurd, Earl of Lade, and both Vestlandet and Trøndelag fell into their hands and thus under indirect control by the Danish king.

At one point, Harald Bluetooth became dismayed with the way his nephews were ruling Norway, probably because they were becoming too independent. He therefore entered into an alliance with their greatest enemy, the son of Sigurd, Earl of Lade, Hakon Sigurdsson (c. 935–995), who had gone abroad after his father was killed by the Eriksons. A Danish-Trønder army under Hakon Sigurdsson's leadership defeated the Eriksons in a battle in the Limfjorden in Jylland in 970. After this, Hakon not only became the ruler of Trøndelag, to which he was the rightful heir, but he was also given leadership of Vestlandet by the Danish king. Viken remained directly ruled by Harald Bluetooth himself. During this period, Trøndelag was Norway's political center. This was not only because of the elevated position of the earls of Lade, but also because Trøndelag was the richest, best organized, and most populous area along the "Northway," and as such, a natural residence for the leader of the realm.

Hakon Sigurdsson remained earl of Lade and leader of Vestlandet, for many years, until his death in about 995, after which Olaf Tryggvason became king of Vestlandet and Trøndelag from around 995 to 1000. The year before Olaf returned to Norway, he and Svein Forkbeard had attacked London with a fleet of ninety-four ships. Because of this cooperation, it has been suggested that it was Svein who sent Olaf to Norway as a Danish sub-king of the Vestlandet kingdom. Olaf had other plans, however, and his ambition for power in the north led him into immediate conflict with Denmark, especially because he challenged the Danes for control of Viken. Olaf was the first Norwegian king to make some headway in that region. His ambitions were a threat to the balance of power in Scandinavia and were eventually curtailed in a battle near Svolder (actual location unknown), circa 1000. There, Olaf fought the dominant powers of his generation: the Danish king, Svein Forkbeard; the Swedish king, Olof Skötkonung; and two sons of Hakon, Earl of Lade, Svein (c. 970–1017) and Erik (c. 964–1024). Olaf died in the battle, and the Danes once more secured the rule of Viken and Vestlandet, where they appointed the earls of Lade as rulers of Vestlandet. To solidify the Svolder alliance, the young earls of Lade, Svein and Erik, married the daughters of Svein Forkbeard and Olof Skötkonung, Gyda and Holmfrid, respectively.[27]

In 1013, Svein Forkbeard was also made king of England, only to die a few months later. His son, Cnut the Great, then had to fight for the English throne. It looks as though he had the support of the Norwegian prince Olaf Haraldsson, who was probably sent to Vestlandet as a Danish sub-king in 1015.[28] The year after this, Olaf had Svein, Earl of Lade, driven from Norway; since Svein's brother Erik had already left for England, this marked the end of the power of the earls of Lade in Norway. Cnut was crowned king of England in 1017, and two years later, he became king of Denmark as well. Because Cnut spent his time securing control over the English and Danish kingdoms, Olaf Haraldsson was essentially free to expand his power in Norway.

Cnut the Great had great ambitions regarding both the North and the Baltic Seas. His fellow kings—Olaf Haraldsson; Yaroslav, who ruled in Russia from 1019 to 1054; and the Swedish king, Olof Skötkonung—all understood this. In 1019, Olaf and Yaroslav each married one of Olof Skötkonung's daughters; the year before, Yaroslav had probably married his son to Cnut's daughter. This shows us that he was a man wise enough to protect himself from several angles. Another of Cnut's in-laws was not as prudent. Around 1015, Ulf Thorgilsson, a chieftain from Skåne, married Cnut's sister, Estrid Svendsdatter. Ulf was a central participant in Cnut the Great's invasion of

England and had been proclaimed earl of Denmark, designated to rule the country on Cnut's behalf while he was abroad. In addition, he was the foster father of Cnut's son, Harthacnut. Olaf Haraldsson and the Swedish king, Anund Jacob—who had succeeded to the throne after his father Olof Skötkonung—used Cnut's stay in England as an opportunity to attack Denmark. Ulf then had Harthacnut made king, making himself de facto ruler of the country. When he learned of the attack, Cnut immediately returned to Denmark. In 1026, he and Ulf engaged in battle at Helgeå in Skåne against Olaf and Anund, who lost the fight. Not long afterward, Cnut had Ulf killed because of his treasonous attempt to make Harthacnut, and by extension himself, king of Denmark.

The reason Yaroslav did not participate in Olaf and Anund's attack on Denmark was that through his son's marriage, he was Cnut's ally and therefore could not attack him. He could not support one friend against another. When Cnut arrived in Norway in 1028 and went after Olaf Haraldsson, Olaf then fled to his brother-in-law Yaroslav in Russia.[29] Olaf tried to take back his kingdom in 1030 with help from the Swedish king, but failed and died in the battle of Stiklestad. After this, Cnut made his son Svein king of Norway (Vestlandet and the realm of the earls of Lade) and Viken, with Svein's mother Alfifa as his legal guardian.

The Agreement that Ended the Viking Age

Svein Alfifason's rule was very unpopular, and in 1035, Magnus the Good, son of Olaf Haraldsson, was brought back from being fostered in Russia and made king of all of Norway. Svein fled to Denmark without a fight. His father, Cnut the Great, died on November 12, 1035; within a few years, all of Cnut's sons died as well, with Svein passing on as early as 1036. Harald Harefoot succeeded to the throne of England at Cnut's death and ruled until his own death in 1040. His younger half brother, Harthacnut, whom Cnut had fathered with his wife, Queen Emma, also made claims to Cnut's realms as his rightful inheritance. A conflict therefore arose between Magnus and Harthacnut over the rule of Norway. Both thought they had legitimate claims to the throne. Magnus insisted that Norway was his inheritance as the son of Olaf Haraldsson, but Harthacnut believed that since his father Cnut had acquired the kingdom, he was entitled to rule it. Both kings mustered large armies and planned to meet at the Göta River to fight. This did not happen, however, because peace negotiations between the kings were arranged instead. Their agreement not only was crucial for the later political development in Scandinavia, but also was a main factor contributing to the decline of the Viking raids. Because of the importance of this meeting, we shall take the time to examine its description in various sources.

According to the *Historia de antiquitate regum Norwagiensium* (*The History of the Old Norwegian Kings*), written by the Benedictine monk Theodoricus Monachus in Norway circa 1180, the chieftains persuaded the kings to reach an agreement whereby if one of them died heirless, the other would inherit the kingdom. As a result, they parted not only with mutual satisfaction, but also as good friends.[30] The overview of Norwegian kings, *Ágrip*, written in Norway circa 1190, tells the story of wise men traveling between the two parties and creating the pact in which the one who outlived the other was to inherit both kingdoms. Additionally, it says that to make sure this deal was upheld, the kings exchanged hostages.[31] The collection of kings' sagas known as *Fagrskinna*, probably written in Norway about 1220, is a bit more detailed than *Ágrip*. Here "the best men from both sides" secured the deal, which is described as a world peace that would last for all eternity. Both kings swore an oath to be like brothers to each other and to inherit each other's kingdoms if they died without heirs. Twelve of the most powerful men in each realm swore that this agreement should be upheld as long as they were alive. *Fagrskinna* adds that this pact was based on the deal made between Cnut the Great and King Edmund of England.[32] After the battle of Assandun on October 18, 1016, Cnut and Edmund agreed that they would divide England between them, and that at the death of one, the other would inherit the remaining part. Edmund died just over a month after the deal was agreed, making Cnut king of the whole of England. In *Morkinskinna*, written in Iceland about 1220, the householders were the ones to ensure the peace between Magnus and Harthacnut; otherwise, the story is identical to the one found in *Fagrskinna*. *Morkinskinna* says that the deal was made as though they were brothers of the same parents.[33] Saxo Grammaticus, in his *Gesta Danorum* (*Deeds of the Danes*, finished sometime between 1200 and 1220), states that the king who died first was to leave his kingdom to the other. This was because old traditions of rule were not to be destroyed, and because Harthacnut was keen to maintain the integrity of the realm.[34] In Snorri's *Heimskringla* (written in Iceland c. 1230), we read the following:

> The following spring [1036,] both the kings called up levies, and the word got around that they would be engaging in battle by the Göta River. But as the two armies advanced on each other until they were close to meeting, the *lendir menn* from each army sent intelligence to their relatives and friends, with the message that people were to make peace between the kings. And because the kings were both immature and young, the government of the land was in the hands of powerful men who had been appointed on their behalf for this in each country. So it came about that a peace meeting was arranged between the kings. After that they met in person and a settlement was discussed, and the terms of it were that the kings were to swear oaths of brotherhood and establish peace between them for as long as both were alive, but if one of them died without leaving a son, then the other was to inherit his territories and subjects. Twelve men, the best men from each kingdom, swore along with the kings that this agreement should be kept as long as any of them lived. Then the kings parted, and each went back to his kingdom, and this agreement was kept as long as they lived.[35]

In other words, all of the sources agree about the most important features of the meeting. Very seldom are events such as this described in as much detail, which tells us how important the agreement was thought to be in the 1100s and 1200s.

When Harthacnut died in 1042, everyone involved respected the settlement, and Magnus was made king of Denmark that same year, thus turning the relationship between Denmark and Norway upside-down. The year after, Magnus led the defense of Denmark against the Wends, a Slavic people, in a famous battle at Lyrskoghede, a little south of the Danevirke. Shortly after this, however, Svein Estridsson, son of Cnut the Great's sister Estrid and Ulf Thorgilsson, was made king of Denmark. This immediately led to conflict with Magnus. However, Magnus died in 1047, and shortly before his death he bequeathed the Danish throne to Svein. According to Snorri, Magnus thought it fair that Harald Hardruler, who had ruled alongside him since 1046, be made king of Norway, and Svein, king of Denmark. Harald, though, believed that with Magnus's passing he had inherited the Danish kingdom as well, and he attacked it several times without succeeding in killing Svein or gaining control of the throne. In 1064, Svein and Harald came to an agreement that they would not attack each other's kingdoms, which was crucial for Harald's ability to complete his attack on England. This happened in 1066, but his ambitions were stopped in the battle of Stamford Bridge, near York, where he died.

The long-term consequence of the settlement of 1036 and the succeeding events was the incorporation of Viken into the Norwegian kingdom, though the Danish kings long believed they were entitled to the area. This is evident in the attacks on Viken by Erik the Memorable in 1137, King Valdemar the Great in 1165 and 1168, and Valdemar the Victorious in 1204. It was not until Valdemar's death in 1241 that Norway entirely escaped the "Danish power field."[36] The loss of Viken played a part in weakening the Danish kings' power in Scandinavian politics and in their inability to reconquer England—but as to the latter, it must also be noted that the new Norman royal power base there improved England's defenses. The Norwegian kingdom was strengthened by these proceedings, having gained control of Viken as well as Vestlandet and the realm of the earls of Lade. In Sweden, the movement toward a unified kingdom was also well underway. The strengthening of the Norwegian and Swedish kings' powers helped solidify the borders between the three kingdoms. In a meeting between the three Scandinavian kings at the Göta River in 1101, the country borders were first officially drawn. It is really only after this meeting took place that there were three essentially equal kingdoms in Scandinavia.[37]

The royal families in Norway and Sweden lived in the shadow of the Danish kings during the Viking Age, although it looks as though the Danish kings were more active in Norway than in Sweden. This is probably because the threat to them from the Vestlandet kings was greater than that from the chieftains in Götaland, and control over the trade route to northern Norway was especially important. Between the royal families in the Nordic region there existed a robust strategy of arranged marriage that could simultaneously heighten or reduce the pressure exerted by the other kingdoms. The kings normally ruled for only a short while, which made long-term planning impossible. As a result, politics in Scandinavia was in some measure subject to chance. Crucial to what little stability existed was how long the kings, or chieftains, were in power, the resources they had access to, and how they used these resources to establish and maintain their sociopolitical networks.

Danish control of Scandinavian politics diminished after about 1040 for two principal reasons. The Jelling dynasty disappeared from the political scene in the 1040s, and Svein Estridsson did not manage to fill the void they left. At the same time, both the Norwegian and the Swedish kings strengthened their power—the unification of the areas of the Swedes and the Geats under one king began at the end of the Viking Age and was completed at the beginning of the 1100s. Because of this, the power balance between the three kingdoms became somewhat more equal.

One question we need to ask before leaving the discussion about Scandinavia's political development is this: How did the Danish kings manage to maintain their power for such a long time? The best explanation is probably that as long as there were no kings able to challenge them, the Danish kings could rest comfortably. In addition, the kings of Denmark had access to resources that made it possible for them to establish friendships with the most important political people in the region. There was also a rather significant stability regarding the question of succession, and many Danish kings enjoyed long reigns, such as Horik (c. 814–854) and the king who succeeded him, also named Horik (c. 854–870), Gorm the Old (c. 930–958), Harald Bluetooth (c. 958–986), Svein Forkbeard (c. 987–1014), and Cnut the Great (1018–1035). The length of the kings' reigns and the strength of their relationships with the chieftains influenced political stability.

Further Reading

Bolton, Timothy. *The Empire of Cnut the Great: Conquest and the Consolidation of Power in Northern Europe in the Early Eleventh Century*. Leiden: Brill, 2009.

Dobat, Andres Siegfried. "The State and the Strangers: The Role of External Forces in a Process of State Formation in Viking-Age South Scandinavia (c. AD 900–1050)." *Viking and Medieval Scandinavia* 5 (2009): 65–104.

Goetting, Lauren. "*Þegn* and *drengr* in the Viking Age." *Scandinavian Studies* 78 (2006): 375–404.

Jansson, Sven B. F. *Swedish Vikings in England: The Evidence of the Rune Stones*. London: H. K. Lewis, 1966.

Jesch, Judith. *Ships and Men in the Late Viking Age: The Vocabulary of Runic Inscriptions and Skaldic Verse*. Woodbridge, UK: Boydell Press, 2001.

Krag, Claus. "The Early Unification of Norway." In *The Cambridge History of Scandinavia*, vol. 1, *Prehistory to 1520*, edited by Knut Helle, 184–202. Cambridge: Cambridge University Press, 2003.

Lincoln, Bruce. *Between History and Myth: Stories of Harald Fairhair and the Founding of the State*. Chicago: University of Chicago Press, 2014.

Lindkvist, Thomas. "Early Political Organisation. Introductory Survey." In *The Cambridge History of Scandinavia*, vol. 1, *Prehistory to 1520*, edited by Knut Helle, 160–67. Cambridge: Cambridge University Press, 2003.

———. "Kings and Provinces in Sweden." In *The Cambridge History of Scandinavia*, vol. 1, *Prehistory to 1520*, edited by Knut Helle, 221–34. Cambridge: Cambridge University Press, 2003.

Line, Philip. *Kingship and State Formation in Sweden, 1130–1290*. Leiden: Brill, 2007.

Ljungkvist, John, and Per Frölund. "Gamla Uppsala—the Emergence of a Centre and a Magnate Complex." *Journal of Archaeology and Ancient History* 16 (2015): 3–29.

Price, T. Douglas, Karin Margarita Frei, Andres Siegfried Dobat, Niels Lynnerup, and Pia Bennike. "Who Was in Harold Bluetooth's Army? Strontium Isotope Investigation of the Cemetery at the Viking Age Fortress at Trelleborg, Denmark." *Antiquity* 85 (2011): 476–89.

Chapter 3

Networks of Power

In studying power in the Viking Age, we need to focus on the social networks of the chieftains and kings: it was through these they gained and exerted their power. The political game consisted of establishing networks and/or being included in already existing ones—one had to make friends. There was a clear connection between power and the size of the network, whereby the most powerful leaders possessed the largest networks. In this respect, the kings stood out. Their networks included foreign rulers, local chieftains, householders, and *hirðmenn*. In this chapter about the networks of the kings and the chieftains, we shall look at the two main elements of all Viking Age networks: friends and family.[1]

"To His Friend a Man Should Be a Friend / and to His Friend's Friend Too"

The collection of poems known as the *Hávamál* is the most important source regarding the friendships of the chieftains and the kings. The dating of the collection is uncertain, but large parts of it probably originate from the last years of the Viking Age.[2] The most important stanzas about friendship in the poem are as follows:

> *34. It's a great detour to a bad friend's house,*
> even though he lives on the route;
> but to a good friend's house the ways lie straight,
> even though he lives far off.

> *39. I never found a generous man, nor one so unstingy with food,*
> that he wouldn't accept what was given;
> or one so open-handed with wealth
> that he disliked a gift when offered.

> *41. With weapons and gifts friends should gladden one another,*
> those which can be seen on them;
> mutual givers and receivers are friends for longest,
> if the friendship keeps going well.

> *42. To his friend a man should be a friend*
> and repay gifts with gifts;
> laughter men should accept with laughter
> but return deception for a lie.

> *43. To his friend a man should be a friend*
> and to his friend's friend too;
> but no man should be a friend
> to the friend of his enemy.

> *44. You know, if you've a friend whom you really trust*
> and from whom you want nothing but good,
> you should mix your soul with his and exchange gifts,
> go and see him often.

> *45. If you've another, whom you don't trust,*
> but from whom you want nothing but good,
> speak fairly to him, but think falsely
> and repay treachery with a lie.

46. Again, concerning the one you don't trust,
and whose mind you suspect:
you should laugh with him and disguise your thoughts:
a gift should be repaid with a like one.

48. Generous and brave men live the best,
seldom do they harbour sorrow;
but the cowardly man is afraid of everything,
the miser always worries when he gets gifts.[3]

Hávamál describes two kinds of friendships: the good ones and the bad ones. The main difference between these is loyalty. When entering into war, one ought to stand beside an old and faithful friend, since he does not abandon you. One should not trust the disloyal friend, but use him as a piece in one's power games, and return his gifts with corresponding gifts. One should not maintain connections with the bad friend for too long, because the peace with him will break down. In other words, one ought to nurture all one's friends, but be careful not to be in contact with the bad ones for too long, and use them for one's own purposes. Whether the friendship is good or bad, one should never be the one to end it.[4] A bad friend is, after all, better than no friend, as he is obligated to provide help in a crisis or lose his honor.

Stanza 43 is probably the most important stanza about friendship in *Hávamál*: "To his friend a man should be a friend / and to his friend's friend too."[5] Two individuals' entering into friendship also entailed commitments to each other's friends, as one had to support the friends of one's friend. Establishment of friendship therefore affected not only the two people becoming friends, but all of their friends as well. In conflicts and wars, this meant that their friend's friends could become involved. For chieftains and kings this was particularly important, especially when it came to war and they needed large numbers of supporters. The second part of the stanza highlights that one should not establish friendships with the enemies of one's friend— advice not always heeded. We shall examine this point more closely later.

Chieftains wanted to secure their own interests first and foremost and ensure that no other chieftains became too powerful. Friendships between chieftains were easily made and easily broken. For this reason, a network was a convenient tool to increase power and social standing. The chieftains entered into friendships with other chieftains they thought were beneficial to have as allies, and ended those same friendships if they proved unfruitful. The degree of loyalty in the friendships between chieftains was, in other words, low. Pragmatism characterized these relationships.

Not everyone was able to establish a tie of friendship. Only kings, chieftains, members of the upper level of society, and householders (those who were leaders of a household, both male and female) had this opportunity. These groups seem to have constituted about 15 percent of the total population. Members of a household normally could not establish friendships such as these but were included in the friendship between the householder and the chieftain, which led to the chieftain's having to protect them. As a consequence, nearly all of the people in Viking society were part of a friendship network.

The friendship discussed here can be characterized as a political friendship, as opposed to the religious friendship one could establish with the gods, which will be discussed in chapter 7. In a political friendship, it was usually the person of higher social standing (i.e., the person who could offer protection) who initiated it. The relationship between the chieftains and their friends can thus be described as a patron-client relationship, an alliance between two individuals of different social status, power, and wealth. Both found it advantageous to become allies, and both had something to offer. The client could provide loyal support and esteem, while the patron supplied protection and help. It was the patron who decided the different tasks his clients undertook, which meant he had *mannaforráð*, or power over people.

Women from higher social strata could also establish friendships, but the largest group of women who were able to do this was the widows. As we will examine in more detail in chapter 6, widows who ran the farms on behalf of their children held a special place in society. They were leaders of households, and as leaders, they could enter into friendships. This means that the role one played, rather than one's sex, defined one's position.

Chieftains could be friends with several other kings and chieftains at once. In disputes between their friends, these chieftains tried to negotiate a resolution but were not always successful. We see this clearly expressed in the conflict around 1050 between King Harald Hardruler and Einar Bowstring-Shaker, the most powerful chieftain in Trøndelag. A thief who had formerly been connected with Einar was caught in Nidaros (Trondheim). King Harald attended the meeting where this case was to be discussed, and according to *Heimskringla*, Einar was worried that the king might punish the thief. He therefore summoned his men and freed him. This was an insult to the king, and the friends they had in common attempted to settle the dispute between them. The king agreed to meet with Einar at the king's farm, but against all conventions, instead of settling the matter between them, he ordered his men to kill Einar and his son.[6]

The relationships between chieftains and kings were characterized by opportunism. A good example of this is the way Cnut the Great secured control of Norway. Snorri Sturluson tells us in the *Heimskringla* about how, in the autumn of what was probably 1027, Erling Skjalgsson, the most powerful chieftain in Vestlandet, traveled from England to Norway with his entourage. Before he left, he received great gifts from Cnut. Cnut's envoys, who also possessed great riches of the king's, journeyed together with Erling. During the winter, with Erling's support, the envoys traveled around and shared Cnut's treasures with those who pledged loyalty to him. In this way, many became friends with Cnut and promised him service in the fight against Olaf Haraldsson. Many people did this publicly, but several kept their allegiance secret.[7] When Cnut arrived in Norway in 1028, he was made king of the whole country, and Olaf fled to Russia. Olaf attempted to win his kingdom back but was ultimately unsuccessful; he was killed at the battle of Stiklestad in 1030. One of the main reasons Cnut became king and Olaf lost was that Cnut had utilized the English silver in the way he did: to establish friendships with all the most powerful chieftains in the country. As a result, Olaf really had no chance of winning the battle.

Gift giving was a useful means for Cnut to gain support, and indeed, the importance of gifts in the Viking Age cannot be overstated. Through gifts, friendships were forged and maintained. The chieftains could not refuse Cnut's gifts, as that would be seen as an insult. They probably also understood that Olaf's rule was coming to an end and therefore thought it sensible to accept the friendship of the rich and powerful King Cnut. It is also worth noting that Snorri Sturluson does not criticize the Norwegian chieftains for their change in allegiance, despite their betrayal of a king who would be venerated as a saint only a few months later and who, in Snorri's time, was the most popular Scandinavian saint. In fact, Olaf had not maintained his friendships with the chieftains through giving them gifts, and as such, according to Viking Age political culture, he had already terminated the friendships.

At this point, Cnut went against *Hávamál*'s advice about establishing friendships with one's enemy's friends. In the political game, this could be a sensible strategy. It would undermine the opponent's power, because those who were friends of both parties could not participate in the event of a war, and in the best-case scenario—which Cnut managed to make happen—one's opponents' friends would change their alliance. But otherwise, the episode in the *Heimskringla* fairly reflects the political climate in Scandinavia. To secure control over their kingdoms, kings needed to establish friendships with chieftains. Without their support, ruling was problematic. Getting rid of the chieftains by force and replacing them with loyal supporters was not a fitting strategy, since this would signal to other chieftains that their positions equally were not safe. In addition, resistance from the previous chieftains' family and friends would not make it easy for the new chieftains to build a power base. This tension was an important aspect of Scandinavian politics in the Viking Age.

Reciprocation was another key factor in the relationships between the king and his friends. In the saga about Harald Hardruler, we are told that in exchange for "grace and friendship" (*vægð ok vináttu*) one could gain Harald's "protection and fidelity" (*traust ok trúnað*).[8] In order to be the king's friend, one was expected to accept his right to rule, to be faithful, to support him in his battles, and to complete tasks on his behalf. In return, the king was expected to protect and be loyal to his friends.

The kings' and the chieftains' groups of friends were not in any way homogeneous. What bound the groups together was the friendship with the leader: the king or the chieftain. Some people were friends with only one leader, while others were friends with two. The leaders trusted those from the former group in any dispute. Support from the latter group varied from case to case, according to who the opponent was. The leaders themselves controlled the recruitment of their friendship groups. It was the leader's ambition that characterized the group and affected recruitment to it. For this reason, there could be opposing interests and even full-out conflicts within the friendship groups. Therefore the kings and chieftains highly prioritized solving the disputes between their friends, since doing otherwise risked alienating one of the parties.

However, the kings did not always form these friendships face to face. For example, Harald Fairhair and Athelstan were friends despite never having met. Another good example, albeit from a later period, is the friendship between Hakon Hakonsson (1217–1263) and the German emperor Frederick II (1212–1250). The gift exchange between these two was extensive and took

Figure 3. A royal network: Sigurd Syr (d. c. 1018), his wife Asta Gudbrandsdatter
(d. c. 1020/30), stepson Olaf (later King Olaf Haraldsson and St. Olaf), and Rani
(the Wide-Faring). Source: *Snorre Sturlason kongesagaer,* trans. Gustav Storm
(Christiania: J. M. Stenersen, 1899).

place over a long period of time. It seems that Hakon employed a man solely
to carry gifts to and from the emperor. This exchange of gifts resulted in a
"great friendship" between the two.[9] To the king and the emperor, this friendship was of great importance, because it increased their prestige in their re-
spective realms.

Regarding relationships between chieftains and householders, there are
hardly any helpful sources from Scandinavia or about Scandinavia. Iceland,
however, is another matter, and thus we will use the situation there as a model
for what such relationships probably looked like in Scandinavia. In contrast
with the more ephemeral horizontal friendships between chieftains (and between chieftains and the king), the vertical friendship between chieftains
and householders was durably loyal. To secure and renew the friendship of
the householders, the chieftains needed to give protection, distribute gifts,
and, in particular, organize feasts. If the chieftains did not meet these responsibilities, the householders were free to choose the friendship of other chieftains. This freedom of choice is also found in Early English laws from the
early 900s that state that a lord could not stop a free man from seeking a
new lord if the original lord had not fulfilled his duties to the free man.[10] In

return, the chieftains received the support of the householders, without which they did not possess any real power. It was this reciprocity that created the great strength of the bond of loyalty, to the point that in many cases, householders sacrificed their lives for their friend the chieftain.

Householders could be friends with two chieftains at the same time. This increased overall socictal security. In conflicts between their chieftains, such householders were put in the difficult position of deciding whom to support. They could not help one friend in a conflict against another, and therefore they had to attempt to negotiate. For society, it was clearly advantageous that these householders with multiple loyalties existed. They contributed significantly to creating the basis for the peace that existed in Iceland and Scandinavia during the Viking Age.

When a king or chieftain died, his networks fell apart. His sons, if there were any, did not automatically inherit their father's network. Instead, in many cases the sons organized a funeral for their father, to which they invited his friends. The burial feast or inheritance feast functioned as a way to transfer friendship ties from their father's friends to the new leader.[11] When the guests left, they often received gifts from the hosts, establishing friendship with the new leader. In other words, the burial feast was used not only to say goodbye to a father, leader, or friend, but also to reinvent his networks. If there were no heirs to pick up the networks, they would dissolve.

The funeral feast also had other functions, one of which was making promises. Svein Forkbeard is supposed to have drunk a memorial toast to his father at his burial feast and sworn that within three years, he would go to England with his army and kill King Æthelred or drive him from the country. This memorial toast had to be joined by all the guests at the inheritance feast.[12] For the king's sons and chieftains, it was important to set themselves greater goals than what their fathers had achieved. Nobody wanted to live in their father's shadow. To make sure their supporters did not shy away from these plans, the supporters also had to make the same promise.

Whether the householders or the chieftains had the most to gain from the friendship is highly debatable. I would claim that friendship was equally necessary to both parties. The strong reciprocation was its key. Without the support of the householders, the chieftains were all but powerless, and without the protection of the chieftains, the situation was very uncertain for the householders.

The importance of friendship is also indicated by the mention in the Norse sources of about forty different types of friends, a breadth of vocabulary that is unique in medieval Europe. Some of the modifiers used with *vinr* (friend) are: *alda-* (old), *alúðar-* (dear), *atgerða-* (agency), *einka-* (private), *forn-* (old), *gjaf-* (gift), *guðs-* (God's), *göfgr-* (great), *höfuð-* (main), *konungs-* (king's), *leyndar-* (secret), and *trúnaðar-* (confided in).[13] The importance of friendship is most evident in the term that was used almost without exception to describe a person with power in Viking Age society: *vinsæll*, one who has many friends.

Kinship

The kinship ties between the kings' and chieftains' families probably stretched across all of Scandinavia.[14] The marriage patterns among the elite made sure of that. But Norway, Sweden, and Denmark were relatively isolated from non-Scandinavian countries. In the west, the family ties across the North Sea with England, Scotland, and Ireland were probably not extensive. Even though there was a great deal of trade contact between the Sami people and the Swedish and Norwegian elites, and Sami women were mistresses to Swedish and Norwegian chieftains and kings, there is no reason to believe they married their children to each other. It is therefore unlikely that extensive family ties between the Sami people and Scandinavians existed. There is a good deal of evidence to indicate that this was also the case across the Baltic Sea. With regard to the southern border, marriages did occur across the Danevirke, but these were probably not very common either.[15] In many ways, then, Scandinavia was its own universe when it came to kinship.

Kinship ties within Scandinavia were still not especially strong, however. This was because of the bilateral kinship system, in which one's kin was traced through both the mother's and the father's sides of the family. Only legitimate children had identical kinship groups. Their parents each had their own, and the same went for grandparents, and so on. It is important to note that the bilateral kinship system in Scandinavia had clear patrilineal features, best expressed through the patronymic name custom. Children's last names were usually based on their father's given name, as for example with *Haraldsson* (Harald's son) or *Haraldsdottir* (Harald's daughter).

Kinship overlaps were extensive (figure 4), which resulted in unclear obligations of support. The terms "kin" (*frændi, æt, køn/kyn*) and "kinswoman"

Figure 4. Kinship: Gunhild the King-Mother and her sons. Source: *Snorre Sturlason kongesagaer*, trans. Gustav Storm (Christiania: J. M. Stenersen, 1899).

(*frænka, frændkona*) were primarily used to describe the relationship to a son, daughter, father, mother, grandson, granddaughter, grandfather, grandmother, brother, sister, nephew, niece, uncle, aunt, or cousin. Kinship, in other words, usually extended for three generations, counted from the same paternal grandfather. Because of all these overlaps, it was impossible to maintain the same contact with all one's kin. It was therefore important to nurture relationships with distant, powerful kinship members. For this reason, chieftains' families were larger than normal families, and they counted five generations back instead of three. This expansion was also advantageous to the powerful family members, since they controlled the marriages of both their male and female kin and were able to use them as pieces in their power games.

In many cases, friendship ties were also necessary to reinforce the bonds of kinship. This is most clearly shown through the sagas' formulation of friends and relatives. That friends were regarded as a more important support group than family members is evident in *Hávamál*. The poem provides a detailed description of how friendship is to be nurtured, but no such advice is given when it comes to kinship. We could presume that family loyalty was so obvious a given that it did not need mentioning, but if kinship were that important to the political game, we would expect it to be featured in a poem whose purpose was to guide people through life.

Exchange of Information

We do not know much about what relationships between members of different networks were like. Contact between members of chieftains' networks was probably more frequent than in the kings' networks. This is because the chieftains' networks were more circumscribed by local and regional boundaries than the kings' networks, which stretched across the whole of the realm as well as beyond its borders. We can suppose that in the smaller chieftains' networks, most of the members were able to see each other regularly at local *þing*, at meetings, or in the chieftain's hall. Even though the smaller size of the networks meant a lesser degree of power, we must not forget that the mobilization of the smaller networks was quicker, and in some cases that was just as important as size.

The different parties in these networks had different tasks or roles, and the power they acquired depended on their relationship to the leaders of the networks. Kings and chieftains surrounded themselves with counselors, and we can assume that in many cases, the royal advisers were in fact chieftains themselves. In this way, they were part of the king's network at the same time they were the leaders of their own. One person could have several roles in the same network, including adviser, friend, kinsman, and *hirðmaðr*.

Interplay in a network largely depended on what was exchanged. Support, protection, gifts, and feasts were all necessary currency in the networks we have examined. However, the exchange of information was also critical. In all networks, there were people whose position was distant. Nevertheless, there is no reason to underestimate their importance, especially when it came to maintaining the flow of intelligence to the leader. For the leaders of the networks to make the right decisions, they needed to be well acquainted with the political situation within their chiefdoms and in the kingdom at large. The political landscape could change radically overnight—for example, with the death of a king—and therefore information was crucial to the political elite. In addition to one's networks, *þing*, meetings, and religious gatherings were essential arenas for gathering intelligence and passing it on. Merchants and travelers were also valuable informants. It is partly because of this that we find so many trading sites near the kings' and chieftains' residences, and it is also among the reasons that kings established towns near their farms. When Ohthere of Hålogaland traveled to Kaupang, then to Hedeby, and then to the English court, he did not just bring goods. Equally important was the knowledge he brought with him, not only from his local home area, but from all the places he had visited along the way to England. It was not easy to keep secrets in Viking Age society. All decisions were made publicly, in the hall or at the *ping*. It was therefore easy for visitors to gain information about the latest news, especially if they belonged to the social elite.

Not every member of the social elite had their own network. Rather, only the sons and daughters whom the chieftain or the householder thought promising merited one. Daughters considered suitable for marriage could set up networks, establishing friendships through gift giving with men outside and inside the family. When these girls were married, they thus brought to the marriage not only a dowry, but also their own networks, which usually supplemented their husbands'. If these women became widows, or ran their farms while their husbands were away, they controlled both networks.

Viking Age society was a network society, in the sense that power was built and exerted through networks. We should differentiate between network power, the collective power of the members of a network to execute actions and plans, and agent power, the power of an individual to influence the network's decisions. Network power depended on the overlaps between the agents in a conflict. All of the most powerful agents during the Viking Age belonged to several networks, including that of the king. Kings' networks included the networks of most if not all of the chieftains in their kingdoms. In addition, they featured prominent members such as other kings or members of royal families (including queens, who had their own networks). Because of its size and composition, the king's network was usually a great deal stronger than those of the chieftains. The overlapping friendship and kinship ties within these various networks affected the development and results of conflicts. The kings and chieftains held these networks together, and their opinions were crucial when important decisions were to be made. But to the network leaders, it was important to obtain as high a level of assent as possible, as this increased the likelihood of their success.

Further Reading

Ashby, Steven P., and Søren M. Sindbæk, eds. *Crafts and Social Networks in Viking Towns.* Oxford: Oxbow Books, 2020.

Buko, Andrzej, ed. *Bodzia: A Late Viking-Age Elite Cemetery in Central Poland.* Leiden: Brill, 2014.

Carrington, Peter J., John Scott, and Stanley Wasserman, eds. *Models and Methods in Social Network Analysis.* Cambridge: Cambridge University Press, 2005.

Castells, Manuel. "A Network Theory of Power." *International Journal of Communication* 5 (2011): 773–87.

Jesch, Judith. *The Viking Diaspora.* London: Routledge, 2015.

Kenna, Ralph, and Pádraig MacCarron. "Character Networks of the *Íslendinga Sögur* and *Þættir.*" In *Nordic Elites in Transformation, c. 1050–1250,* vol. 2, *Social Networks,* edited by Kim Esmark, Lars Hermanson, and Hans Jacob Orning, 144–68. New York: Routledge, 2020.

Lind, John H. "Nordic and Eastern Elites: Contacts across the Baltic Sea: An Exiled Clan." In *Nordic Elites in Transformation, c. 1050–1250,* vol. 2, *Social Networks,* edited by Kim Esmark, Lars Hermanson, and Hans Jacob Orning, 104–24. New York: Routledge, 2020.

MacCarron, Pádraig, and Ralph Kenna. "Network Analysis of the *Íslendinga Sögur*— the Sagas of Icelanders." *European Physical Journal B* 86 (2013): 1–9.

———. "Viking Sagas: Six Degrees of Icelandic Separation: Social Networks from the Viking Era." *Significance* 10 (2013): 12–17.

Missuno, Marie Bønløkke. "Contact and Continuity: England and the Scandinavian Elites in the Early Middle Ages." In *Nordic Elites in Transformation, c. 1050–1250,* vol. 2, *Social Networks,* edited by Kim Esmark, Lars Hermanson, and Hans Jacob Orning, 125–43. New York: Routledge, 2020.

Östborn, Per, and Henrik Gerding. "Network Analysis of Archaeological Data: A Systematic Approach." *Journal of Archaeological Science* 46 (2014): 75–88.

Sigurðsson, Jón Viðar. *Viking Friendship: The Social Bond in Iceland and Norway, c. 900–1300.* Ithaca, NY: Cornell University Press, 2017.

Sindbæk, Søren M. "Networks and Nodal Points: The Emergence of Towns in Early Viking Age Scandinavia." *Antiquity* 81 (2007): 119–32.

———. "The Small World of the Vikings: Networks in Early Medieval Communication and Exchange." *Norwegian Archaeological Review* 40 (2007): 59–74.

Chapter 4

PEACE AND CONFLICT RESOLUTION

The introduction of this book claimed that Scandinavia was a peaceful region during the Viking Age. Of course, conflicts did happen between kings, between pretenders to the throne, between kings and chieftains, and between chieftains, and people must have been killed in connection with battles of honor—which is why *Hávamál* advises that no one set forth without his weapons.[1] There is nevertheless no reason to believe that such conflicts were commonplace. The most important factor contributing to the generally peaceful situation was the social networks that stretched across the whole region. Without close collaboration among the social elite, it would have been difficult, if not impossible, for them to plunder and trade extensively abroad. Additionally, resolving conflicts mostly revolved around creating new social networks. In this chapter we will look at this and other methods, but before we get there, let us first have a look at the limitations the social networks created for armed conflict between kings.

Kings and Wars

Let us once more return to *Heimskringla*'s description of the peace agreement between Harthacnut and Magnus in 1036.

> The following spring [1036] both the kings called up levies, and the word got around that they would be engaging in battle by the Göta River. But as the two armies advanced on each other until they were close to meeting, the *lendir menn* from each army sent intelligence to their relatives and friends, with the messages that people were to make peace between the kings. . . . Twelve men, the best men from each kingdom, swore along with the kings that this agreement should be kept as long as any of them lived. Then the kings parted, and each went back to his kingdom, and this agreement was kept as long as they lived.[2]

Here, the overlapping network ties are clearly visible. The leading men of both armies had strong kinship and friendship ties to each other. Such bonds extended across all of Scandinavia; it is therefore probable that similar issues of conflicting obligations and loyalty applied in other cases of conflict or internal warfare in Scandinavia. Such circumstances obviously contributed to reducing societal tensions and internal strife. With close social bonds that crisscrossed the battlefield, not only was it difficult to find an enemy to fight, but one also risked killing the friend or the kinsman of the good friend one fought alongside. During and after battles, men could give *grið* (truce) to their friends and kin, an oath which signified that they guaranteed their personal security. Having a kinsman or friend on the opposite side of an armed conflict was thus a kind of life insurance.

These social overlaps were problematic for the kings, however. To solve this, they recruited men to their *hirð* from outside the networks of the social elite—men of low social status and foreigners. These men's loyalty was not divided, and they could kill anyone with a clear conscience. Apparently, this distinction between the social elite and men of lower status and foreigners in the *hirð* became institutionalized at some point. As we have seen, Olaf Haraldsson was the first king in Scandinavia to divide the *hirð* into *hirðmenn* and *gestir* (guests). The *hirðmenn* were usually from good families and consequently had a higher social status and carried out different tasks from the guests, who could be used as something similar to police.

Figure 5. Viking ships in battle. Source: *Snorre Sturlason kongesagaer,* trans. Gustav Storm (Christiania: J. M. Stenersen, 1899).

The Viking Age battles described as the bloodiest are usually those where we find the highest percentage of foreigners. At the battle of Helgeå in Skåne, between Cnut the Great on one side and Olaf Haraldsson and Anund Jacob on the other, we can presume that a great part of Cnut's men came from England and the Baltics. These men therefore had no friends or kinsmen on the other side of the battle, and were able to fight for their king without taking into consideration whom they were fighting.

In the story about the 1036 agreement between Magnus and Harthacnut, the narrative focuses on the leading men in the kings' parties and their networks, but no relationship between the kings themselves is mentioned. This is somewhat surprising, considering Scandinavian royalty's use of marriage to further its goal of establishing alliances. A good example of this policy is the marriages used to create peace between the Danish and Norwegian kings around 1069. We have seen how Harald Hardruler and Svein Estridsson agreed not to attack each others' kingdoms, which allowed Harald to attack England in 1066. He died in the attempt, and his two sons, Magnus and Olaf Kyrre, succeeded him to the Norwegian throne. Svein believed that the agreement had ceased to exist with Harald's death, and he traveled to Norway with an army. Magnus and Olaf also gathered a large army between them, but before the battle began, envoys traveled between the two parties to try and negotiate for peace. The Norwegians said they wanted the same agreement that Harald had made with Svein, or else they would fight for their kingdom in battle. Svein accepted their demand, and the kings settled the dispute. To seal the deal between them and create lasting peace, Olaf married Svein's daughter, Ingerid, and one of Svein's sons married Olaf's sister, Ingegerd.[3] Olaf's mother, Tora, probably married Svein himself. In other words, double or triple marriage deals were made. Such alliances were useful primarily to the reigning kings. Their descendants were usually not greatly affected by the alliances made by their predecessors. Marriage alliances between the Scandinavian royal houses were therefore continually made and remade to stabilize the relationships between them.

These marriage alliances were still no guarantee of peace. If the conflicts continued, they created a great problem for the women. Whom were they to support—their husbands or their original families? A good example, though a later one, is Margrete Skulesdatter. In 1217, the young Hakon Hakonsson was chosen as king of Norway instead of Skule Bardsson, Margrete's father. Two years later, Margrete was promised to King Hakon to confirm the alliance between him and Skule, who was the acting ruler of the kingdom. After a while, Hakon began to act more on his own, and in the 1230s, the relationship between the two men increasingly worsened. In 1239, Skule was crowned a king and started a rebellion against Hakon. This rebellion was brought down the year after, and Skule was killed. The year before Skule began his rebellion, Margrete had given birth to her second son. If her father had become king, it could have resulted in her son missing out on the throne, and in a worst-case scenario, possibly being killed. Thus, we presume that Margrete probably supported her husband in this conflict.

Olaf Kyrre's mother, Tora Torbergsdatter, belonged to the powerful Giske line. It is uncertain whether she was married to Olaf's father, Harald Hardruler, or was his mistress, as Harald was already married to a Russian woman, Elisiv.[4] Kings and chieftains having mistresses in addition to their wives was not unusual. Polygamous relationships such as these were entered into with the complete acceptance of the women's fathers or brothers; to what degree the women themselves were consulted in the decision is not known. But to the women and their families, the relationships (whether marriage or concubinage) were beneficial, because the women became part of the king's household and were thus under his protection. This established strong relationships between the families and the kings. If the women gave birth to sons who later became kings, as Tora did, it not only brought honor to their families but also gave them access to the riches of the royal seat. Whether Tora was Harald Hardruler's mistress or wife, the relationship was important to him as well because it afforded him the support of one of the most powerful families in the whole nation. In chapter 3, about network societies, we argued that kinship ties were not as strong as friendship ties. This does not mean, however, that kinship was inconsequential to the political game, especially among the social elite.

The hazards of demography were always a problem for the reigning dynastic power, since an heir born within wedlock was never guaranteed. Kings had to produce royal heirs to maintain their authority, which they often did through so-called polygynous reproduction, meaning that they fathered children by several women.[5] The kings of Norway, as well as other kings in Scandinavia, were promiscuous, as the sagas make clear. In fact, in contrast to most of the mothers of the local lords or kings elsewhere in Europe, the Norwegian kings' mothers usually were women of low birth. This emphasized the male dynastic line.[6] But it also meant that a king could not expect any support from his mother's side of the family, as they might not be in a position to offer any. In the dialogue between Magnus Olafsson, the son of St. Olaf Haraldsson, and his mother Alvhild, Magnus complains about his mother's family: "Many people owe a great deal to their fathers, and none more than I in most matters, but he did not choose a good mother for me." She said, "You should not blame him regarding this account because he has made a lesser choice, but you should rather honor me more for the father I found for you."[7]

One way to establish or enforce alliances among kings and chieftains was for them to foster one another's sons. Fosterage, a "method of childrearing whereby adults, other than the biological parents, undertook to raise a child for a particular period of time," was an important element of alliance building and established strong ties of loyalty between families.[8] It was "therefore a useful diplomatic tool within the network of chiefs and kings"—a kind of "peace-weaving."[9] Many kings in the Viking period let noble families foster their sons. As we saw, Hakon Adalsteinfostre was sent to Wessex to be fostered at one of Europe's most influential courts. By letting noblemen foster the kings' sons (daughters were almost never fostered), the kings both gave their sons another family and built them a power base at the same time. The foster parents often had sons of their own, and those sons were expected to support the king who had been their foster brother once he took over his father's holdings. The future king could also use his foster family's networks. Fostering was obviously beneficial to the foster families, as it increased their social status, but more importantly, these ties gave the families better access to the royal treasury.

Marriage and fostering were not the only method of reconciling conflict. Hostages were also exchanged to create peace. In the *Ynglinga saga*, Snorri tells us how Odin set out with an army against the Vanir, but they defended themselves well. After a long war in which the parties took turns winning battles, both sides grew weary, and so they arranged a negotiation where they established peace and exchanged hostages. The Vanir offered up their best men, Njord and his son Freyr, and the Aesir offered the promising future chieftain Haenir and the wise Mimir (girls were not given as hostages).[10] Such an exchange of hostages to ensure both sides honored an agreement also happened in conflicts between the Scandinavian kings.

Without exception, hostages were drawn from among those held in the highest regard and were undoubtedly treated well while in the enemy's care. In this way, one ensured the good nature of future relationships. The difference between being a king's hostage and a king's foster son was primarily the greater degree of compulsion or force in the former situation. But although the starting point was different, the boys exchanged as hostages were never mistreated, and they became important members of the household. And the goal remained the same in both cases—creating positive relationships among all those involved: chieftains and/or kings, the boys who were fostered, and often the sons of their foster parents.

Of course, the headstrong chieftains did not always accept the decisions made by the kings, and they often acted without consulting them, as, for example, when Ulf the Earl made Harthacnut king of Denmark. In conflicts between the chieftains and the kings, it was not unusual for the chieftains to give the king *sjálfdæmi* (self-rule), which is to say that he alone was to decide the outcome of the disagreement. The saga episodes relating to these conflicts do not always use the term *sjálfdæmi* explicitly, but there is no doubt that the kings were indeed afforded this option. Giving one's opponent the right to decide the outcome of a conflict was a sign that one recognized him as the more powerful person. This was an important signal, not only to the

king but to all of society, of one's understanding of the hierarchical order; at
the same time, it signaled a desire for resolution and eventual friendship. To
the king, it was essential that the chieftains accept him as their superior, and
in return, he was expected to make his generosity known by being considerate and demanding only a small tribute from the chieftains.

Chieftains and Conflicts

Chieftains naturally came into conflicts with other chieftains. But how were
these conflicts brought to an end? Here, as in many other important areas,
the Scandinavian sources cannot help us, and we have to seek answers from
territories outside of Scandinavia to get some idea of how such disagreements
were resolved.[11] In conflicts where both chieftains were friends of the king,
he needed to find a solution that was agreeable to both parties. Otherwise,
he risked losing the support of one of them, possibly to another king or pre-
tender. The kings, in other words, were in the same situation as the chieftains, who needed to resolve conflicts between their friends with agreements
that all involved could accept, or risk not only losing the support of one of
the parties, but even worse, losing face. To the chieftains, it was crucial to
maintain the peace in their chiefdoms. The chieftains thus had the same obligations to their friends as the kings had to theirs. In disputes between two
chieftains where only one was a friend of the king, the king had to support
his friend against the other chieftain.

In many cases where no royal power existed, such as in Norway in the
early Viking Age, or where kings had few opportunities to become involved
in local disputes, which was the case for most of the Viking Age, the local
community needed to find a way to settle disagreements between their chieftains. There are many indications that most conflicts in Scandinavia were
resolved privately, for example through the use of settlement meetings in
which the intention was to reach a compromise. To settle a dispute, the social networks needed to become involved: friends, friends' friends, and kin.
The Viking Age and High Middle Ages in Norway saw the use of the *dómr*,
a twelve- or six-man *nefnd* (committee). Each of the disputing parties named
half of the *dómr*, whose primary purpose was to act as a commission for arbitration or settlement and to find a solution acceptable to both parties.[12] Settlement was the best way of preventing the polarization of the local

community. It was perceived as more solid and more of a commitment than a verdict, which would be difficult to enforce—for who would do the enforcing? This emphasis on compromise is well known from Europe during the period of around 500 to 1100. Most people went to the courts, if they existed in some shape or form, only if there were no other options for ending the disagreement. Neither Roman nor Germanic laws restricted mediation or compromise—far from it. On the contrary, the courts often encouraged people to settle their own disputes. It was the most successful way of restoring peace.

The significance of arbitration and compromise is clearly visible in Iceland during the Free State period (930–1262/64). Householders who felt their rights had been violated or who had gotten themselves into conflicts—related to killings, allegations of murder, or disputes over inheritance, for instance—appealed to their chieftain for support. Because of the strong friendship ties between the chieftains and householders, the chieftains needed to support their friends, no matter what. When a conflict arose, mediators usually got involved. They were very frequently friends with both of the two involved chieftains and were therefore unable to support one friend against the other. The main aim of the mediators was to get the opposing parties to call a temporary truce so they could attend a meeting of settlement, or, even more importantly, to make the chieftains consent to arbitration and remain at peace until the arbitration award was announced. Letting cases such as these enter arbitration usually meant that the parties appointed an even number of arbitrators, similar to the Norwegian *dómr*—private judges who were to decide on the outcome.

The arbitrators were bound by procedure but were expected to make their judgement based on common sense. If the arbitrators did not come to an agreement, they were supposed to draw lots. The person who won the draw was to swear an oath before he made the award known. Chieftains were typically chosen to decide arbitration awards. The arbitrators were therefore people whose influence was equal or superior to that of the involved parties. Most of the arbitrators were also friends and/or kin of the party they represented. The arbitrators were under immense pressure not only because of their relationships with the opposing parties, but also because it was necessary to reach an agreement that both sides would accept and not consider an insult, since the arbitrators had reason to imagine that the roles would be reversed at a later date. It was important that the opposing parties obeyed the arbitration agreement, since doing otherwise would have been considered an insult to the arbitrators and could develop into hostile relations. Most conflicts in Iceland were ended through arbitration over the duration of a few weeks or months. In this way, chieftains were able to avoid conflicts that were drawn out for decades. A central aspect of arbitration was that it made it possible for the involved chieftains to withdraw from a conflict with their honor intact. After the case had been settled to the satisfaction of both parties, they often exchanged gifts and thus established friendships. The resolving of a conflict could therefore completely change the political landscape. Those who had previously been enemies became friends and allies.[13]

A small number of cases in Iceland were treated in the courts. In most of these cases, one of the parties was a chieftain and the other a man without the support of a chieftain. In cases such as these, the outcome was already clear—the man without support would be declared an outlaw. Because there was no central government in Iceland to uphold justice, the chieftain was supposed to execute the verdict. If two chieftains of equal power came into conflict, and one of them secured the conviction of the other chieftain or one of his clients at the *Alþingi*, the national assembly, there was a possibility that the chieftain who had won the case would be unable to execute it because of resistance from his enemy. The judicial system was for this reason unsuited to resolving disputes. The system for ending conflicts used in Free State Iceland was developed in accord with this political structure. Its main purpose was to reach solutions that the chieftains would find acceptable, and at the same time, to create peace in the local community. The goal was not justice and obedience according to the law, but rather peace and the honor of the chieftains.[14]

Þing and Laws

What laws were valid in which parts of Scandinavia during the Viking Age is unclear. Most of the surviving laws from the Middle Ages are from the thirteenth and fourteenth centuries. The oldest of the law codes is the *Gulaþing* law, which was probably written at the end of the eleventh century, though the oldest preserved handwritten fragments of it date from the twelfth century. The *Gulaþing* law is divided into the Magnus text (after King Magnus Erlingsson), which is a revision of the law probably dating to 1163 CE, and the Olaf text, which possibly originates from King Olaf Haraldsson. As we have seen, it was most probably Hakon Adalsteinfostre who laid the foundations for royal law in Norway.

It is evident that it was important for the kings to make laws, or at least to be portrayed as doing so. We know nothing about the topics the earliest laws covered, but they probably included trade, marriage, inheritance, and fines for killings. However, since the royal administration was not strong enough to enforce these laws, it was down to each individual to protect his rights—which is where the local chieftains enter the picture. The householder and his household were in a particularly vulnerable position without help and protection from the chieftain. In other words, having rights was one thing, but claiming and protecting them was another. The *þing* were likely very important arenas for the resolution of conflicts, since the social networks were able to exert pressure on the parties involved and see that the disputes were resolved to everyone's satisfaction.

There is a general consensus that local and regional *þing* were fundamental parts of Viking Age society, and that both free men and women participated in them. At the *þing*, participants made decisions concerning the public, for example in connection with conflicts. The *þing* were also essential for spreading news from both inside and outside the realm. Parents could find spouses for their children there, and the *þing* were also important trading sites. It is the combination of the different functions that made the *þing* natural centers of Scandinavia's social structure. The term *þing* was generally only used to describe *þing* meetings, with *mót* and *fundr* often used for other official meetings. This somewhat clear distinction between *þing* and *mót* and *fundr* is not known from Europe, where the terms *placitum, curia, synodus,* and *conventus* were used to refer to both types of gatherings.[15]

In Scandinavia there were probably about fifteen larger regional administrative regional lawthings (*lögþing*) by the end of the Viking Age.[16] The saga about St. Olaf Haraldsson tells of an old Swedish custom from pagan times, that there should be a *blót* (sacrificial feast) in Uppsala sometime between mid-February and mid-March. At this time, according to the saga, people from all across Svealand would gather there and *blóta* (sacrifice) in the hopes of a good harvest, peace, and victories for the king. The occasion was also used to hold a *þing* for all Swedes, and at the same time, there would be a market and a fair for the duration of a whole week. After Christianization, Uppsala continued to host the *þing* and the market, but the date was changed to February 2.[17] That Uppsala was regular host to a *þing* for the Swedish kingdom, similar to what Frosta in Trøndelag was to the *Frostaþing* in Norway, there is little reason to doubt. What is surprising is that the meeting places for most of the *þing*s are unknown to us. This is probably because of the tendency of power centers to change location, and because a rotation of the *þing* sites evened out the expenses of the participating householders.

In addition to the fifteen or so great regional lawthings, there existed a number of local *þing*. In the *Gulaþing* law, we read that the *einvirkjar* (householders who ran their own farms with the help of a person under the age of sixteen) were required to attend three *þing*—*manndrápsþing* (manslaughter *þing*, assembled in connection with killings or murders), *konungsþing* (king's *þing*, assembled when a king was to be declared), and *manntalsþing* (assembled when an overview of the population eligible to be draft into the *leiðangr* [naval levy] was to be made)—while for "all other *þing* the *einvirki* should sit at home."[18] What "all other *þing*" refers to is unclear, but we can at least ascertain that there were many local *þing*, and that they must have been organized on an ad hoc basis in different places at different times. There is little reason to suppose that the situation was any different in other parts of Scandinavia. This means that we know of only a very small number of *þing* sites from the Viking

Figure 6. The king (Olaf Haraldsson) speaking at a *þing*. Source: *Snorre Sturlason kongesagaer*, trans. Gustav Storm (Christiania: J. M. Stenersen, 1899).

Age. Those few we do know of were located close to the chieftains' centers, such as the Trondenes-*þing* near Harstad, close to the chiefdom's main seat at Trondenes.

The *þing* were not very democratic. Chieftains and kings ruled on just about everything. They were the ones who spoke first:

> King Hakon came to Frostaþing, where a large group of householders had gathered. When the þing was assembled, the king made a speech. He started by stating that it was his message and plea to householders and tenants, wealthy and poor, and the whole of the population, young and old, rich and poor, women and men, that they should let themselves be baptized and believe in one God, Christ, son of Mary, and turn away from all sacrificing and heathen gods, honor the weekend and not work every seventh day, and fast the seventh of each day. But as soon as the king had said this, loud protestations arose from the gathering. The householders complained that the king would take their work from them, and said that with such an arrangement, the land could not be maintained. Workmen and thralls shouted that they could not work were they not fed.[19]

Yet, the chieftains and kings needed to obtain the consent of the participants of the *þing*, since this was the best way of ensuring peace in the chiefdom or kingdom. This is clearly expressed in Rimbert's chronicle of Ansgar and the town *þing* at Birka, where as we have seen, the missionary Ansgar asked the Swedish king Olof for permission to work as a missionary. The king called his chieftains to consult with him. They agreed on drawing lots, which means that the gods were to decide on the outcome. The result turned out to be positive for Ansgar. Afterward, the case and the result of the draw were proclaimed to the *þing* at Birka, and the *þing* participants agreed to allow Ansgar to carry out his mission.[20]

Conflicts are an unavoidable part of any society. In scholarly work, disputes have often been interpreted as disruptive to social development, and not as a stabilizing process that actually helped uphold the social structure. Yet the conflicts in Scandinavia led to a unity between the involved parties, and as such, created an identity. The conflicts were important to chieftains because they could use the difficult situations to show off their power, determination, and suitability to maintain order within their chiefdoms. It is unlikely that the kings got involved in local disputes on any large scale, but they did involve themselves in conflicts between their chieftain friends. Much evidence points to the existence of set rules for how the conflicts were to be handled, which contributed to cementing the social structure. Greater overlaps between the chieftains' and kings' networks proved advantageous to ensuring peace in Viking Age society. Under those circumstances, there would always be individuals who needed to negotiate.

Further Reading

Barnwell, Paul S., and Marco Mostert, eds. *Political Assemblies in the Earlier Middle Ages.* Turnhout: Brepols, 2003.

Brink, Stefan, Oliver Grimm, Frode Iversen, Halldis Hobæk, Marie Ødegaard, Ulf Näsman, Alexandra Sanmark, et al. "Comments on Inger Storli: 'Court Sites of Arctic Norway: Remains of Thing Sites and Representations of Political Consolidation Processes in the Northern Germanic World during the First Millennium AD.'" *Norwegian Archaeological Review* 44 (2011): 89–117.

Iversen, Frode. "Concilium and Pagus: Revisiting the Early Germanic Thing System of Northern Europe." *Journal of the North Atlantic* 5 (2013): 5–17.

Pollington, Stephen. "The Mead-Hall Community." *Journal of Medieval History* 37 (2011): 19–33.

Riisøy, Anne Irene. "Eddic Poetry: A Gateway to Late Iron Age Ladies of Law." *Journal of the North Atlantic* 8 (2015): 157–71.

———. "Performing Oaths in Eddic Poetry: Viking Age Fact or Medieval Fiction?" *Journal of the North Atlantic* 8 (2016): 141–56.

———. "Sacred Legal Places in Eddic Poetry: Reflected in Real Life?" *Journal of the North Atlantic* 5 (2013): 28–41.

———. "Vǫlundr: A Gateway into the Legal World of the Vikings." In *Narrating Law and Laws of Narration in Medieval Scandinavia*, edited by Roland Scheel, 255–74. Berlin: Walter de Gruyter, 2020.

Semple, Sarah, and Alexandra Sanmark. "Assembly in North West Europe: Collective Concerns for Early Societies?" *European Journal of Archaeology* 16 (2013): 518–42.

Sigurðsson, Jón Viðar. "The Role of Arbitration in the Settlement of Disputes in Iceland c. 1000–1300." In *Law and Disputing in the Middle Ages: Proceedings of the Ninth Carlsberg Academy Conference on Medieval Legal History 2012*, edited by Kirsi Salonen, Per Andersen, Helle Møller Sigh, and Helle Vogt, 123–35. Copenhagen: DJØF Publishing, 2013.

Storli, Inger. "Court Sites of Arctic Norway: Remains of Thing Sites and Representations of Political Consolidation Processes in the Northern Germanic World during the First Millennium A.D." *Norwegian Archaeological Review* 43 (2010): 128–44.

Chapter 5

Honor and Posthumous Reputation

In all societies, ideologies convey the "right" world order, and prescribe what power relations are supposed to look like.[1] This was also the case during the Viking Age. The ideology was dynamic and constantly changing, its development closely connected with politics and the economy. This was particularly the case when it came to religion, which was the main element of all ideologies in premodern societies. We will return to the Norse religion in chapter 7. In this chapter, we will concentrate on four visible, concrete tools used during the Viking Age to shape the ideology of the population: feasts, gifts, skaldic poetry, and monumental burial mounds. Through the use of these, the ideology became public, something that everyone could experience. At the same time, the feasts, skaldic poetry, and burial mounds helped bring honor to the members of the social elite and ensure a good posthumous reputation for them. Ideologies are therefore about legitimizing not only the power structures of their society, but also the duties and expectations that accompanied those power structures.

The Feast

The farms used as residences by the kings and chieftains were the centers of society. They were favorably situated to facilitate communication, with trading posts and *þing* sites frequently located nearby. These farms usually performed administrative, ceremonial, economic, military, judicial, religious, and ideological tasks. They therefore needed to be distinguishable from the landscape, through the size of the farm itself, for example, as well as by having a hall, burial mounds, and boathouses. Powerful men in Scandinavian society competed with each other to build the greatest hall. In the 700s, the average hall was around thirty-seven yards long, whereas forty-four yards was common in the 800s, and in the 900s the average had grown to forty-nine yards. Some of the most important halls known to us from the Viking Age, such as those in Uppsala, Leijre, Tissø, and Uppåkra, were as long as around fifty-five yards. The largest of these was Borg in Lofoten, at ninety-one yards (map 7).[2]

Competition between the chieftains also revolved around who could organize the greatest feasts. The feasts were public events that created a common experience for the participants and were probably the most straightforward and fundamental way of materializing an ideology. Political rituals, with their symbols and actions, define power in two ways. The group that participates in them has identical values and goals, while the rituals themselves show off the connection between the leaders and a divine order. The feasts were without a doubt the most important political ritual of the Viking Age, comprising the core of the political game. With them, social differences were created and re-established. Hosts could show off their generosity, not only to the participants but to the whole of society. Many different rituals were connected with the feasts; let us begin by looking at the seating arrangements.[3]

In the first stanza of *Hávamál*, a guest arrives at an unfamiliar farm. The poem states that he should be cautious, because he does not know whether his enemies are seated inside. A guest was under the protection of the householder, and an attack on him would therefore be an insult to the host and his hospitality. Nevertheless, the guest needed to be wary of enemies; he would have to guard his tongue when it came to people and business, and be careful about how much he should brag about his own accomplishments.

Hávamál then turns to the hosts and asks: Where should the guest sit?[4] Seating arrangements replicated the social hierarchy, so that those who were seated closest to the chieftain or king were the most important. If a king visited a chieftain, the king was to sit at the high seat, the most prestigious seat in the hall. The host then needed to move to the second most prestigious place, the place beside where the king was sitting. If the host knew his guest, he could be shown directly to his rightful seat in the hall. The problem arose when an unfamiliar person showed up. The guest needed to tell the host about his family background, his home, and his achievements. His clothes would also reveal his social position.[5] When all these elements had been assessed, the guest was shown to a seat. The person already sitting in that seat then needed to move one place down. This resulted in a sort of chain reaction, which culminated in the person sitting the furthest from the high seat needing to stand up and leave their position at the bench. The seating arrangement was, however, not set in stone, and by earning an upgrade, one could move up a seat. This was especially the case with the king's or chieftain's warriors.

After the guests had been seated, the feast could begin. First the food was served, with the most prestigious person offered the first helping.[6] We can assume that the leaders did not give their guest everyday food like loaf of bread or porridge, but instead more prestigious food, such as roasted meat. In one of the skaldic verses about Harald Fairhair, it is said that he would rather eat roasted meat than boiled, because it was more warrior-like. The same idea also appears in *Rígspula* and elsewhere in Eddic poetry. After the food was served, ale, mead, or wine was poured. Many sources suggest that it was the hostess who initiated the festivities. An Old English poem written in the second half of the tenth century states that she should first greet her lord (husband) and then place a full cup in his hand.[7] As the hostess poured the first cup for her husband, she also drew attention to the social hierarchy. The remaining guests were served according to their seat on the bench.

Hávamál advises the guest not to brag about himself, so as to avoid eventual confrontation and competition with other guests.[8] Such competition could take different forms. This is clearly seen in the tale of Thor and Loki's visit to Utgarda-Loki in *Snorri's-Edda*, also known as the *Younger Edda* or *Prose Edda*.[9] On their arrival, they were challenged in the sports they were best at. Loki chose eating, and Thor, drinking. Loki bragged that there was no one who could eat food faster than he could. Utgarda-Loki doubted this and called for Logi, who was sitting further down the table, to compete against Loki. A tray of meat was fetched and placed on the floor of the hall. The two contestants sat down on either side of the tray and "ate as fast as they could, and met at the middle of the tray. Loki had eaten all the meat from the bones. Logi had also eaten all the meat, as well the bones and the tray. Everyone could see that Loki had lost the game."

For Thor's drinking competition, Utgarda-Loki asked his *skutilsveinn* (table man) to fetch the horn that the *hirðmenn* usually drank from and give it to Thor. Utgarda-Loki said that it was thought to be well drunk when one could drain the horn in one go. Some could drain it in two attempts, but none were so poor at drinking that they could not empty it in three. Thor did not think the horn especially large, although it was long. He was thirsty and raised it to his mouth and drank heavily from it. When he stopped and examined how much he had drunk, there was little or no noticeable difference. Utgarda-Loki saw this and commented: "You have drunk well, but not very much. I would not have thought that Thor was not better at drinking if someone had told me so, but I now know that you will empty the horn on the second attempt." Thor did not reply to the taunt but drank "as deeply as he could. Still the other end of the horn did not raise itself as high as he wanted." When he stopped and looked, he thought the difference to be even smaller than before. Utgarda-Loki goaded Thor to make one last attempt at draining the horn. Thor became angry and "put the horn to his mouth. He drank as forcefully possible and made it last for as long as he could. When he went to examine it, the contents of the horn had sunk a little, but now he did not want to drink any more." The day after the competition, Utgarda-Loki saw Thor and Loki on their way and told them that they had been deceived. Loki had competed against a flame, and the horn that Thor had drunk from had been sunk in the ocean, and "when you look next, you will notice how much it has sunk. It is called low tide."

Drinking in the hall—who drank with whom and for how long—depended on custom. The *Ynglinga saga* tells us that when the Swedish king Granmar learned that the Viking king Hjorvard had arrived in his kingdom with an army, he sent word to Hjorvard and invited him and all his men to a feast. Hjorvard accepted the invitation. At the feast, Granmar's guests were expected to drink in the style called *tvímenningr*, with men paired off and drinking together with as many women as were available, and the remaining men drinking alone. But the custom of the Vikings, which Hjorvard's men were subject to since they were on a raid, said that even if they were feasting as guests, they should drink together as a group (*sveitard-rykkja*). This meant that it was unclear whether the drinking should be

Figure 7. A feast. Source: *Snorre Sturlason kongesagaer,* trans. Gustav Storm
(Christiania: J. M. Stenersen, 1899).

done as *tvímenningr* or as a group. King Granmar then told his daughter, Hildegunn, who was exceedingly beautiful, that she should serve ale to the Vikings. "She took a silver chalice [*silfurkálk*], filled it, and walked to King Hjorvard and said: 'To the luck and fortune of all Ylfings [Hjorvard's family], in memory of Hrolf Kraki.'" She drank the silver chalice half empty before giving it to Hjorvard. He took the chalice and her hand and told her to sit with him. "She replied that it was not Viking custom to drink *tvímenningr* together with women. Hjorvard said that he would reject the Viking custom and drink *tvímenningr* with her." Hildegunn sat with him and the two of them drank together all evening. The day after, Hjorvard asked for Hildegunn's hand in marriage, and after Granmar had taken the council of his wife and other powerful men, Hildegunn was married to Hjorvard.[10]

Let us acknowledge that the *Ynglinga saga*, which tells the stories of Scandinavian kings prior to the 800s from a thirteenth-century perspective, is a very unreliable source for political realities and happenings. However, there are still some aspects in the tale of Granmar and Hjorvard worth noting. First, there is no reason to doubt that kings, both hosts and guests, were seated in their own high seats during a guest feast. It is also certain that women participated in feasts. Thirdly, we can remark that the king's daughter was responsible for pouring ale for the Vikings, and of course she started by serving their leader and king first. This is one of the very few tales in the sagas that tell us of such a ritual. Rituals such as these are not known in the Nordic countries from the twelfth and thirteenth centuries, by which time society had moved toward segregating the sexes at such feasts. It is therefore tempting to connect this ritual with the Viking Age in which the saga is set, rather than the period in which it was written. It is also important to note that the term *silfurkalkr* (silver chalice) is not found in other sources. The drinking customs of *tvímenningr*, *sveitardrykkja*, and *einmenningr* (where each person drank on their own) are, however, well documented in other written sources.[11]

Feasts functioned to create and maintain the prestige necessary to act and be acknowledged as a leader in societies lacking formalized leadership. Here we can speak of three different types of feasts. Entrepreneur feasts revolved around a leader who gained new supporters through sharing their table, where all the guests are involved. The goal of the feast was to accrue symbolic capital that could be transformed into informal political power and to influence the group to make decisions and take action. In patron feasts, the demand for equal exchange was not present. Rather, the feast was used to showcase the differences in power and social esteem; as such, it also had ideological elements. A distinction between those who always hosted and those who were always guests was established, and the current leader was expected to arrange such feasts. These two types of feast were exclusively for the social elite, who used them to set themselves apart from the rest of the population.[12] The third kind of feast, the diacritical, is connected with a pattern of consumption different from the first two.

If we use these three models to analyze the feasts of Viking Age chieftains and kings, we need to concentrate on the first two, but especially on the second one. Patron feasts had a very clear structure when it came to who was the host and who was the guest. The host demonstrated his wealth primarily through feasts and gift giving in the hall: his expenditure on food, drink, and valuable objects, and his willingness to share them with his friends, testified to his largesse and aptitude as a leader. The significance of food can be clearly seen in the description of some of the Norwegian kings as generous with gold but cheap with food. The feasts contributed to creating and re-creating the social hierarchy, not just for those who participated but also for those who were not invited. Those who participated were the householders, *hirðmenn*, and women. The feasts also contributed to a sense of community: those who ate and drank together, belonged together.[13]

From the Kawakiutl people in nineteenth-century Canada, we know of the potlatch feast, which was characterized by a large-scale destruction of blankets and copper plates. The Kawakiutl used the crushing of these items as a way to show off their wealth and humiliate their rivals. This was a battle of possessions. Economic power is all about elevating oneself above necessity, for example by destroying possessions and through ostentatious consumption and use.[14] Viking chieftains did not destroy objects, but they needed to display their power and riches through as excessive a use as possible.

Hosts in the Viking Age also utilized the feasts to make meaningful decisions and to create the greatest possible consensus among their friends, who needed to feel that their advice was heard. However, in the end, it was still the host's word that carried the most weight. After all, he was the chieftain and/or king of the guests. Here again, we can look to Svein Forkbeard, who at the funeral feast after his father's death is supposed to have drunk a toast to his memory and made an oath to either kill the English king Æthelred or drive him out of his kingdom within three years. All the guests at the funeral feast joined in this memorial toast. Important decisions were made in full public view—there was no back room where deals were made in secret.

There were also other kinds of feasts in Viking society, such as guest feasts between householders or between chieftains, and feasts for local people or weddings, to mention a few. But these, especially those between householders, did not have the same clear-cut political-ideological profile of the feasts of the social elite.

Religious feasts, which we will discuss more thoroughly in chapter 7, had a somewhat different character than the other feasts. It appears that the chieftains led these, and that it was they who sacrificed to the gods on behalf of their friends. However, we can assume that the participants themselves brought what they were going to eat and sacrifice to the gods. Thus, the chieftain did not become a host, even though he led the feast. Sometimes the chieftain paid for all expenses; in such cases, he played a role similar to the one he enjoyed at his own feasts. There is also reason to believe that both women and children participated in the sacrificial feasts, and that it therefore became a feast for the whole of society, not just for the chieftain's friends.

The Gift

The hosts in the *Hávamál* are called *gefendr*, meaning "those who give." The poem here refers not only to food and drink, but to other gifts as well. There was, as mentioned earlier, an ongoing rivalry between chieftains and kings over who could organize the greatest feasts, but also who was able to give away the finest gifts. In addition to signifying the wealth of the host, this was also a marketing trick to acquire more friends and thus expand one's power base. For the kings and chieftains, it was a matter of giving the right types of gifts—jewelry, good horses, gold, rings, clothes, and weaponry—to the right people at the right time.

Three parties participated in the gift-giving process: the giver, the receiver, and the spectators, who were probably the most important of the three. The gift giving occurred openly, and to the kings and chieftains, it was imperative that as many people as possible witness the event, hear about it, or come to behold the gift itself, either as it was bestowed or when it was displayed at a later time. Those who received the gifts were supposed to show them off, according to the *Hávamál*. The friendship between giver and receiver should be visible to everyone. Being mentioned positively was the best form of publicity. However, the kings and chieftains understood that their generosity was going to be compared with the generosity of other chieftains and kings— and not just their contemporaries, but also leaders of the past.

The gifts were deeply symbolic, with custom dictating who gave what to whom. Weaponry was usually given to a recipient lower in the social hierarchy, by kings and chieftains to *hirðmenn* and householders; that is, those who received a weapon were subordinate to the giver. King Athelstan in England supposedly sent a man to Harald Fairhair. He approached the king with a "sword ornamented with gold on hilt and handle, and the whole scabbard was decorated with gold and silver and set with precious stones." The messenger held out the hilt of the sword to the king and said: "Here is a sword, which King Athelstan said you were to receive." The king took the hilt in his grip, and then the messenger is supposed to have said: "Now you have accepted it as our king wished, and now you shall be his subject, since you have received his sword."

To balance the books, the following summer Harald sent his man Hauk Long-Leg to England, along with Harald's young son, Hakon. Hauk traveled to King Athelstan in London, was greeted, and then, as Snorri tells it:

Hauk took the boy Hakon and put him on King Athelstan's knee. The king looks at the boy and asks Hauk why he does that. Hauk replies: "King Harald bade you foster a handmaid's child for him." The king became very angry and grasped at a sword that was by him and drew it as if he were going to kill the boy. "You have now put him on your knee," says Hauk. "Now you can kill him if you like. However, by doing that, you will not destroy all King Harald's sons." Hauk then walked out with all his men. They went to the ship and sailed out to sea as soon as they were ready to do so, and returned to Norway to see King Harald. He was pleased, because it is a common saying that a person who fosters a child for someone is of lower rank. In such exchanges between the kings, it was evident that each of them wanted to be greater than the other, and even so, no disparity between their status came about as a result. Each sat as supreme king over his realm until his dying day.[15]

There is no reason to put too much trust in the truth of this story, but it nevertheless highlights the symbolic nature of certain objects and practices and illustrates how gifts were used to signal superiority and inferiority. The gift-giving process was publicly staged, and it was crucial to follow the rules of the game; otherwise, the purpose of the gift might be misinterpreted and

Figure 8. A gift: King Athelstan with Hauk and Harald's son, Hakon. Source: *Snorre Sturlason kongesagaer,* trans. Gustav Storm (Christiania: J. M. Stenersen, 1899).

the recipient could take offense. Leaving aside gifts to the gods for the time being, gifts usually traveled downward through the social hierarchy. It would have been almost unthinkable for a householder to approach his chieftain or king and hand him a gift. This would have been a clear breach of the rules and in a worst-case scenario could be interpreted as an insult punishable by death. Of course, such a misunderstanding could be created on purpose as well. One could bestow a gift that both the giver and the receiver would see as an insult. The rules of the game could be changed and bent.

Honor and Poems

The kings and the chieftains sustained an intense competition over honor and posthumous reputation. For this reason, it was important to have poems composed about one's achievements, so that they would be retold not only in the present, but from generation to generation, ensuring that one's heroics were eternally known. Our continued study of these poems in the present day confirms that the poems could perpetuate the posthumous reputation of great men. The skaldic poems were, in a way, a manifestation of the ruler ideology and served as proof that the kings and chieftains lived up to society's expectations.

The importance of honor and a good posthumous reputation in the Viking Age is most clearly expressed in two of the most famous stanzas of *Hávamál*:

> 76. *Cattle die, kinsmen die,*
> the self must also die;
> but the glory never dies,
> for the man who is able to achieve it.

> 77. *Cattle die, kinsmen die,*
> the self must also die;
> I know one thing which never dies:
> the reputation of each dead man.[16]

Honor comprised the basis of Viking Age society's ethical value system. The quest for honor ruled individuals' actions, and the individual's status was dependent on their honor. It therefore had to be established and protected. Honor could also be part of a type of social calculation. In a conflict or battle, the losing party lost their honor, which was transferred to the victor. In certain disputes that ended in honorable ways, both parties could still increase their capital of honor. Honor took on different forms; it interfered with people's lives in different stages and at different times. Young people were expected to be aggressive and show off, to showcase what they were capable of. Young people could of course participate in Viking voyages and raids, and through their deeds abroad acquire both honor and wealth. But when they later married, and often became leaders of their own households, they took on a new role. They should no longer challenge but rather contribute to keeping peace and order, and prudently calm down the rising generation of young warriors.[17]

Honor was very much a part of maintaining the social hierarchy. Chieftains, householders, and slaves played on the same field, but the roles they had were very different, as discussed in chapter 6. In a battle, the fiercest fighting took place around the banners of the chieftains and kings, and it was the great men together with their *hirð* who usually brought an end to the battle. Chieftains and kings were also supposed to hand out bounty when the battle was finished, and those whose efforts and deeds had been heroic were expected to receive better gifts than other members of the *hirð*. The word and gift of the chieftain carried a lot of weight, and it became a sort of tag that followed their warriors for as long as they lived.

It was important to pay close attention to what was being said in the local community. A person needed to respond to the smallest hint of loss of honor, no matter the circumstances or truth of the accusation. Those who did nothing to counteract the rumor effectively accepted its truth.

The honor we have talked about so far can be characterized as social honor, which could be used to assert oneself socially and thus climb the social ladder. But there was also another type of honor, more understated: the personal one, which was about completing one's tasks in a satisfactory way without having to challenge others.[18]

As we have mentioned, one way to accrue honor was to have poems composed about one's deeds. Most chieftains and kings in Scandinavia probably employed skaldic poets in their *hirð* in the early Viking Age, but in the later Viking Age, it seems that the skalds were mainly connected with only the most powerful of chieftains and kings. Poems about the heroes of the past were part of oral culture, performed in the hall so that everyone could listen to them, learn them, and retell them later. A good skaldic poem was the result of a complex, taxing type of poetic construction with strict rules regarding form, and linguistic flexibility and elegance were required. There were also different genres. For instance, a *drápa*, which is characterized by having a refrain, was more difficult to compose than a *flokkr*, and as such, it was a more honorable poem.[19] When the skalds composed a poem about a king, it was important that it be a *drápa* and not a *flokkr*. Chieftains, however, could receive a *flokkr*.

The *Skáldatal*, an Icelandic list of skalds from circa 1200, mentions mostly Icelandic skalds. They became an inseparable part of Norwegian courts from the reign of Harald Fairhair until well into the thirteenth century. They did not have as strong a connection with the courts of the Danish and Swedish kings. However, the oldest skald whose poems have survived to this day is Bragi Boddason the Old, who was probably Norwegian and lived during the first half of the 800s. He composed poems about Swedish and Danish kings, and a *drápa* about Ragnar Lodbrok, in return for an elaborate shield given to him by Ragnar. In its first stanza the poem refers to the shield as the "leaf of the footsoles of the thief of Þrúðr," and in the second as the "resounding boss-hubbed wheel of the maid Hǫgni."[20]

Vilið, Hrafnketill, heyra,	*Do you wish, Hrafnketill, to hear how I*
hvé hreingróit steini	shall praise the leaf of the footsoles of the
Þrúðar skalk ok þengil	thief of Þrúðr, bright-planted with colour,
þjófs ilja blað leyfa?	and the prince?
Nema svát góð ens gjalla	*Unless in such a way that the famous son of*
gjǫld baugnafaðs vildi	Sigurðr [Ragnar] should want good
meyjar hjóls enn mæri	recompense for the resounding boss-hubbed
mǫgr Sigvarðar Hǫgna.	wheel of the maid Hǫgni.
Knátti eðr við illan	*Jǫrmunrekkr then awakened with an evil*
Jǫrmunrekkr at vakna	dream among the blood-stained troops in the
með dreyrfáar dróttir	eddy of swords [battle]. There was tumult in
draum í sverða flaumi.	the hall of the chief kinsmen of Randvér,
Rósta varð í ranni	when the raven-black brothers of Erpr
Randvés hǫfuðniðja,	avenged their injuries.
þás hrafnbláir hefndu	
harma Erps of barmar.	

Such multilayered metaphors (known as "kennings"), which often included references to Norse mythology, are a hallmark of skaldic poetry. Clearly this poetry was a common feature in Scandinavian culture, since the kings and their *hirðmenn* had no trouble understanding complicated kennings when the skalds performed their poems. It is still an open question why Icelanders came to dominate skaldic poetry in the later Viking Age to such a degree. One explanation could be that they were considered more neutral because they observed the happenings in Scandinavia from the outside, and their poems were thus considered more trustworthy. The kings often bestowed lavish rewards on the skalds for their poems, and it conferred great prestige in Iceland to return home with gifts from a king.

Skalds came from the top rank of the social hierarchy, and many of them were chieftains themselves. The court skalds were all male, but this does not mean that women could not compose poems. We know of a few female poets from the Viking Age, such as Hild Hrolfsdottir and Jorunn Poet-Maiden.[21] The skalds were held in high esteem. Harald Fairhair was said to have respected his skald most among the members of his *hirð* and honored his skald with the high seat opposite his own. Many of the skalds had especially personal relationships with the kings and could criticize their actions more directly than other *hirðmenn* could. In many ways, skalds held a freer position than most others in the Viking Age society and could jump from court to court, as did Sighvatr Thordarson, whom we can link to Olaf Haraldsson, Cnut the Great, and the chieftain Erling Skjalgsson from Sola in Rogaland. Sometimes they also served as counselors or as agents on important missions.

The skalds were expected not only to compose poems of praise about the kings and chieftains, but also to entertain. To become a skald required a long period of training and tutoring. Such an education included the study and memorization of old poems, royal lineages, and stories about past and present heroes. The skalds were the traveling libraries of the Viking Age.

The Burial Mound

Beowulf, the Old English heroic poem, possibly dates from the mid-700s; its oldest preserved manuscript is dated to about 1000. In it, the hero Beowulf from Götaland asks to be buried in a burial mound on a headland so that seafarers will use it as a landmark and call it "Beowulf hill."[22] That is, the burial mound would become a point of recognition on seafaring journeys, thus memorializing Beowulf for as long as ships sailed past the headland.

There are burial mounds all across Scandinavia, but it is only the larger ones that we can identify as public monuments with a mainly, though not exclusively, ideological purpose. Viking Age great mounds (that is, mounds between twenty-two and thirty-three yards in diameter) or king's mounds (thirty-three to fifty-five yards in diameter) do not seem to have been erected in Denmark, although the Danish kings and chieftains built other types of public monuments that we can identify as "administrative symbolic-demonstrative monuments."[23] These include not just the Danevirke, but also the *trelleborg* ring fortresses, roads, and bridges. The great burial mounds are instead known from Norway and Sweden. When it comes to the eleven great ship mounds (burial mounds larger than twenty-two yards in diameter, containing remains of a ship over fifteen yards long), nine of these are within the borders of present-day Norway (map 6). Smaller boat graves are found all across Scandinavia and in areas where the Vikings settled, however. However, it must be underlined that ships and ship motifs were very important to Vikings from all over Scandinavia, as we see in the 387-yard-long ship

Figure 9. A burial mound: King Björn the Farman's howe, near Jarlsberg. Source: *Snorre Sturlason kongesagaer*, trans. Gustav Storm (Christiania: J. M. Stenersen, 1899).

formation that is part of Harald Bluetooth's grave monument to his father, the Danish king Gorm the Old.[24]

The ships were the Vikings' main tool; without them, the Viking Age would have been completely different. It seems that regular Viking ships could be made in great quantities in only a short period of time, which worked well since they needed a large quantity of them. The *Anglo-Saxon Chronicle*, which regularly records Viking ships being destroyed, abandoned, or disappearing at sea, makes it clear that the Viking ship's life span was typically short. Of course, building ships for the kings and chieftains took a longer time, because their ships needed to display their wealth and power. This is clearly expressed in the saga of Harald Hardruler:

> King Harald stayed the winter in Nidaros [Trondheim]. He had a ship built during the winter out on Eyrar. It was a *buss*-type ship [large and wide]. This ship was built after the form of Orm the long [the most famous warship in Scandinavia in the Viking Age, built for King Olav Tryggvason] and made with the finest craftsmanship. There was a dragon's head at the prow, and in the rear a curved tail, and the necks of both were all decorated with gold. It numbered thirty-five rowing benches, and was of a proportionate size, and was a most handsome vessel. The king had all the equipment for the ship carefully made, both sail and rigging, anchor and ropes.[25]

Ships that were placed inside graves look as though they were old and probably no longer in use.

In Vestfold, there are about 150 known great burial mounds. The great mounds from the Viking Age are usually larger than those raised before 800 CE. At the same time, the average diameter of the burial mound changed from 10.4 yards to 8.7 yards. This means that the contrast between the smaller and the larger burial mounds increased over the course of the Viking Age. For this reason, and because they were placed closer to the coast, the larger ones thus became more visible against the surrounding terrain. To build the great burial mounds, such as Storhaug (Great-mound) by the royal seat Avaldsnes at Karmøy in Rogaland, chiefdoms needed knowledge and control over people and material. Storhaug, which was probably constructed around the year 779, was about fifty-five yards in diameter and sixteen to twenty feet high and was made up of around 140,000 cubic feet of mass. If we suppose that a person with the tools available in the Viking Age was able to build

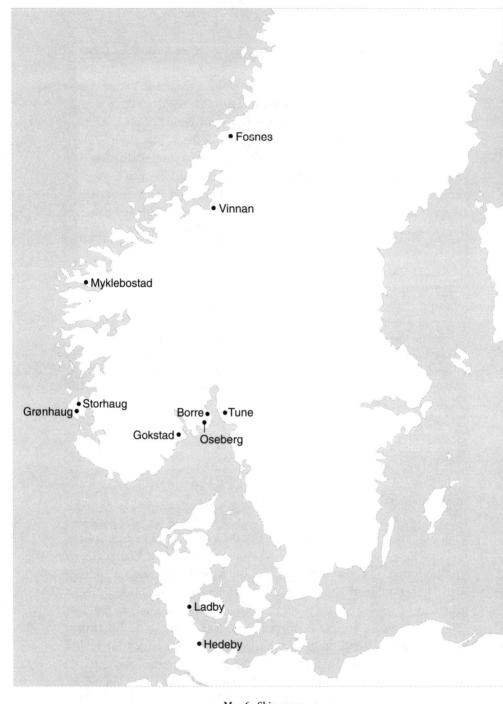

Map 6. Ship graves

about thirty-five cubic feet of mass per day, it would have taken one hundred men forty days to build the mound. The location of Storhaug resembles the one suggested in *Beowulf.* It is north of the narrowest part of the strait called Karmsundet, about twenty-seven yards above sea level.[26] These public symbols, and the excavation and re-forming of the landscape entailed by the construction of the mounds, displayed the power and wealth of these chieftains and their families: they were able to reshape nature, usually a constant in the Vikings' worldview.

Much suggests that the building of burial mounds, both large and small, followed a set ritual. Marilyn Dunn observes, "For the soul to secure admission to the world of the dead, it is necessary for the correct funerary rites to be performed." In many societies, funeral rites are "extensively elaborated" and of the "greatest importance."[27] This is clearly seen in the Oseberg mound in Vestfold. First the place was chosen, and a pit dug where the ship was to be placed. The burial chamber was constructed behind the mast, after which objects, dead animals, and people were laid in their places before being covered with earth and finally with turf (figure 8). The building of the great burial mounds took a long time, and the different steps of the process, from the leader's death to the closing of the grave, were completed in accordance with specific rituals in which the different parties—not least the leader's heirs—played central roles. It was important that the deceased be accompanied by their most valuable items, as these were to be displayed in the afterlife. At the same time, their display before burial underlined the wealth of the deceased's family.[28] There was an obvious distinction between building a large burial mound and throwing a slave into a grave.

Funerals, like weddings, are a rite of passage. Such rites commonly have three phases. The first is *parting* from one's earlier status; the next is transition, the threshold or *liminal phase*; and the third and last is the *incorporation phase* in which the person has achieved a new status. There can be some variation as to which of the three phases is the most developed or the longest. A phase can consist of a single rite and last for one day, while another might comprise a series of complex rites and stretch across several months or years. The rites of passage connected with death are aimed at both the living and the deceased. Already separated from society by their death and the subsequent funeral rites, the deceased enters the liminal phase, travels to the land of the dead, and is finally integrated into it. The living, those left behind, are first separated from the dead and then go through a period of grieving, which is the liminal phase. When the grieving period is over, the mourners need to be reintegrated into society. If the deceased person was a ruler, the liminal phase is pertinent not just to their kin but to the whole of society. Included among the separation rites at the highest levels of the social hierarchy was the moving of the dead from the place where they had been lying to the place where they were to rest, whether that was a grave, a burial mound, a coffin, or another burial place. Physical separation was accompanied by the killing of the deceased's slaves and favorite animals and the laying down of weaponry. The meal or inheritance feast that took place after the funeral was probably the most important integration rite. Its intention was to reunite all the living members of the group with each other.[29]

Archaeologists have discovered a significant amount of destruction of the mounds, often carried out relatively shortly after the burial took place. In some cases, this was connected with common pillaging. In other instances, mound break-ins were done to retrieve symbolic artifacts that could justify the successors' position of power. Alternatively, a new ruler might have wanted to show off their power by destroying the power symbols of the previous ruling family. Later, in connection with the introduction of the new Christian religion, people wanted to move their deceased relatives to churchyards.[30]

The feasts, skaldic poems, and burial mounds were all part of one common goal: displaying and memorializing the kings' and chieftains' generosity and achievements. The farms that the kings and chieftains used as residences were not just power centers, but the most important places of consumption. They allowed the kings and chieftains to display their power, wealth, and honor from their high seats in the hall. The kings and chieftains lived their lives in the public eye, and to acquire a good posthumous reputation, they needed to have done heroic deeds. The saga about St. Olaf says that Olaf's mother wanted him to become king of Norway and die young, rather than to die an old man no greater than a petty king. Though we cannot put too much trust in this saga, there is little reason to doubt that Olaf and other leaders actively cultivated a good reputation, and that in many instances they were goaded on by their own mothers. Olaf himself made a desperate attempt to regain his honor when he returned to Norway in 1030 and fought in the Battle of Stiklestad. For him, it was better to die in an honorable way than to live with shame. And in his case, we see that his death and its aftermath contributed greatly to his immortality.

Further Reading

Carstens, Lydia. "Powerful Space: The Iron-Age Hall and Its Development during the Viking Age." In *Viking Worlds: Things, Spaces and Movement*, edited by Marianne Hem Eriksen, Unn Pedersen, Bernt Rundberget, Irmelin Axelsen, and Heidi Lund Berg, 12–27. Oxford: Oxbow Books, 2014.

Dietler, Michael. "Feasting and Fasting." In *The Oxford Handbook on the Archaeology of Ritual and Religion*, edited by Timothy Ingersoll, 179–94. Oxford: Oxford University Press, 2011.

———. "Feasts and Commensal Politics in the Political Economy." In *Food and the Status Quest: An Interdisciplinary Perspective*, edited by Polly Wiessner and Wulf Schiefenhövel, 87–125. Providence, RI: Berghahn Books, 1996.

Enright, Michael J. *Lady with a Mead Cup: Ritual, Prophecy and Lordship in the European Warband from La Tène to the Viking Age*. Dublin: Four Courts Press, 1996.

Goeres, Erin Michelle. *The Poetics of Commemoration: Skaldic Verse and Social Memory, c. 890–1070*. Oxford: Oxford University Press, 2015.

Kjær, Lars, and A. J. Watson. "Feasts and Gifts: Sharing Food in the Middle Ages." *Journal of Medieval History* 37 (2011): 1–5.

Vedeler, Marianne. *Silk for the Vikings*. Oxford: Oxbow Books, 2014.

Chapter 6

CLASS AND GENDER IN VIKING SOCIETY

Viking Age society had clear-cut social classes: kings/chieftains, householders, and unfree thralls, or slaves. We do not know how large the social elite was compared to the rest of society, but it could not have been a particularly large group, possibly around 1 to 2 percent of the population. Householders and their families made up the largest group of Scandinavians. Between these two classes, the economic and social differences were significant. Socioeconomic differences within the householder class were also stark: some possessed great riches, while others had just "two goats" and lived in a "rope-raftered hall."[1] At the bottom of the social hierarchy were the unfree thralls, or slaves, with almost no rights, who probably made up about a fourth of the population. Land and birth (family background) were the foundation for power and prestige and laid the ground rules for the social hierarchy. Therefore, there was usually a visible connection between an individual's status, the size of the farm they owned, and the family they were born into. Despite these social divisions, there were opportunities to climb the social ladder or be brought up into the elite by kings and chieftains. Social demotion also occurred. In this chapter, we shall look at different aspects of the social stratification. We begin with the poem *Rígspula* and its picture of the social hierarchy. We then continue by looking at which abilities members of the elite were expected to possess. Finally, we will turn to women's roles in the various social ranks, first by getting to know the Oseberg chieftain better, before we look at how women are portrayed in *Hávamál*.

Chieftains, Householders, and Thralls

In *Rígspula*, one of the Eddic poems, we find an explanation of how the three classes of the Viking Age—the ruler, the householder, and the thrall—came into being, and the skills and tasks connected to the different positions. We will use the poem as a source demonstrating how the people themselves explained social divisions and the organization of power in Viking society. We will, in other words, study the poem as an *ideological* source. But first, a few comments on the dating of the poem. Scholars have suggested that it was composed between the late 800s and the late 1200s.[2] In my opinion, much points toward *Rígspula* dating from the Viking Age. The most important point supporting this argument is that the society described in the poem is not reconcilable with the social hierarchy we know from Scandinavia in the 1100 and 1200s. By that time, for example, most of the householders had become tenants, and slaveholding had disappeared.

Rígspula tells the story of the god Heimdall traveling disguised among the humans and going by the name of Rig (Rígr). The first people he visited were Great-Grandmother and Great-Grandfather, and he stayed with them for three nights. They served him "loaf of bread, thick and heavy" and "boiled calf-meat, the best of delicacies" in a bowl. Every night he slept between them. Nine months later, Great-Grandmother gave birth to a son. He was "swarthy" and called Thrall (Þræll).

> 8. *He began to grow and to thrive well;*
> on his hands there was wrinkled skin,
> knotted knuckles, . . .
> thick fingers, he had an ugly face,
> a crooked back, long heels.

Thrall wove "bast rope to make bundles" and carried home "brushwood" the whole day. Eventually, Thir (Þír), a slave girl, came to the farm. She had "mud on her soles," her arms were "sunburned," and her nose was "bent." Thrall and the slave girl were not married, because they were the property of their master, but they had a number of children. Their tasks were, among others, to make fences, fertilize the fields, raise pigs, herd goats, and dig turf, and from them all the families of thralls are descended.[3]

Rig continued his travels and came upon a hall where a fire was burning on the floor.

> *15. The man was carving wood for a loom-beam.*
> His beard was trimmed, his hair above his brows,
> his shirt close-fitting, a chest was on the floor.

> *16. There sat a woman, spinning with a distaff,*
> stretching out her arms, ready to make cloth;
> a curved cap was on her head, a shirt on her breast,
> a kerchief round her neck, brooches at her shoulders.
> Grandfather and Grandmother owned the house.

Rig again slept between the couple for three nights. Nine months later, Grandmother had a son, Householder (Karl), who was "red-haired and rosy" with "lively eyes." Householder grew up, and among other tasks he "tamed oxen," "made a plough," "built houses," and "drove the plough." He was married to Daughter-in-Law (Snær), who kept keys on her belt, and they made a home together. They had several children, and from them all of the householders' families (*karla ættir*) are descended.[4]

Rig traveled further and arrived at a hall with the door facing south. He entered and met the married couple, Father (Faðir) and Mother (Móðir), who were "playing with their fingers."

> *26. There sat the householder and twisted bow-strings,*
> strung the elm-bow, put shafts on arrows,
> and the lady of the house was admiring her arms,
> stroking the linen, smoothing the sleeves.

> *27. She straightened her head-dress, there was a coin-pendant on her breast,*
> a trailing dress and a blue-coloured blouse;

her brow was brighter, her breast more shining,
her neck was whiter than pure fresh-fallen snow.

Here Rig was served "roasted birds" and "dark and light pork-meat" on a plate "chased with silver," and downed the food with wine.

The same chain of events repeated itself one more time, and nine months later, Mother delivered a son who was swathed in "silk." He was named Earl (Jarl). His hair was blond, his cheeks were bright, and his eyes were "piercing," like a "young snake's."

> *35. Earl grew up there on the benches;*
> he began to swing linden shields, fit bow-strings,
> bend the elm-bow, put shafts on arrows,
> hurl a javelin, brandish Frankish spears,
> ride horses, urge on hounds,
> wield swords, practice swimming.

Rig taught him "runes," gave him his name, and called him his son. Earl owned eighteen farms and gave generous gifts. He married Erna, and together they had twelve sons. The youngest of Earl's sons, Konr, had exceptional abilities that his father did not possess. For example, he was able to calm the sea, dull sword-edges, and save lives, and he was as strong as eight men. In addition, he had an even greater knowledge of runes than his father did. Konr therefore elevated himself above the level of his father, the earl, and became a king.[5]

Earl had to learn important warrior abilities: wielding a shield, fitting strings to his bows, fletching arrows, shooting with Frankish spears, riding horses, swimming, and sword fighting. His sons were taught a variety of "sports" (*íþróttir*): swimming, board games, taming horses, carving arrows, shaping shields, and swinging spears.[6] That these abilities were perceived as important in the Viking Age is demonstrated by the number of saga episodes and skaldic poems that depict them. Here is how *Heimskringla* describes the most powerful chieftain in Norwegian history, Erling Skjalgsson:

> Erling came from a large and great family, wealthy and powerful [*vinsæll*, with many friends]. He always kept a large following as if it was a royal *hirð*. Erling often spent the summer on raids acquiring wealth, for he carried on his conventional custom of grand style and munificence, though he now had

fewer and less profitable incomes [*veizlur*] than in the time of King Olaf, his brother-in-law. Erling was the handsomest [*fríðastr*] of all men, and the tallest and strongest, better than anyone at fighting and in all accomplishments most like King Olaf Tryggvason. He was a wise man and zealous in all issues and a very great warrior. [The skald] Sighvatr speaks of this:

> *There was no-one among*
> the district chieftains
> other than Erlingr, who,
> bold, deprived of support, held more battle.
> The generous man deployed his stamina
> to the utmost in onslaughts,
> because he went into many a fight,
> and out as the last.[7]

Erling possessed all the qualities that a great chieftain should have. He had a good family background, was powerful, and had many friends. He was also generous, handsome, and large and strong, and he was very skillful in wielding weapons. The description of Erling in *Heimskringla* was penned in the 1230s, some two hundred years after his death. It is self-evident that we have to be critical of this story, and *Heimskringla* cannot be used as a reliable source of knowledge about Erling Skjalgsson's life and deeds. However, along with other saga episodes and skaldic poems, it gives an idea of the ideals most appreciated in Viking Age society.

In the tale of Erling, there are several elements worth closer consideration. Let us start with sports. Erling was almost as good an athlete as Olaf Tryggvason, who was the greatest Norway had ever seen. But what is meant by the word "sports" (*íþróttir*)?[8] In two nearly identical poems, which either King Harald Hardruler or Ragnvald Kale, earl of Orkney, are supposed to have composed about themselves, we read that among those sports the two mastered were the skaldic arts, riding, swimming, skiing, shooting, rowing, playing the harp, playing chess, writing in runes, and forging.[9] Most of the skills that Earl in *Rígspula* had to learn are on this list. Even if more cultural pastimes such as playing the harp and carving runes could be thought of as sports in the Norse era, it meant first and foremost that one was good at physical exercises that were meaningful in battle. It was about being strong, swift, and good with weapons.

Returning to the larger question of social hierarchy in the Viking Age, we can say that the social division created by the gods in *Rígspula* is based on three elements: looks, abilities, and power. Rig has children with three different mothers of unequal birth status, Great-Grandmother, Grandmother, and Mother. These women's sons, in turn, marry women of birth status equivalent to their own, and these three couples become the ancestors of the three different classes. We notice that the abilities of Rig's offspring depend on who their mother is; a godly patrimony is not enough to elevate one's social status, in this case. Another important aspect of this imagery is the inherent *power* of the three couples visited by Rig. Great-Grandmother and Great-Grandfather are the oldest and therefore the weakest, whereas Father and Mother are the youngest and strongest. Father and Mother's son is Earl, who is not only a son of the god Rig but also is named and acknowledged by the god himself. In addition, Rig teaches Earl about runes. It is then Earl's youngest son, Konr, who becomes king. He is the youngest of them all, and therefore also the most powerful. Finally, the difference in the diets of the rich and the poor characters in the text is also seen in archaeological finds. In a study from Flakstad in Lofoten, the householders and thralls had the same diet (fish/marine protein), whereas the chieftain consumed more meat (protein from land animals).[10]

Beauty and the Social Hierarchy

An important aspect of *Rígspula*'s model is the strong correlation between looks, ability, and power. The thralls are presented as ugly, the householders are ruddy, and Earl is beautiful, with light hair, fair cheeks, and sharp eyes. This idea was integral to the Vikings' understanding of people's division into different social ranks and of the differences between the gods and the common people.

The Norse gods had divine abilities, of course, and these were connected to their looks. In *Gylfaginning*, we find the following description of the god Balder: "Balder is another son of Odin, and there is much good to be said about him. He is the best and all praise him. He is so beautiful [*fagr*] in appearance and so bright it shines from him; there is a plant so white that it is compared to Balder's eyelashes. It is the whitest of all flowers, and from this you can tell his beauty both of hair and body. He is the wisest of the Aesir and most beautifully spoken and the most merciful."[11] Balder is beautiful (*fagr*), so white that the whitest of flowers is compared to him, and he is also the wisest and most eloquent of all the gods. Balder is, however, not the only god who is beautiful: they are all beautiful.[12] Beauty is used as an explanation for their outstanding abilities. The same idea greets us in the description of Jesus Christ in the *Icelandic Homily Book* from the 1100s. It states that a "godly ring was discovered around the sun," which signaled that in the realm of the emperor Augustus, a boy would be born whose "strength, beauty and brightness, wisdom and bravery, and power will become superior and control everything and rule the sun and the moon and all things."[13] This boy was Jesus, the most powerful of all gods ever to have existed. If one combined all the Old Norse gods, they would become Jesus.

The kings' looks are also remarked on in the sagas, but with a significant difference in the vocabulary used to describe them. One of the most famous Viking kings is Harald Hardruler. In *Heimskringla*, he is described as "a handsome [*fríðr*] and noble-looking man; his hair and beard, yellow. He had a short beard, and long mustaches. One eyebrow was somewhat higher than the other. He had large hands and feet; but these were well made."[14] Harald is handsome (*fríðr*) but not beautiful (*fagr*), which signifies that he is powerful but does not have any divine powers. Gorm the Old, the founding father of the Jelling dynasty, was apparently more handsome than any other man.[15] Cnut the Great was particularly handsome, apart from his nose. He was light in color and had beautiful hair and eyes.[16] Most of the kings who ruled in Scandinavia during the period covered in this book, and who are described in the Norse sources, are described as handsome. The exceptions include the Danish king Svein Knutsson, who ruled Norway for a short period. The reign of Svein and his mother was unpopular, and so Snorri and the other saga authors did not describe him favorably.

Even though the kings were never described as beautiful, parts of their bodies were. Cnut the Great, as we have seen, had beautiful eyes, as had Olaf Haraldsson.[17] In this way, the sagas stressed that these kings had greater powers than the other kings, who were only referred to as handsome. The weather was beautiful during the battle of Stiklestad, and after St. Olaf's death, not only his face but also his wounds became beautiful. In the place where Olaf's body had lain, there came to be a beautiful well with healing powers.[18] By using the word beautiful in this way, Snorri underlines that as

Olaf was transformed into a saint, parts of his body become divine. Sometimes landscapes, ships, and weapons are also described as beautiful. The
beautiful landscape has exceptionally fertile abilities, beautiful ships and
weapons have some extra qualities, and we understand that when the sagas
use the word *fagr*, they do it to highlight the exceptional abilities of
something.

But what about the women? Let us look at an episode from Snorri's *Heimskringla*. It states that when King Harald Fairhair was almost seventy years
old, he had a son with a woman named Thora Pole. She was from Moster in
Hordaland and of good kin. "She was fair and handsome [*fríð*]" and was
referred to as the king's handmaid. Their son was Hakon Adalsteinfostre,
and he was "handsome [*fríðr*] and well built and much like his father."[19]
Harald was one of the handsome kings, and when such a king had a child
with a beautiful or handsome woman, their offspring became exceptional.
As we have seen, Hakon is recognized as one of the most important kings
in Norway in the Middle Ages. We find similar descriptions in several other
sagas. Women from all strata of society are handsome or beautiful, and the
children they have with kings or chieftains are exceptional. These women
also possess abilities that other women do not have. For instance, in *Krá-
kumál*—a poem from the point of view of the legendary Viking king Ragnar Lodbrok, probably composed in a Nordic community on the British
Isles—a mother's looks tell us all we need to know about her worthiness.
Ragnar, as he is lying in the snake pit his opponent had put him in, says that
he is unafraid of death because his sons will avenge him. He had given them
"such a mother that their hearts were capable."[20] This mother was no other
than Aslaug, daughter of Sigurd the dragon slayer, and in the saga she is
described—exactly—as beautiful.[21]

The Norse gods and some exceptional women are beautiful, and the kings
handsome, but what of the earls and the chieftains? When it comes to the
earls, we need to divide them into two groups. In Norway, as mentioned, the
earls of Lade were perceived as royalty and were therefore described as handsome.[22] We know of the high rank of the earls of Lade and the Fairhair
dynasty, kings of Vestlandet, from the poems *Háleygjatal* and *Ynglingatal*,
which explain their descent from the Norse gods. If we turn to the earls in
the Orkney Islands and how they are described in the *Orkneyinga saga*, only
one of about twenty is described as handsome.[23] The same pattern is found
when we move downward through the social hierarchy and look at how

Scandinavian and Icelandic chieftains are described. Of about 150 chieftains whose appearance is mentioned in any detail, fewer than ten are referred to as handsome.[24] One step further down, the householders are handsome on only very rare occasions.[25] When it comes to the thralls, most, as we saw in *Rígspula*, are unattractive, but interestingly, some of the female thralls are said to be beautiful or handsome.

Thus, we clearly see the connection between looks and social status in the Scandinavian Viking Age: the gods were imagined as being beautiful, the kings handsome, the earls and chieftains not handsome or beautiful, but still more attractive than the householders, and at the bottom were the thralls, who were mainly depicted as being unattractive. This is of course a general model, and there are exceptions. Such ideas also exist in other cultures. In the Old Testament, beauty is one of God's attributes, and when God bestowed his blessings, beauty was part of it. This was especially the case with kings and queens, but he could also bestow beauty on ordinary people, albeit in the form of actions such as beautiful work or words.[26]

It is unclear when this practice of using particular words to refer to gods and rulers was established in Scandinavia. It might have happened in connection with the development of kingship. What we should note, however, is that this way of talking was perhaps the most important element of the Viking Age ruler ideology. The greater part of the population had probably seen a chieftain, but only a select few had beheld a king, and no one had met a god. Because of this, linguistic customs were a significant marker of the differences between the gods and the common people, and between different types of rulers and the population at large. When a householder described a king or a chieftain, he simultaneously underlined the abilities he himself did not possess. Linguistic conventions were part of cementing the social structure and people's places within it.

The Oseberg Chieftain and Other Widows

One of the best-known monuments from the Viking Age is the Oseberg mound in Vestfold, in modern-day Norway. Everything points to it having been more than thirteen feet tall and about 130 feet in diameter. From dendrochronological studies of the wood in the burial chamber, the grave's construction has been dated to the summer of 834. When the Oseberg mound was excavated in 1904, it contained the remains of two women, around seventy and fifty years old.[27] This came as a surprise, especially since the sagas describing Nordic history in the period circa 850 to 1000 do not mention any women being buried in a mound. But it evidently did happen, as this great mound was constructed for a woman. This circumstance underlines the esteem in which women were held in Viking Age society and, as we shall see, indicates that they could take on roles we have traditionally attributed to men.

Traditional notions of gender also inform the vocabulary typically used to describe the Oseberg mound inhabitants. In the scholarly debate about the mound and its contents, one of the women is usually called a queen, the other her slave. But why is she referred to as a queen and not a king or a chieftain? According to the traditional notion of kings and queens, the king is usually aggressive, engaged in plundering and fighting battles, while the queen is commonly thought of as more submissive and staying at home. By calling her a queen, we are reducing her to a rather passive individual relying on the support of men. By using the term queen, we are also making another mistake. In the ninth century, there were only two royal families in Scandinavia—those in Denmark and Sweden. If a man and a woman or two men were lying in the Oseberg mound, the man would be called a chieftain. I think we should show the leading woman in the Oseberg mound the respect she rightly deserves and call her a chieftain, in the same way we call her colleague in the Gokstad mound, also in Vestfold some miles away from Oseberg, the Gokstad chieftain.

In the written sources, women never lead an army; they are never talked about as *dróttinn* or *konungr*; and on only a few occasions are they labeled *höfðingi* (chieftain).[28] The main reason women are not talked about as *höfðingi* more frequently in the sagas is that these sources usually deal with the period after the end of the Viking Age. In addition, the sagas describe a society whose power structure only slightly resembles that of the Viking Age. Not least, Christianity, with its hierarchical gender model, had been shaping Scandinavian society for almost two centuries by the time the sagas were written down.

However, both genders could take on almost any social role in the Viking Age society. This can clearly be seen in the term *maðr*. During the Viking Age, the word *maðr* was used to describe both men and women, a fact whose import has been overlooked until now. In the *Dictionary of Old Norse Prose* we find approximately 1,500 words that end with -*maðr*. Some words, due to different spellings in different sources, are listed more than once. A rough count of all the words that end with *-maðr* that excludes this doubling leaves us with somewhere between around 1,100 and 1,300 individual words. Among the words we find, for example:

> *afbragðs·maðr* (outstanding person), *bana·maðr* (killer), *banda·maðr* (ally, confederate), *bardaga·maðr* (warrior), *eignar·maðr* (person of wealth), *einvígis·maðr* (dueling person), *fylgðar·maðr* (retainer), *íþrótta·maðr* (sporting person), **karl·maðr** (man), *konungs·maðr* (king's person), **kven·maðr** (woman), *orrustu·maðr* (warrior), *sæmðar·maðr* (honorable person), *valds·maðr* (powerful person), *virðinga·maðr* (person of honor)

If we look at these words from a contemporary Scandinavian viewpoint, where *maðr* means "man," we are inclined to place the women on the farm, cooking and looking after the children. However, if we use the Viking Age definition of the word *maðr*, then we are looking at a different society, where women could take on all of the "classic" male roles except for king. A good example is when the *Gulaþing* law states that "no one, either man or woman, has a right to claim compensation more than three times, unless they have taken revenge in the meantime."[29] When discussing the Viking hall, we tend to think of the chieftain as a man. However, if we accept that the leading woman in the Oseberg mound was a chieftain, then we should also put her, and other female warlords, in the high seat, even though it is important to recognize that the warrior "profession," for lack of a better term, was dominated by men.

The grave goods laid in the Oseberg mound are unique. The mound contained, among other things, fifteen horses, four dogs, an ox, seven beds, four sleighs, a chariot, axes, tapestries, a burial chamber, and a decorated Viking ship, which was approximately fourteen years old when it was placed in the mound during the summer of 834. Let us look briefly at some of these objects, starting with the horses.

It was common to bury horses with deceased people during the Viking Age, as well as in the centuries before. However, the number of horses in the Oseberg mound is exceptional. One of the few comparable graves with respect to horses is that of the Merovingian king Childeric (d. 481 or 482), in which twenty-one horses were buried in three different pits.[30] In stanza 35 of *Rígsþula*, the earl is trained in "riding horses," and in stanza 37, he makes

"his horse gallop," hurling "the shafted spear," wielding his "sword," starting a "war," and fighting for "lands."[31] The association between horses and
warlike behavior seems clear, indicating that the Oseberg chieftain was considered a great warrior by her contemporaries.

Another artifact found in the Oseberg burial mound was a chair, a classic symbol of power.[32] In the saga about Olaf Kyrre, Snorri writes that an
old custom in Norway was for kings to have their high seat in the middle of
the long bench. But why did the high seat become a symbol of kings and
chieftains, when householders had something similar on their farms that
symbolized the husband's power over his household? It is not unusual for
rituals and power symbols to have their origin in something familiar to most
people that was elaborated on and expanded.[33] A symbol of power such as
the high seat could also be connected with the gods, particularly Odin's seat,
Hlidskjalf.

Another traditional symbol of power was the ship within which the
women were placed. It is almost impossible to interpret this as signifying anything other than the chieftain having been a war leader, even though there
was no typical weaponry found in the grave. We cannot rule out the possibility that weapons had been there and later were removed from the
mound, since some believe that it was subjected to grave robbery. Of the
approximately 150 boat graves we know of from Norway in the Viking Age

Figure 10. Viking ship. Source: *Snorre Sturlason kongesagaer,* **trans. Gustav Storm
(Christiania: J. M. Stenersen, 1899).**

where the gender of the deceased can be determined, about forty were women. In addition, we have twelve graves where man and woman are lying together.[34] These numbers support the assumption that women were significantly more active in the typically male areas than traditionally believed, and that some of them also mastered the sports of the war leaders. Finally, we can again raise the question: How would we have interpreted the findings of the Oseberg mound if it had contained a man and a woman or two men, and not two women?

When the Oseberg burial mound is discussed, scholars often ask which of the two women was the queen and which was the thrall.[35] We shall pose a somewhat different question here, which is whether the leading woman in the mound could have been a widow, since widows had a different role than wives in medieval society. Let us have a look at some of them. One of the most famous women in the sagas is the Icelandic settler Aud the Deep-Minded. She was the daughter of the Norwegian *hersir* (chieftain) Ketill Flatnose, and married to a Norwegian chieftain who had conquered the Viking town of Dublin. After losing her husband in a battle in Ireland, Aud probably traveled with her son Thorstein to the Hebrides. Thorstein died in a battle in Scotland a few years later. Aud was in Caithness in the very north of Scotland when news about her son's demise reached her. She then secretly commissioned a ship to be built. Thereafter, she gathered her friends and her great riches and sailed to the Orkneys. According to tradition, she is supposed to have married off one of Thorstein's daughters there. After this, she went to the Faroe Islands, where she married off another granddaughter. Then she sailed to Iceland, since two of her brothers had settled there. When Aud reached Iceland, she sought one of them out. He invited his sister and ten of her people to stay the winter at his farm. Aud, however, declined this invitation and called her brother an ungenerous fellow. She then traveled to her other brother, Bjørn, who knew her imperious demeanor well and invited her to winter in his home with all of her entourage. She accepted and spent the winter there. The next spring, she traveled across the fjord from the place where her brother lived and claimed the land there. Her settlement (*landnám*) stretched from Dögurðará to Skraumhlaupsá. She lived at Hvammur, the first farm built in the area. Much points to Aud running a large, extensive farm, including the names of the neighboring locales: Skerðingsstaðir and Hofakur both hint at the growing of crops; Kýrunnarstaðir means the place where cattle are pastured; Knarrarhöfn, bay of the *knarrs* (merchant vessels);

and Rauðbarðarholt, which hints at iron mining. Aud began giving, or selling, land to her companions, family members, and household members
shortly after Hvammur was first founded.[36]

Aud was one of thirteen women among the original settlers of Iceland,
most of whom were widows. Another widow who should be mentioned is
Frakokk (c. 1064–1138) of the *Orkneyinga saga*. She was deeply engaged in the
power struggles in the Orkneys and Caithness, which finally resulted in an
attack on her own farm in which her house was burned down with her in it.[37]
It is also worth noting that among the Swedish rune stones there are many
which were raised by women, most of whom were probably widows.[38] The
woman who in memory of her daughter erected the Dynna stone in the mid-
1000s, a rune stone from the farm Dynna in Gran municipality in Hadeland,
Norway, is also believed to have been a widow by that time.[39] Another phenomenon that shows the high status of widows is that their children are often
named after them. The best example of this, even though the woman in this
case was not a widow, is that Christ was called "Jesus Mariason."

Viking Age society distinguished between two types of widows. If a
woman became a widow without having had a child by her husband, she
usually had to move back to her father's home and was therefore once again
part of his household and had to accept his authority. If, however, the woman
did have children, as Aud and Frakokk did, she was often made guardian
of their property until they were of legal age, and as such she could claim
nearly all the positions in society which her husband had held. The status of
the widows shows us that it was the social role, not the biological sex, that
determined one's status, and that the gender boundaries were in no way as
strict as we often imagine. But how many widows were there? Here we unfortunately do not have any reliable information, but given Scandinavian
society's extensive Viking raids, we believe that widows would have been
quite common.

Despite, or perhaps because of, their power, widows were generally subject to a great deal of pressure to remarry. They were attractive partners, not
least because the new husband would become the head of the household
ruled by the widow and would thus control the estates administered or owned
by her. Chieftains and kings therefore wanted influence over who married
wealthy widows and daughters who were sole heirs to great fortunes. The
lords could marry off these women to faithful men and thus gain control of
riches they otherwise would not have been able to access. To the families of

Figure 11. Widowed: Åsta Gudbrandsdatter learns of the death and unfaithfulness of her first husband, Harald. Source: *Snorre Sturlason kongesagaer*, trans. Gustav Storm (Christiania: J. M. Stenersen, 1899).

the widows and young girls, this often seemed a sensible plan, since they secured support and protection from the most powerful people in their society. We cannot rule out the possibility that the Oseberg chieftain was a princess who had inherited her father's realm, but the likelihood is that a woman of such an elevated societal position was a widow, and that she inherited the position of her late husband and became a great warlord.

From Norse mythology we are all familiar with the idea that warriors who fell in battle were supposed to go to Odin in Valhalla. What is less well known is that, according to *Grímnismál* (*The Sayings of Grímnir*, one of the poems of the *Poetic Edda*), Freyja, the goddess of love, fertility, and war was supposed to choose half of all the dead warriors and take them to her farm, Folkvang. We never give her the same credit as Odin, mainly because of *Völuspá* and its description of Ragnarok. However, why should Freyja choose half of all the fallen warriors if she was not leading them in the final battle?

We have two medieval sources mentioning women as warriors. The Byzantine historian John Skylitzes "reports women fighting as part of Rus forces in the 970s," while a less reliable Irish source, *The War of the Irish with the Foreigners* (*Cogadh Gaedhel re Gallaibh*), records a "fleet of the Red Girl

[Inghen Ruaidh]" operating against Munster during the tenth century.[40] There are also legends about shield-maidens, and according to thirteenth-century Danish historian Saxo Grammaticus, three hundred of them participated in the legendary battle at Brávalla in eastern Götaland around 750 CE. Most scholars do not believe that the stories of these women, which are all from Christian times, are very reliable.[41] In other words, there is not much suggesting that women participated in acts of war to any great degree, although there were probably exceptions. This conclusion is supported by archaeological examinations of women's graves. Only a small percentage of these contain weapons, and these were usually axes, which were also found in the Oseberg mound. There is debate whether these axes should be interpreted as weapons or as tools used in the daily running of the farm, but most scholars lean toward these axes being used as tools first and foremost.[42]

Yet there is evidence implying that the opposite is true. In 2017, an article reassessing the Birka chamber grave Bj. 581 suggested that previous interpretations that assumed it was a high-status male grave were wrong, and that the person lying in it was a woman.[43] This theory, based on genomic technology, raises questions about earlier interpretations of burials. The theory that women were a part of the Viking Age fighting force is also partly supported by the "growing number of so-called 'Valkyrie' brooches and pendants depicting females bearing weapons and shields, such as those from Wickham Market, England, and Hårby, Denmark, which demonstrate that the concept of armed females was familiar to Viking Age Scandinavians."[44]

There is an ongoing discussion about gender and gender roles in the Viking Age.[45] Social roles are the parts people play as members of a social group. With each social role you adopt, your behavior changes to fit both your own and others' expectations of that role. On this stage, you play the role in accordance with both your "cultural" and "national" repertoire; you have a "'tool kit' of symbols, stories, rituals, and world-views," to use Ann Swidler's words.[46] There is reason to believe that many roles in the Viking Age were not as gender-specific as in the High Middle Ages, from which we have most of the written sources about the Viking Age.[47] We should keep this distinction in the back of our minds when we try to understand both gender roles and the relationships between men and women in the Viking Age, especially when interpreting archaeological findings. From Viking Age Norway, we know of about eight thousand graves. Archeologists have gendered the graves depending on the grave goods—that is, whether they are considered to be

typical of men or women. The graves containing "oval buckles" have traditionally been interpreted as female graves, while graves containing weaponry
have been understood as male graves.[48] Using this criterion means that we
have one female grave for every five male graves. The question arising from
these numbers is, where are the rest of the women? This has made archaeologists question how gender is being identified.

Women's Lives per *Hávamál*

It looks as though women enjoyed greater freedoms during the Viking Age
than they did during the High Middle Ages. The women in *Hávamál* act
independently, and they are single-handedly able to choose whom they want
to have as their lovers and husbands. It is important to note that where women
are mentioned in *Hávamál*, their men—fathers or guardians—are not ref-
erenced. There was, therefore, nothing to hinder men from approaching a
woman. She was not under any protection. However, it is also worth noting
that a woman's or her family's honor does not seem to be in any way diminished by such an approach.

According to *Hávamál*, there are two things worth achieving for a man:
wealth and the love of a woman. To secure this love, the man must give the
woman gifts. A poor man therefore had no opportunity to gain a woman's
love. Even if one had access to riches, though, winning a woman's favor could
be problematic. The men were expected to compete for women's favor and
love, but the women also needed to be careful. The men of the Viking Age, as
in our times, were not always honest; they spoke "the most beautifully" when
they thought "the most falsely."[49] We notice the use of the word beautiful—as
we have seen, it denotes something exceptional. To deceive a woman, one required truly exceptional words. Yet the young maiden and the wife could also
deceive, so men needed to be vigilant as well. According to *Hávamál*, the un-
wise man becomes full of himself when he has acquired riches and a woman's
love. The poem does not specify who the man is; he might be a young unmarried man or a married and settled husband, both longing for love.

In the sources from the twelfth and especially the thirteenth century, the
picture is different. In Norwegian laws from the 1100s and 1200s, marriage
was to be arranged by a woman's guardian, usually her father or another
male relative. In the *Frostaþing* law, a woman could marry off her daughter,

but only if there were no male relatives who could do so. In some cases, the arranging of marriages happened without the young woman and man being consulted, but the choice of spouse was probably often made with the young ones involved. Love was not a factor, however. The goal was to find a spouse whom the young people, both the son and the daughter, could bear to live with. Furthermore, the marriage was a pact between two families, not just the individuals in question. The intention was both to establish a joint economy and to expand the family network, and in this way gain greater political and economic security.[50]

But what was it really like in the earlier period? Where does the "free" woman of *Hávamál* fit in? Was she able to choose her husband without her parents' consent? As we will discuss in chapter 8, one can claim that Viking Age society was run by women to a certain degree. A large percentage of the men left on Viking raids, and many of them never returned. Some of those who did come back had been severely injured, and because of this, their ability to complete the tasks required of an adult was limited. The unmarried injured men were unable to marry; the married ones presumably were enfeebled and had to hand over many of their responsibilities to their wives. Thus a lot suggests that the daily responsibilities of running the farm fell to the women and that they were required to perform both the "female" and "male" roles to a much greater extent than in the High Middle Ages. This situation probably resulted in the young women of the Viking Age having many more liberties in their everyday lives than later women did, including a say in whom they were to marry and take as lovers.

In stanza 81 of *Hávamál*, it is said that when evening comes, the day shall praise the woman when she is "burnt."[51] In other words, when a woman is buried, her legacy is duly recounted. Honor was thus also of great importance to women. Of course, women were under the watchful eye of society, just as men were, particularly with regard to how they looked after their farms. In addition, many of them, especially the queens and the wives of the chieftains, possessed prestigious secret knowledge their men did not. In *Hávamál*, we are told that Odin knew invocations unknown even to a king's wife.[52] This strengthens the impression that the honor of Viking Age women, at least the wives of the social elite, was distinct from that of their husbands.

Women were also guardians of their family's honor: if a woman thought her family had lost honor, she could stir her husband and sons into recovering it.[53] There are a number of episodes in the sagas where women goad their husbands and sons into defending the family's honor. As mentioned above, *Heimskringla*, for example, tells us that Olaf Haraldsson's mother, Åsta Gudbrandsdatter, chided her son for being insufficiently ambitious: "For my part, my son, I am pleased at your arrival, but much more at your advancing your honor. I will spare nothing within my power for that purpose, although my advice will be of little help. But if a choice could be made, I would rather that you should be the supreme king of Norway, even if you should not sit longer than Olaf Tryggvason did [five years], than that you should not be a greater king than Sigurd Syr [Olaf's stepfather] and die the death of old age."[54] It is impossible to miss Åsta's point: she would rather lose her son in the hunt for honor than have him be no more powerful a king than his stepfather. The person doing the goading, female or male, was often of lower social standing than the one being goaded, meaning that goading offered a way for those of lower standing to influence politics.

The relative freedom of women in *Hávamál* seems to disappear after the Viking Age, not just because of the introduction of Christianity and its ideas about the roles of the sexes, but also as a consequence of a different political situation, in which war, battling, and trade abroad were of less importance. Nevertheless, even though the view of women in *Hávamál* is significantly more liberal than the one in sources from the 1100s and 1200s, there is no reason to exaggerate women's freedom in the Viking Age. This was a society dominated by men. Most of the important positions of society were filled by men, and even if women acquired a higher position as widows, we do not hear of their being very significant participants at the *þing* or in places where important decisions were made. That widows and other wives kept the wheels turning in Scandinavian society is a whole different matter, however.

Further Reading

Amory, Frederic. "The Historical Worth of *Rígsþula*." *Alvíssmál* 10 (2001): 3–20.

Androshchuk, Fedir. "Female Viking Revisited." *Viking and Medieval Scandinavia* 14 (2018): 47–60.

Borovsky, Zoe. "Never in Public: Women and Performance in Old Norse Literature." *Journal of American Folklore* 112 (1999): 6–39.

Friðriksdóttir, Jóhanna Katrín. *Valkyrie: The Women of the Viking World*. London: Bloomsbury Academic, 2020.

Gardela, Leszek. "'Warrior-Women' in Viking Age Scandinavia? A Preliminary Archaeological Study." *Analecta Archaeologica Ressoviensia: Rzeszow* 8 (2013): 273–309.

Hedenstierna-Jonson, Charlotte, Anna Kjellström, Torun Zachrisson, Maja Krzewińska, Veronica Sobrado, Neil Price, Torsten Günther, Mattias Jakobsson, Anders Götherström, and jan Storå. "A Female Viking Warrior Confirmed by Genomics." *American Journal of Physical Anthropology* 164 (2017): 853–60.

Jesch, Judith. *Old Norse Images of Women*. Philadelphia: University of Pennsylvania Press, 1996.

———. *Women in the Viking Age*. Woodbridge, UK: Boydell Press, 1991.

Naumann, Elise, Maja Krzewińska, Anders Götherström, and Gunilla Eriksson. "Slaves as Burial Gifts in Viking Age Norway? Evidence from Stable Isotope and Ancient DNA Analyses." *Journal of Archaeological Science* 41 (2014): 533–40.

Præstgaard Andersen, Lise. "On Valkyries, Shield-Maidens and Other Armed Women in Old Norse Sources and Saxo Grammaticus." In *Mythological Women: Studies in Memory of Lotte Motz, 1922–1997*, edited by Rudolf Simek and Wilhelm Heizmann, 291–318. Vienna: Fassbaender, 2002.

Price, Neil, Charlotte Hedenstierna-Jonson, Torun Zachrisson, Anna Kjellström, Jan Storå, Maja Krzewińska, Torsten Günther, Verónica Sobrado, Mattias Jakobsson, and Anders Götherström. "Viking Warrior Women? Reassessing Birka Chamber Grave Bj.581." *Antiquity* 93 (2019): 181–98.

Raffield, Ben, Claire Greenlow, Neil Price, and Mark Collard. "Ingroup Identification, Identity Fusion, and the Formation of Viking War Bands." *World Archaeology* 48 (2015): 1–16.

Chapter 7

Religion and Power

The Norse religion was an *ethnic* religion, not a universal religion like Christianity. That it was ethnic signifies that it belonged to a certain people, and like many such religions, it encompassed a great number of male and female gods and powers. The Norse religion was tolerant in the sense that there were no rules or laws about *what* and *how* the people were to believe. This is reflected in the use of the term *siðr* (habit, custom) to describe the religion. During the later Viking Age, the term *heiðinn dómr* (heathendom) was used to draw a distinction between it and *kristinn dómr* (Christianity). Because the Old Norse religion was all encompassing, it could not be separated from politics or daily life. Yet, the lack of a central organizing body that might train priests (or their equivalents) led to local variations. There was no need for any religious control. Summonses to the sacrificial feasts were part of the routine of the year and one's life, as commonplace as planting and harvesting.[1]

The pre-Christian religion can be characterized as an elite religion, meaning that the upper ranks of society controlled communication with the gods (probably with the help of ritual specialists for the greatest feasts) as well as who could establish friendships with them. In the Norse religion, the role and tasks of the king were ambiguous (apart from in Svealand). This was an important factor in the kings eventually choosing Christianity as their kingdom's new religion. With this innovation, they became the protectors and leaders of the church. Harald Bluetooth, as we have seen, has been credited with introducing the new religion to his realm. In Norway, Olaf Haraldsson proclaimed Christianity as the official religion of the country around 1020. Sweden was first officially Christianized in the late 1000s.

The Kings and Odin and Freyr

The Norse gods were made up of two groups: Vanir and Aesir. Freyr and Freyja, among others, belonged to the first group, who were all gods of fertility and wealth. The best known of the Aesir, the larger group of gods, are without doubt Odin, Thor, and Balder. The division between the Aesir and Vanir seems to date to the beginning of the Merovingian period (c. 550–800). They appear to have been two warring groups who after a long period of unrest came to a settlement and sealed the peace by exchanging hostages. This explains why there are Vanir among the Aesir. In addition to these groups of gods, there were many mythological categories, including *völvur* (prophetesses), *jötnar* (giants), *Nornir* (Norns, similar to the Fates), *fylgjur* ("fetches" who accompany people to their fates), *dísir* (ghosts, spirits, or deities, perhaps of fertility), and *Valkyrjur* (Valkyries).[2]

As we have seen, kingship in Denmark developed at an early date. It is however uncertain when royalty became connected with Odin, the greatest of the Aesir and the one who "ruled" all things. The Danish kings claimed they were descended from Odin's son Skjoldr, and were consequently referred to as *Skjoldungar* (Scyldingas). This assertion might date from the same time that the early English kings had ancestral genealogies drawn up showing their descent from Odin.[3] Of the Scandinavian royal families in the early Viking Age, only the Danish claimed such a history. Later, after the Danish kings had converted to Christianity, the skaldic poem *Háleygjatal*, composed by Eyvindr Poet-Destroyer (*skáldaspillir*) in the late 900s, claimed, to legitimize their power, that the earls of Lade were descended from Odin.

Odin has more than 170 names, such as Alfaðir (All Father), Auðunn (Friend of Wealth), Sigmundr (Victory, Protection), Sigtryggr (Sure of Victory), Rúnatýr (God of Runes), and Valfaðir (Lord of the Slain). Only a small number of these names were given to young men—first and foremost, Sigmund and Sigtrygg. No such namesake belonged to the Danish royal family or the earls of Lade. About seventy theophoric (holy, sacral) place-names with Odin as their first element are found in Scandinavia. Of these, forty-nine are found in present-day Sweden, and eleven each in Denmark and Norway.[4] The distribution of the theophoric Odin-names thus cannot explicitly be connected with the areas controlled by the Danish kings and the earls of Lade.

In *Ynglingatal*, composed by Thjodolf of Hvin around 890, the ancestry of the Fairhair dynasty is traced through the Swedish royal family of the Ynglinga in Uppsala back to the god of fertility, Freyr, also called Yngvi-Freyr. We know of thirty-eight "certain" theophoric Freyr-names within the borders of present-day Sweden, twenty-two in Norway, and one in Denmark. The largest concentration can be found in eastern Sweden and the areas around the Oslofjorden, Østfold, Oppland, Hedmark, and Vestfold.[5] The geographical distribution of the theophoric Freyr-names, as with the Odin-names, does not follow any clear-cut pattern, nor is there any evident connection with the royal families.

Only the royal families could claim such an exalted descent from the gods in the Viking Age, but what was the situation like before kingship developed, especially in the parts of Scandinavia where it did not exist before the end of the 800s? The sagas' explanation of the success of Harald Fairhair—his ability to conquer Vestlandet and become a king—is that his luck was greater than that of his opponents. The gods were on his side. The fact that he and his sons managed to establish a kingdom might have been the reason why an attribute that had previously been connected with all chieftains—descent from the gods—now became limited to men from the Fairhair line. This means that the other aristocratic families became desacralized in the process. Something similar probably happened when kingship grew stronger in Denmark and Sweden.

It is uncertain how strong the bonds were between the royal families and the gods they claimed as their ancestors. We can, however, assume that the kings led the sacrifices to these gods, especially in the case of the Swedish kings. For the Norwegian kings, the situation was somewhat more complex. This is because the Norwegian kingdom was first established in the late 800s, and only the founder himself, Harald Fairhair, was not baptized. The same appears to be the case with the Danes, although some think that Jelling might originally have been meant to function as a dedicated location for the cult of Odin. The only centralized religious site in Scandinavia where we know with certainty that the kings played a central role was in Uppsala.

The Holy Kings

A crucial but disputed question is whether the kings were considered sacred (holy). At its most heated, the debate has centered not only on disagreements about the dating of central sources but also on whether Scandinavian kingship can be compared to kingship in other cultures with strong beliefs in the sacred nature of the king. There are two main points of view.[6]

On one side of the debate, scholars claim that both the pre-Christian and the early Christian kings were perceived as a link between the people and the gods, and that this made them holy. As we have seen, the Danish kings claimed to be descended from Odin, and the Swedish kings from Freyr. In Norway, the sagas attributed divine heritage to both the Fairhair dynasty and the earls of Lade—the Fairhair dynasty in *Ynglingatal* and the earls of Lade in *Háleygjatal*. In the first poem, the Fairhair dynasty's lineage is traced through the Swedish royal family of the Ynglinga in Uppsala to the god Freyr. In the second poem, it is the god Odin who is the ancestor of the earls of Lade. We find similar depictions in the lineages of, for example, the early English kings.[7] Such origin stories were part of legitimizing these families' elevated position in society. Above, we discussed that the Norse gods were beautiful (*fagrir*) and the kings were handsome (*fríðir*), and they had abilities other men did not, because they descended from the gods. The myths therefore acquired a clear ideological function. Here we must remember that chieftains could also have special relationships with the gods, which will be addressed later, but that they did not claim divine heritage.

Luck (*hamingja, gæfa, gipta*) was hereditary and connected with divine descent, a power that only certain people possessed. This power was given to the king at the beginning of his reign. Because the king was of divine descent, his luck could bring *ár ok friðr*—that is, a good harvest and peace—to the people of his reign (*öld*). Because of his luck, the king was also supposed to precede his men in battle and in this way demonstrate that he, and by extension they, were supported by the gods. Prosperity in peacetime and victory in battle confirmed that the gods protected the king, since his luck had passed the various tests of his reign and grown. The king's gifts included a transference of his luck. Gifts from kings were therefore important in two ways: they were valuable as items in and of themselves and they carried some of the king's luck to the recipient.

On the other side of the debate are the scholars who claim that such a sacral kingdom did not exist. They insist that the royal family in Uppsala was not considered holy and that although the king in Uppsala most likely led the religious gatherings, his power was fundamentally secular. Their theory is largely based on a different proposed dating of *Ynglingatal*. They do not believe that it was composed by Thjodolf of Hvin around 890, as most scholars do, but instead that it was created in a learned community in Iceland in the 1100s and is basically a reflection of later Christian ideas. By turning *Ynglingatal* into a twelfth-century source, an important puzzle piece in the theory of a sacral kingdom disappears.[8]

Such a dating has not, however, been accepted by philologists. They raise a number of other questions that would need to be answered, such as why Snorri Sturluson, whose knowledge of the skaldic poems was vast and who belonged to the learned Icelandic community, would refer to it as a Viking Age poem if it was not.[9] Even if the situation is not ideal when it comes to the sources due to their scarcity and ambiguity, ideas about sacral kingship are so universal that it is difficult to imagine they do not also apply to Scandinavia.[10]

After the establishment of kingship, Scandinavian reckoning of time was connected with the king's reign (e.g., this battle took place when Harald had been king for ten years). We do not know what kind of system for tracking time was used before the development of kingdoms, however. Possibly it was tied to the reigns of the most powerful chieftains (e.g., this event happened when Thorolf had been chieftain for ten winters). This supposed shift in dating, from chieftains' to kings' time, must have been a strong demonstration of power. From this point on, there would be no question as to who was ultimately in charge: the king. After the development of kingship, each kingdom had its own timeline. This linear, Christian perception of time, from the Creation through to the birth of Jesus Christ and on to the end of days, was first introduced around the year 1000. But this linear dating, which we are using today, was not widely used across Europe until much later; the immediacy of the rulers' time dominated Europe for most of the Middle Ages. The king's timeline in the Viking Age had a strong ideological character in addition to its practical side. It underlined who the top authority in the kingdom was, and at the same time it created a common identity for the people of the realm and finally it made it possible to evaluate his reign and compare it with other times and other kings to determine whether it had been good to the people and brought *ár ok friðr.*

The Chieftains and Thor

Thor occupied a significant place in the consciousness of Viking Age people. Because he ruled over the wind, rain, thunder, and lightning, he was able to offer protection from them. The strong ties between Thor and the chieftains are readily visible in the Icelandic *Eyrbyggja saga.* The settler Thorolf and his wife Unn had a son together, Stein. Thorolf gave the boy "to his friend Thor" (i.e., the god) and at the same time gave him a new name, Thorstein. Thorstein was now the property of the god, but it was Thorstein's father and mother who were entrusted with looking after the gift. Thorstein became a great chieftain. He had two sons, Bork, who was the elder, and Grim, who was the younger. Thorstein offered Grim to Thor and said that he should lead the *hof* (temple) and become chieftain. Thereafter, Thor changed Grim's name to Thorgrim.[11] Much suggests that the sons who were given to Thor were preferred over their other brothers. It was inappropriate to offer Thor a boy who was not expected to become a central figure in society. In the Viking Age, it was important for the chieftains that the positions of power were inherited by their best sons, rather than the oldest or those born in wedlock.

There are many issues connected with the use of the *Eyrbyggja saga* as a historical source, not least the length of time between the events described and the time the saga was composed and recorded—the *Eyrbyggja saga* was probably written in the first half of the 1200s, but the events it describes are set in the 900s. However, much still supports the trustworthiness of its depiction of the aspects we have highlighted—the renaming of boys to demonstrate their connection to Thor, and chieftain families in Iceland systematically trying to establish and maintain such friendships with the god. In Lúðvík Ingvarsson's book *Goðorð og goðorðsmenn* (Chieftaincy and

Figure 12. **King Olaf Haraldsson before a statue of Thor.** Source: *Snorre Sturlason konge-sagaer,* trans. Gustav Storm (Christiania: J. M. Stenersen, 1899).

chieftains), there is a register of names including all those he thought were chieftains during the Icelandic Free State period.[12] In this register, approximately 340 people are listed. About 110 of those mentioned correspond to the period 930 to 1030, and of these, around sixty bore names connected with the Norse gods, such as Asbjorn and Thorstein. A large majority of these sixty chieftains, around fifty people, had names starting with "Thor." We do not know, though, whether all of these men had been offered to

Thor. Additionally, this naming practice was not limited to boys alone. The social elite's most promising daughters were also offered to Thor and given names reflecting this; an example is Thordis.[13] This, more than anything else, shows us that girls were equally as important as boys.

The chieftains were not descended from the gods, but nevertheless, it appears that they attempted to create bonds of friendship with them, especially with Thor. It is tempting, then, to claim that the kings had a monopoly on communication with Odin and Freyr, and that this was part of cementing political differences in Viking Age society.

Worship of the Norse Pantheon

Fixed ritual actions were the core of the Norse religion. It primarily consisted of regular gatherings where sacrificing to the gods (*blót*) and drinking were central. The offering could be a sacrifice made to the gods (a sacrifice of gifts) and/or a communication sacrifice, where the gods participated symbolically in the common feasting and were served part of the same sacrificial animal being eaten by the participants in the *blót*. The *blót* was about holy unification, the conveyance of power between gods and people. When blood from the sacrifice was sprinkled over the participants drinking a toast to the gods, they were symbolically unified with the gods. The *blót* and the sacrifice were meant to gain the support of the gods so they would ensure that there would be *ár ok friðr*, good harvest and peace. The most significant animal that could be sacrificed was the horse.[14]

If the people did not have their wishes fulfilled, it meant that they had not been able to come into contact with the gods through their gifts; the Vikings thought this was because the gods had not showed up to the *blót* and did not want to accept their gifts. In *The Old Icelandic Homily Book* from the 1100s, there is a short comparison of the Christian God and the Norse gods.[15] The difference between them was that the Almighty God was everywhere and heard everything, and one did not need to use many words to come into contact with him. The Norse gods, however, were only able to be in a few places at one time, and therefore needed to choose whom to visit.

Communal drinking and eating especially characterized the *blót*. We have little reason to doubt that drinking ale was an integral part of the *blót*—the drinking of alcoholic beverages was a large part of all types of gatherings in

Viking Age society, both religious (pre-Christian and Christian) and secular. Drink, especially alcoholic mead, was perceived as godly, and the drinking of it symbolized unity with the gods. Those who drank together, belonged together. Communal eating symbolized the same unity. Those who ate together, belonged together; they were part of a fellowship. The first reliable source of *blót* feasting in the Nordic realm is found in the writings of the Andalusian merchant Al-Tartushi. He describes the conditions in Hedeby, where it is said that the inhabitants of the town held a feast to honor the gods and to eat and drink.[16]

The practice of the Old Norse religion can be divided into private worship, which happened at home at the farm, and public worship, which took place more publicly, for example at the chieftain's farm or at the *þing*. The chieftains and householders had a religious fellowship, probably with large gatherings every year: autumn *blót* in the middle of October, when they arranged a *blót* for a good harvest; midwinter *blót* at the end of December for good growth in the coming year; and a summer *blót* in the middle of April for luck in war. The priestly function in this religious fellowship was probably performed by the chieftains, who presumably led the gatherings of the fellowship along with a few ritual specialists (e.g., *gyðja*). Such chieftain priesthoods were not theocratic, as nothing suggests that the chieftains based their power on any sacral organization or religious functions, or on the supervision of property belonging to the Norse gods. It is probable that participants in the general *blót* provided gifts but the chieftains were the ones to sacrifice those gifts to the gods on behalf of the groups they led. The chieftains were not priests; they were leaders who possessed military, religious, and economic power. This double function of the chieftains, as both secular and religious leaders, therefore led to their friends the householders owing them allegiance secularly though friendships and religiously through the common worship of gods. The Norse religion was not a religion for the individual, where the personal experience of faith was the determining factor, but rather a religion for the group and unity within it. To what degree the chieftains and ritual specialists used their own language to control the conveyance of esoteric knowledge, and thus limit the possibility of who could perform the religious rituals, is uncertain, but it was probably a factor.

The chieftains' gifts to the gods were an attempt at establishing friendships with them, thereby securing their support in the chieftains' everyday life. In stanza 43 of *Hávamál*, we read: "To his friend a man should be a friend /

and to his friend's friend too."[17] If we apply this to the relationship between people and gods, the chieftains thus became a link between their friends and the gods. As a repayment for the gifts/sacrifices, the gods supported not only the chieftains but also the chieftains' friends—the householders. The chieftains' role as friend of the gods was a significant part of their power base and a primary reason we are able to label the Norse religion an elite religion. Much also suggests that there was a belief in local godlike figures such as elves, whom the householders and their families turned to with their daily problems.[18]

The *Hof*

Was there a particular building where the *blót* was performed? This is disputed among scholars. Up until the 1960s, most thought that the *hof* was a building specifically designated for religious functions, and that it had been replaced by churches with the introduction of Christianity. Once again, the sagas—and the *Eyrbyggja saga* in particular—provided the main source of evidence in their descriptions of the *hof*. The *Eyrbyggja saga* recounts that the Norwegian chieftain Thorolf had to flee from Norway to Iceland because of Harald Fairhair's conquests. Thorolf settled on Snæfellsnes, where he built for himself a large farm, Hofstaðir, with a *hof* included among the structures. It was a large house, with a door on the long wall, close to the corner. In the *hof*, there were the pillars of the high seat, and within them were the "god's nails" (*reginnaglar*—what this term signifies is the subject of its own debate). Within the *hof* there was an "annex like the choir in the churches, and there in the middle of the floor stood a pallet like an altar," and on it was placed a large, valuable bracelet on which oaths were to be sworn. The chieftain (*hof-goðinn*) was to wear the armband at all gatherings. On the pallet was also the *blót* bowl, which contained the *blót teinn*, a twig used to sprinkle the blood from the animals sacrificed to the gods. All men were expected to pay tribute to the *hof* and to be committed to following the chieftain in all his travels, as all *þingmenn* (thing men) were in the 1200s. But the chieftain himself should maintain the *hof* and organize *blót* feasts.[19]

When the Danish archaeologist Olaf Olsen published his thesis *Hørg, hov og kirke* (Horgr, hof and church) in 1966, he dealt a great blow to the credibility of the Icelandic sagas and their description of the *hof*. According to

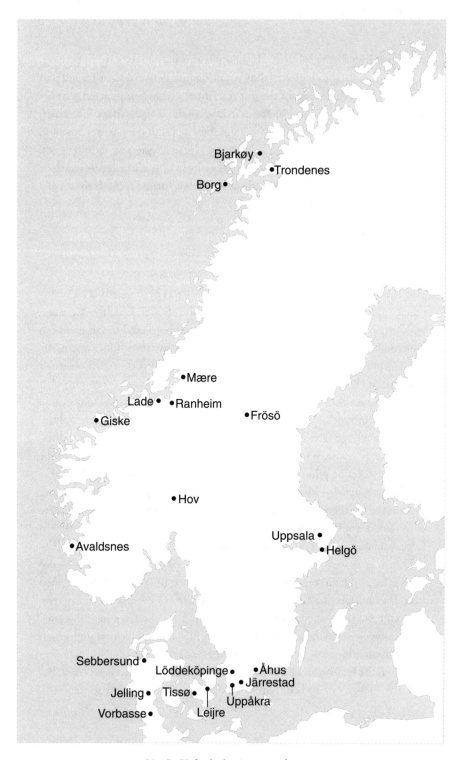

Map 7. *Hof* and other important farms

Olsen, the term *hof* signified not a particular building but a farm where religious gatherings were regularly held for a larger circle than just the farm's inhabitants.[20] For this reason, he claimed there was no continuity in the places of worship used by the old and new religions.

During the last few decades, archaeologists have found on the great farms more buildings that they interpret as places of worship, for example Järrestad in Skåne, Uppåkra in the proximity of Lund, Helgö in Mälardalen, Frösö in Jämtland, Leijre in Tissö, Hov in Oppland, and Ranheim in Trondheim.[21] It therefore looks as though the pendulum is swinging the other way again, and the idea of separate *hof* buildings on the most central farms is gaining support.

Ancestral Worship?

A central aspect of Norse religion was the idea that even if people were physically dead, they lived on in another world. That is, the living and the dead existed in different parts of a common whole. Through certain rituals, the living were able to communicate with the dead and gain access to their knowledge. The ability to communicate with the deceased was dependent on an individual's social position, meaning that only chieftains, kings, and *völvur* (prophetesses or seeresses, who were often older women) were able to do it. Through magic, which was called *seiðr* (spells), the *völva* gained knowledge and power over life and death. This knowledge could sometimes be used to give people bad luck or conjure a silent storm or snowy weather. The knowledge of the *völva* was sought after, and she was often called on in times of crisis.

It is commonly believed that ancestral worship comprised a central part of the Norse religion. The family buried their dead in burial grounds closely connected with the farm, and the ancestors could secure the fertility of the earth and thus the livelihoods of their descendants. A great number of farms had their own burial grounds, and it seems there was only one mound built per generation. If the farm was taken over by another family, they built their mounds in an area separate from the older burial grounds. The householders were probably placed in these mounds, while other members of the household were likely placed in regular graves elsewhere.[22]

Not all people could gain the status of an ancestor—only those who had held prominent positions in society. However, it is problematic to call this an ancestral cult. If these mounds were to become the centers of an ancestral cult, the bilateral kinship structure, in which each individual was a member of the lineages on both their maternal and paternal sides, would have meant each person had to deal with a great number of different burial mounds in various places. The cult revolving around the farm burial mounds should instead be understood as a farm cult, where the existence of the farm and fellowship within the household were central tenets. The differences between an ancestral and a farm cult are not great in many cases, but they still constitute important distinctions. In any case, we need to take into consideration varying degrees of family loyalty as well. Since people at the top of the social hierarchy merited more loyalty, the burial mound cult at a chieftain's farm could take on the form of an ancestral cult and/or a cult based around a heroic chieftain.[23]

Kings and the Christian God

In the written sources, the Christianization of Scandinavia is attributed to the decisions of the kings. Despite the significance of his father Gorm in the process, it is Harald Bluetooth who is credited with bringing Christianity to the Danes.[24] On the large Jelling stone from around 965, we read that it was Harald who "made the Danes Christian." This inscription has been used to date when Christianity became the official religion of Denmark, and it is often thought of as the baptismal record of Denmark. In Norway, the credit for introducing Christianity is shared among three Christianizing kings: Hakon Adalsteinfostre, Olaf Tryggvason, and Olaf Haraldsson. The Christianization of Sweden was a more complicated process. Erik the Victorious was the first Swedish king to be baptized, but when he returned to Uppsala he converted back to the Norse religion.

The first truly Christian Swedish king was Erik's son Olof Skötkonung, who, as previously mentioned, ruled over both the Swedes and the Geats. His son, Anund Jacob, continued his father's mission, but was overthrown by his supposed half brother Edmund the Old in the mid-1000s. Edmund died around 1060 and was replaced by Stenkil, who was probably Christian or at least kindly disposed toward the faith. After his death, practitioners of the Norse religion seemed to have pushed back against Christianity. Around 1080, the Christian king Inge succeeded to the throne. He did not participate in the traditional *blót* in Uppsala, and as a consequence was driven out to West Götaland, while *Blót*-Svein rose to power in Svealand. But the Christianizing process was unstoppable, and in about 1090, the temple in Uppsala, the last bastion of the Norse religion, was torn down and Christianity firmly established. To complicate this story further, Jämtland (in Norway) was Christianized by a local chieftain. On the so-called Frösö rune stone in Jämtland, dated circa 1050, it is written that Ostman Gudfatsson Christianized Jämtland.

The introduction of Christianity was a political decision, and the kings were the ones who championed it. But why were the kings so set on promoting the new religion? The short answer is that the church legitimized their claim to power, and the church administration could be both controlled by the kings and used as a role model for their own administrations. There is a broad consensus among scholars today that the social elite of kings and chieftains played an exceedingly large role in this religious transformation;

Figure 13. Christian priests. Source: *Snorre Sturlason kongesagaer*, trans. Gustav Storm (Christiania: J. M. Stenersen, 1899).

thus, the process of Christianizing mainly happened from the top down. Kings and chieftains were the well-wishers of Christianity, building churches and providing them with land.[25]

Contact between the Nordic realms and the rest of Europe was extensive during the Viking Age, and the Nordic elite undoubtedly knew about the development of the relationship between church and state in Europe. The Carolingian Empire in France and Germany and the West Saxon kingdom in southern England were probably the Nordic rulers' role models. The ruling concept among the European elite in the 900s and 1000s was that the king should be the head of the church and the lord of the clergy. It became obvious to the kings in Scandinavia that the new religion could be used as an ideological-religious basis for breaking down resistance to the kingdom and could legitimize the subjugation of local chieftains. In other words, Christianity could be used to create a religious fellowship with a common frame of reference where the king was in the top position. The connection between secular and spiritual power was as evident as it had been previously, but now it was a connection between one God and one king.

The relationship between church and king was mutually beneficial. The hierarchical structure of the church worked best when it was supported by a central power, and the kings could secure the church economically through donations and politically by ensuring peace. Without the kings' protection, Christianity would not have enjoyed the favorable conditions that presumably were necessary to the institutionalization of a new faith, new ethics, and a new nationwide organization. In exchange for this protection, the king became leader of the church. Beneath him were the bishops, who in turn kept an eye on the priests. As such, the organization of the church was a powerful consolidating element in society. It was of great importance to the kings to support a religion that visibly showed their elevated position in the world order. It was advantageous for the church to present kingship as God's preferred form of government, though the church's greatest concern was its own continued survival.[26]

The kings used a simple method when introducing Christianity. If they managed to baptize the chieftains in the different parts of the country, then the rest of the population would follow. The Norwegian Christianizing kings, especially Olaf Tryggvason and Olaf Haraldsson, were brutal in their efforts to Christianize the country, or more precisely, to enforce the process of baptism. If someone refused to be baptized, they were tortured or murdered. Chieftains who accepted the new religion probably believed it was in their best interests to do so, indicating that this was a strategic change of faith. In this way, they established or maintained a friendship with the king and could later count on both political and economic support from him. It was better to be the king's friend than his enemy and lose both landed goods and positions of power. But the transition to a new religion also had obvious disadvantages for the chieftains. By accepting the new religion, their status as subject to the king was even more visible, as we have seen above. The king was the leader and protector of Christianity. It was therefore empowering for the kings to have the chieftains accept the new faith; opposition to Christianization functioned as a form of political resistance against the kings. The kings could not override the most powerful chieftains in this process, however, and occasionally had to admit defeat in the face of resistance.

After the elite had been baptized, the common people were next. This was usually done through mass baptism. We see the same pattern all over Western Europe during the early periods of Christianization. Conversion to a new faith was first and foremost a social phenomenon, and not a matter of individual conviction. It was about adapting one's religion and religious behavior to fit with that of one's friends and relatives. This signifies that one's network played the determining role; people did not begin to actually believe in the new doctrine until *after* they converted.[27]

Social networks influenced the adoption of the new faith in lower levels of society too. A householder needed to follow in the footsteps of his chieftain. Otherwise, he would not only earn his chieftain's wrath, but even worse, lose his position in his network and the support it provided. According to *Hávamál*, lacking a social network was the worst thing that could happen in the Viking Age. The householders were the leaders of their farms, and their household was under their protection; if they changed their faith, their household needed to do the same. This was probably not always a smooth process. Not all householders would have been ready to stop believing in the Norse gods, and many probably continued to practice their old religion at home at their farms. The determining factor, however, was that one *publicly* belonged to the same religion as one's network. This underlined loyalty and fellowship. Like kings and chieftains, the householders had political motives for changing their faith. The householders probably did not know what it actually meant to be a Christian—the first attempts at Christian education were not well organized or explained, and a mass baptism was of little significance without the proper context. No sources suggest that the introduction of the new faith was to meet the demands of the people.

Even though the chieftains used the pre-Christian religion to sanction their position in society, their ties with the Old Norse gods were not necessarily strong. Chieftains and kings changed friendships to improve their power. This same attitude doubtless applied to their relationships with the Old Norse gods. If the gods did not fulfill their side of the bargain by protecting one's friends, it was perfectly permissible to simply change one's god. A change of religion was thus nothing more than a simple shift in allegiance from the Norse gods to the Christian God, as depicted in the poem of Hallfredr Vandræðaskáld (Troublesome Poet).[28]

The Christianizing process and Christianity differed greatly across the various regions of Scandinavia. Western Christianity already had regional variations, and when these were fitted into the different versions of the Norse religion, the diversity became even greater. There were many "micro Christianities."[29] Only in the 1100s and 1200s, with a strong pope in place, did the church acquire a more unified character.

St. Olaf

Olaf Haraldsson fell at Stiklestad on July 29, 1030, and the year after that, he was venerated as a saint. The royal and religious powers united in support of the cult of St. Olaf, and both institutions used it to further their causes. Olaf quickly became popular in all of Scandinavia, based on the number of churches dedicated to him. In Scandinavia, we find around four hundred such churches. Only the Virgin Mary was more popular. Olaf was the first Scandinavian saint, and there is much reason to believe that the cult around him helped pave the way for the new religion. In addition, the cult of St. Olaf quickly spread to other, non-Nordic countries. Even the *Anglo-Saxon Chronicle*, written around 1050, and English religious books from around 1060 refer to Olaf as a saint.[30]

It is difficult to date when the Nordic people first came into contact with the cult of saints. During the Viking Age, raiding Vikings commonly robbed monasteries and churches, though not because they were trying to fight Christianity. Rather, powerful local men often stored valuable objects at these

Figure 14. The death of Olaf Haraldsson at the Battle of Stiklestad. Source: *Snorre Sturlason kongesagaer,* trans. Gustav Storm (Christiania: J. M. Stenersen, 1899).

religious institutions, similar to the way we use banks today. The Vikings also stole religious books and relics, and these were sometimes returned in exchange for hefty ransoms. In other words, they knew how important these items were to the local populations. After the northerners settled in the British Isles, they quickly became familiar with the cult of saints. The English king Edmund was killed by Danish Vikings in 870; some twenty years later, he was acknowledged as a saint by his killers. By all accounts, the word "church" had entered the *dönsk tunga* (Danish tongue) before the missionaries reached Scandinavia, and it seems likely that the Vikings were familiar with the well-established tradition in Europe that all churches should be dedicated to one or more saints.

The cult of saints played a central role in the introduction of Christianity in Europe, and there is little reason to doubt that this was also the case in Scandinavia. The saints were instruments of God whom He used to display His power through miracles. When a church was established, it—and often the accompanying landed property—was given to its dedicatee, who was regarded as the legal owner of the church and its lands. However, the founders of the churches often made it a condition of their gifts that they and their heirs be put in charge of the churches' management. Through these gifts, the givers attempted to establish friendship ties with the saints. In the Norse sources, the saints are often referred to as God's friends (*guðsvinir*), and as such they were committed to support their friends, and their friends' friends. Most saints had a specific area of influence. For example, they helped merchants, or people in need at sea, or women giving birth. As a consequence, the saints were perceived as the helpers or protectors of the people.[31]

Religion manifests in three main ways in politics: (1) power can be directly based on the religion, as in theocracies, where the political authority is awarded to a god, but a priesthood manages that political authority on behalf of the deity; (2) religion can be used to legitimize the power of the ruling elite; (3) religion can, with its fundamental structures, beliefs, and traditions, be used to secure power.[32] Even if it is problematic to clearly differentiate between these three categories, they can help us study central aspects of the relationship between power and religion in the Viking Age. Here, the relationship between religion and power clearly cannot be characterized as a theocracy. However, religion was used to legitimize the power of the kings and chieftains at the same time that the internal religious structures were used to maintain the social and political structures.

We have claimed that the Norse religion was an elite religion—that is to say, it was the elite who controlled communication with the gods. The householders actively participated in the *blót* and probably contributed with gift offerings, but it was the chieftain who sacrificed these on behalf of his friends. The control the kings and the chieftains had over religion (both old and new) was important to their position in society and to legitimizing their power. They became a link between their friends and the gods. Yet, friendships between the kings, the chieftains, and the gods were unstable. The rulers were as loyal or disloyal to the gods as they were to their friends in the real world. To their way of thinking, if another more powerful god existed who could offer better protection and help, then the Norse gods had failed and it was therefore necessary to change sides and begin worshipping the new god—in this case, the Christian God. For the elite, maintaining one's control over religion allowed one to maintain one's position of power. This happened for instance through the rulers' building of churches. These were usually dedicated to saints, who in the Norse sources are referred to as the friends of God.

Further Reading

Andrén, Anders. "The Significance of Places: The Christianizaton of Scandinavia from a Spatial Point of View." *World Archaeology* 45 (2013): 27–45.

Brink, Stefan. "How Uniform Was the Old Norse Religion?" In *Learning and Understanding in the Old Norse World: Essays in Honour of Margaret Clunies Ross*, edited by Judy Quinn, Kate Heslop, and Tarrin Wills, 105–36. Turnhout: Brepols, 2007.

——, ed. *New Perspectives on the Christianization of Scandinavia and the Organization of the Early Church*. Leiden: Brepols, 2004.

Garipzanov, Ildar H., and Rosalind Bonté, eds. *Conversion and Identity in the Viking Age*. Turnhout, Belgium: Brepols, 2014.

Goeres, Erin. "The Many Conversions of Hallfreðr Vandræðaskáld." *Viking and Medieval Scandinavia* 7 (2011): 45–62.

——. *The Poetics of Commemoration: Skaldic Verse and Social Memory, c. 890–1070*. Oxford: Oxford University Press, 2015.

Schjødt, Jens Peter, John Lindow, and Anders Andrén, eds. *The Pre-Christian Religions of the North*. 4 vols. Turnhout, Belgium: Brepols, 2020.

Sundqvist, Olof. *An Arena for Higher Powers: Ceremonial Buildings and Religious Strategies for Rulership in Late Iron Age Scandinavia*. Leiden: Brill, 2016.

——. *Freyr's Offspring: Rulers and Religion in Ancient Svea Society*. Uppsala: Uppsala Universitet, 2002.

——. "The Pre-Christian Cult of Dead Royalty in Old Norse Sources: Medieval Speculations or Ancient Traditions?" *Scripta Islandica* 66 (2015): 177–212.

Chapter 8

Livelihoods

Which was the most important means of subsistence in the Viking Age economy: pillaging, farming, or trade?[1] There is no unequivocal answer to this question. It seems that it was the changing dynamic among these three sources of income that was important. The householders, in clear distinction from their counterparts in other parts of Europe, did not pay taxes to their kings and chieftains. The development of towns was also different in Scandinavia than on the Continent and in England, where many more towns were established. The fundamental element of the Viking Age economy was certainly the farm. In Scandinavia, as elsewhere in Europe, it was local food production that provided the basis for society's continued existence. Yet, pillaging and trade brought great riches to Scandinavia and strongly contributed to shaping the economic system back home. There was tension between these sources of income. Because people in Viking Age society lived a hand-to-mouth existence, plundering and trading claimed human resources that would otherwise be working the farm. At the same time, food production needed to be increased in response to the growth of the population, which was increasing during the whole period.

The Farm

Let us divert our attention for a moment from Scandinavia in the Viking Age to England during the Second World War. At this time, the traditional division of labor between the sexes changed radically. While the men fought on the front, the women had to work not only in the home but also in the factories, in offices, and on the farms. In other words, they took over many of the roles previously filled by men. One can say that England, to a degree, was run by women during the war. In similar fashion, the extent of warfare and trade in Viking Age Scandinavia must have meant that quite a large percentage of the men were absent for long periods—in some cases, several years—and many never returned home at all. This situation must have led to a great number of women being responsible for the running of the farms. Without the efforts of the women, there would have been no Viking Age.

It has been claimed that in the year 847, more than one thousand Scandinavian men were killed in battles in Ireland.[2] If we take this as the low end of the possible number of men killed in raids and warfare abroad during the Viking Age—and I should stress that these are only estimates—then 250,000 Scandinavians were killed in the period around 800 to 1050. If we continue to play with numbers and guess that equally as many Scandinavians settled abroad or drowned on their journeys, then we are talking about five hundred thousand individuals. As previously mentioned, we do not know what the population of Scandinavia was during the Viking Age. However, in chapter 1 we estimated that it would have been around six hundred and fifty thousand in around the year 800, and one million around 1050. Even though all these numbers are uncertain, we do know that many Scandinavians, especially men, died abroad or did not return home. As a result of this situation, women played crucial roles in maintaining Scandinavian society.

Additionally, to compensate for the loss of half a million Scandinavians, thralls had to be either bought or captured—that is, the keeping of thralls became a precondition for the Vikings being able to continue their activities abroad to the degree that they did. In a way, this was a self-intensifying process. The more wealth the Vikings acquired abroad, the more thralls they could buy, and the more free people could leave their traditional tasks on the farms to engage in Viking activities. The number of men who could go on Viking voyages was still limited by factors such as the birth rate, however. It therefore became important to the great men, especially the kings, to secure the support of warriors from outside Scandinavia.

A central aspect of the economic development during this period was demographic growth. Demographic growth is measured as the difference between the number of people who are born and the number of people who die. The number of people being born is related to the birth rate, which is impacted by the average age of women giving birth for the first time. A small shift in women's average age could have major consequences, since a higher average age at first childbirth shortens the childbearing period, whereas a lower average age has the opposite effect. The average life expectancy during the Viking Age, as in the Middle Ages in general, was low—probably thirty to thirty-five years for men and a little lower for women. (By contrast, in Norwegian society today, it is about eighty-one years for men and eighty-four years for women.) One factor that makes the average age at death lower is a high rate of infant mortality. It is likely that 15 to 20 percent of all Viking Age infants died before they reached the age of one, and probably about 30 percent of the population died before they reached their twenties. Those who reached thirty, however, had a reasonably good chance of living for another twenty years. That the population rapidly increased despite such a high mortality rate points to a high birth rate.[3]

To provide for an ever-growing population, forests had to be cleared and new villages and farms established. We can see this development through the study of place-names. For example, those that end in *-stad* (*staðir*, settlement), *-rud* (*ruð*, derived from "clearing"), *-torp* (*þorp*, farm, or gathering of houses) and *-tved* (*þveit*, small piece of land) were among the most dominant types of place-names during the period circa 800 to 1300. This nomenclature was particularly connected with new clearings of woods and outfields— that is, land of somewhat poor agricultural quality. The social elite probably organized most of the clearings. Draining large marshes, damming waterways, and clearing wooded areas required significant labor forces and organization. Only the greater landed lords could coordinate such work. In the Middle Ages, land was valuable only once it could be exploited, and therefore the social elite had an economic interest in making new usable land.[4]

The most common settlement type during the Viking Age in Norway was the single-family farm. In Denmark and Sweden, it was the village—that is, a grouping of farms. The farm's existence depended on what it could produce itself. However, access to varying natural resources forced the farms to specialize their production somewhat. For example, a number of householders based their incomes on extensive fishing or extraction of iron ore. These products were exchanged for other commodities the householders needed to survive. This specialization made it possible to make better use of the natural resources. In the *Voyages of Ohthere*, the author describes his farm and his riches. He was a wealthy man who owned twenty cows, twenty sheep, and twenty pigs, and what little he plowed, he plowed with a horse. In addition to this, he owned six hundred tame reindeer. His riches, however, were mostly based on the tribute paid to him by the Sami people. This tax consisted of animal skins, bird feathers, whale bones, and ship's ropes made of seal and whale skin. The wealthiest of the Sami were taxed "fifteen marten skins, five reindeer skins, one bear skin and ten measures of feathers, and a jacket of bearskin or otterskin and two ship-ropes. Each of these must be sixty ells long, one made from whale-hide the other from seal."[5] However, farm animals and tax revenues were not the only things that provided Ohthere with his daily sustenance. Fishing, hunting, and foraging in the wild were also important sources of income.

Further south, the cultivation of grain was common wherever it was possible. It was extremely important in Trøndelag, Jæren in Rogaland, Eastern Norway, Skåne, the area around Mälaren, and Denmark. During the Viking Age, the development of the heavy plow was a great breakthrough that contributed to increasing the crop yield. The most important types of grain were rye and barley, but oats and wheat were also grown. Grain production was the optimal way of making use of the land. One could gain ten times more calories from an area if it was used for raising crops rather than for meat production.[6]

Both bread and porridge were made from grain, and porridge appears to have been a staple of most Scandinavian people's diet. Another reason for growing grain was the need for ale, which was brewed from barley, oats, and mixed grain. Lighter ale, together with milk and soured milk, was an everyday drink, while stronger ale, mead (which one needed honey to brew), and imported wine were used for feasting. How much alcohol these drinks contained is unknown, but they were probably not very strong.[7]

Figure 15. Harvesting. Source: *Snorre Sturlason kongesagaer*, trans. Gustav Storm (Christiania: J. M. Stenersen, 1899).

Animal husbandry also played a role in farming. The most important animals were cattle (oxen were used as draft animals), sheep and goats (especially in Norway), pigs (especially in the south), and horses. The resources and privileges that belonged to the farm, primarily forests and the rights to hunt, trap, fish, and gather berries and fruit therein, were significant supplements to the primary methods of food production. To utilize these resources, many of the farms, especially in Norway, owned one or more shielings, farm outposts located in more remote areas.

Coastal fishing was also relatively common. Archaeological investigations in Vestlandet indicate that there was an intensification of coastal fishing in the period from around 600 to 1300. For example, a number of fishing villages and cabins were established in Hordaland during this period.[8] It was the combination of cultivation, animal husbandry, fishing, hunting, and gathering from the wild that characterized farming in Viking Age Scandinavia.

The size of villages in Denmark and Sweden varied greatly, ranging from just a few inhabitants in the smallest villages to several hundred people in the largest ones. One of the most thoroughly examined villages in Denmark is Vorbasse (map 7), in southern Jylland. It was already well established by the beginning of the Viking Age; at that time it consisted of seven farms, and that was the case throughout the whole period. The settlement at Vorbasse can be divided into two phases, with a break at the end of the 900s. Up until this point, the main house on each farm had been divided into two, with the family living in one part and the other part being used as a stable. Afterward, the village was completely remodeled and the farms re-established with separate stables. The (re)organization of the village hints at higher-level regulation. However, one cannot interpret this to mean that the seven householders were independent and equal free men. "They were more likely some type of tenant householders subjected to a landed lord, who exerted some degree of control over the conditions in the village."[9] Around the year 800, the lot of each single farm expanded from about 1.4 acres to around 2.2 acres, the average being about 1.7 acres. At the end of the 900s, when the village was reorganized, the lots of some of the farms grew to closer to 6.2 acres.[10]

In Viking Age society, and other agrarian societies, uncertainty about climate, flooding, droughts, and erosion was part of one's everyday life. We assume that there was collaboration between the householders to reduce these worries. Much suggests that an organization existed for just this purpose, probably the one later known as the householders' guild.[11]

The Household

The household, the people who ate at the same table and slept under the same roof, was the fundamental social unit of Viking Age society.[12] There were great differences between the households of the chieftains, which consisted of several dozens, if not hundreds, of people, and the householders' households of four or five persons. But whether the farm was small or large, the work that needed to be done during the year followed a set cycle. It started in the spring, when the men left on raiding or trading voyages. The period up to the beginning of June was hectic, with those who stayed behind tending to both the animals and the fields where crops were cultivated. After this intense period of work, a few weeks of lighter labor followed during which the houses and fences were repaired. In late summer the haying began, and it lasted for the remainder of the summer. The gathering of fodder was very labor intensive and time consuming, as it included both deliberately sown and wild growth fields. The enclosures between farm buildings and the wild

fields in places such as hillsides, mounds, riverbanks, and small islands all
had to be mown. Gathering enough fodder to keep the livestock alive
throughout the winter months was an existential question—this was especially the case in the areas where animals could not be kept outside all year
round. Grain also had to be harvested, and if the crop was good, a large part
of the winter was probably also used for threshing the grain.

The duties of the household varied according to the size of the farm. In a
small community, we presume that most people actively participated in all the
farming, including children, adults, and the elderly, and not least the thralls.
The threat of famine always lurked in the background, and it was therefore
crucial that as many people as possible worked on producing food. The exceptions to this were the chieftains, the wealthiest householders and their families, warriors, and at a later date also the clergy. Industriousness was a virtue,
as clearly expressed in *Hávamál*:

> 59. *He should get up early, the man who has few workers,*
> and set about his work with thought;
> much gets held up for the man sleeping in in the morning;
> wealth is half-won by activity.

And everyone needed to contribute:

> 71. *The lame man rides a horse, the handless man drives a herd,*
> the deaf man fights and succeeds;
> to be blind is better than to be burnt:
> a corpse is of no use to anyone.[13]

The second stanza displays a certain respect for the disabled at the same time
as it reveals another characteristic aspect of Scandinavian warrior society during the Viking Age: many men must have returned home from Viking voyages with severe injuries.

Tasks on the farm were clearly ranked according to their type. Heavy
labor such as tilling, carrying water, grinding grain, and tending to animals
ranked lowest. These tasks were perceived as labor for the lowborn, as seen
in the description of the thralls in *Rígsþula*. That women were thought capable of handling heavy workloads is evident from Norse mythology, where
the female thralls Fenja and Menja, who were both large and strong, were
tasked by their owner with turning grindstones so large that no other

person could move them.[14] A householder and his wife shared a common interest in and a division of responsibility for the success of their farm. The wife usually took care of or led the work inside the house such as preparing, storing, and handing out the food. The householder was in charge of the labor that took place outside of the house. But as we have seen, when the householder was away, for example when he was participating in the *þing* or on Viking or trading voyages, the wife assumed his responsibilities as well as the ones she already had.

We do not know the size of the average household in Scandinavia during the Viking Age. Usually scholars assume that it consisted of five to seven people, which is the number we are going to use here. When it comes to its composition, we are once more on thin ice, but let us presume that it was made up of a married couple, two or three of their children, one or two laborers, and the same number of thralls. Viking Age society had a functional definition of age, and one was considered a child until one could perform the tasks society expected from an adult; one became old once one could no longer complete those tasks. The transition between the different stages was therefore blurred. One probably became an adult sometime between the ages of twelve and sixteen, but the point at which one was considered old is indeterminable. No particular rights were connected with a specific age as in our modern society. Only a few, if any, knew their exact birthday, but even so, people knew how many winters they had endured.[15]

We can also note that in sources from the twelfth and thirteenth centuries, respect for children and the elderly was minimal. They were considered a burden, and there is no reason to believe that the conditions were any different during the Viking Age. This lack of respect is reflected, for example, in the words used to describe the elderly, which almost without exception were negatively loaded. The old were described as stiff, weak, cowardly, ugly, toothless, senile, and unable to eat. The negative attitude toward old people and children is by all accounts caused by the great value placed on work, whether this was labor on the farm or participation in Viking raids. These two groups were unable to work as much as the adults and were thus perceived as burdens, with an accompanying lack of recognition.[16]

To compensate for the loss of workforce when the men were away, the household had to be expanded, and the common solution was to bring in thralls. We do not know how long a history slavery has in Scandinavia, but many things point to it having very old origins. It had without a doubt become a fully developed institution by the Viking Age. There is no information on the number of slaves in Scandinavia at any given time. In the *Frostaþing* law, we read that if a man puts out another man's eye, the victim could be compensated with a farm, twelve cows, two horses, and three thralls (*mannsmenn*).[17] Jørn Sandnes has conducted a quantitative assessment on the basis of this legal provision, estimating that the number of slaves in Norway in the Viking Age was fifty to seventy-five thousand, about 20 to 30 percent of the population.[18] Guesswork for Sweden has resulted in the same number; we do not have any guesses for Denmark.[19]

One of the few concrete numbers concerning the extent of slavery during the Middle Ages is found in the English *Domesday Book* from 1086. According to it, about 10 percent of the total population of England were slaves, and in the parts of the country in where slaveholding was the most extensive, the numbers approached 25 percent. In the "somewhat ill-defined" Danelaw, slavery "did not differ from the rest of England as far as the prevalence of slavery was concerned. It was as much a part of the social structure there as it was in Mercian Warwickshire, where 12.4 per cent of the recorded population were slaves, and in West-Saxon Wiltshire, where 16 per cent were slaves."[20] A number of uncertainties are connected with these figures, and

Figure 16. Thralls and their master: Erling Skjalgsson (d. 1028) sets his thralls to work.
Source: *Snorre Sturlason kongesagaer,* trans. Gustav Storm
(Christiania: J. M. Stenersen, 1899).

much points to the number of slaves having been larger before the Norman invasion in 1066.[21] It is therefore not unlikely that slaves comprised about 15 to 20 percent of the population in England in the Viking Age. Of course, these numbers do not necessarily correlate exactly to conditions in Scandinavia. But if we look at the largest numbers from England, then an assumption of about two thralls on an average farm in the Viking Age is not unrealistic (25 percent, if we believe the household to have consisted of about seven people).[22]

Slaves were crucial for the running of the average farm, not to mention for the production of iron, ships, and sails. Vikings both sold and bought slaves. The "new" big slave market in Scandinavia in the Viking Age and the Vikings' increasing demand for slaves had a great impact. In Ireland, the Irish kings started to capture people from other Irish kingdoms, selling them to the Vikings on the slave markets in Dublin, for example. In 1031, the *Annals of Ulster* record that Uí Néill captured 1,200 people.[23] According to the annals and the chronicles, most of the captives were women. This was probably because it was easier to control women than men, they could work equally as hard as men could, and not least of all, they could be used as sex slaves. Supply of slaves was also organized internally. People in Scandinavia could be enslaved by debtors as penalty for crimes. But the main form of internal supply was that the children of female slaves in most cases became slaves themselves.[24]

The Chieftain's Residential Farm

It is often difficult to determine whether a farm was a central farm (i.e., the residence of a chieftain) or not, due to uncertainties concerning continuity. In Iceland, where we have a good overview of the farms used by the Icelandic chieftains during the period of 930 to circa 1260, only two or three farms continually served as the chieftains' centers during the whole of the period. The development was probably not significantly different in Scandinavia, especially when it comes to the smaller power centers. At the really grand ones, however, such as Borg in Lofoten, Avaldsnes, and Uppåkra, we can assume that the degree of continuity was significantly higher.

In *Rígspula*, we hear that the earl owned eighteen farms, and there is little reason to doubt that the social elite as a whole owned substantial riches.

Typically, in addition to the main farms that served as their base, they owned several smaller farms. In Western Norway, the chieftains' power was economically based on large estates and tenancies. In areas set further away from the chieftains' seats, independent farms were more common. At the beginning of the Viking Age, most householders in Scandinavia probably lived on their own farms and were free. By 1300, this situation had completely reversed. The householders were still free, but a greater proportion of them had now become tenants. Scholars disagree on how to explain this development. For us, it is important to assume that the clearing of land continued at a more or less regular pace from 800 to 1300, and it was probably this pace that influenced the rate of the transition from independent to tenant ownership and farming. This indicates a slow-paced development. It also needs to be stressed that the relationships between land owners and tenants were personal—that is, that the tenants were also the friends of the chieftains.[25]

In the saga about the Norwegian king Olaf Haraldsson, it is written that the most powerful chieftain in Vestlandet, Erling Skjalgsson, always kept thirty thralls in addition to other servants at his farm.[26] He gave the thralls their daily tasks, but during the evenings and nights, they were given leave to work for themselves. Erling is supposed to have provided the thralls with fields where they could plant their own crops, and its harvest belonged to them. He determined a price for each thrall's freedom, and many managed to gather enough money to buy their freedom after a year or two, while those less capable managed it within three years' time. With this money, Erling bought new thralls. His freedmen—that is, the thralls who had become free—were assigned to herring fishing or other industries, and some cleared forests and settled there. While we must again remain critical of the story as a historical source, it does highlight three central aspects of thralls' position in society. The first is the large number of thralls the saga author believed Erling kept on his farm. Another is that it was possible for the thralls to gain their freedom through the process of manumission. Slaves who were granted their freedom remained economically indebted to their former masters, and their offspring would continue to remain so for generations. This relationship could be highly profitable for lords, provided that land was available on which to settle the freedmen. Precisely the same system seems to have been common in the other Nordic countries. The third aspect is that the farm Erling ran must have been exceedingly large. It appears that most of these enormous farms disappeared during the 900s and 1000s and that population growth and, later, diminished access to slaves made maintaining this type of establishment problematic.[27]

The chieftains' farms, especially those in the north, made use of all types of resources found on the varied terrains of their estates, which included forests, quarries (for soapstone), rivers (for salmon), hunting grounds, and areas for trapping and gathering eggs and down. Some of these resources could be used to feed large parties of companions and participants at feasts, while others could be exported, such as the down and feathers found in the Oseberg burial mound.[28] That such wild resources, together with trade in hides, were profitable sources of revenue to the Northern Norwegian chieftains is perhaps best reflected in the greatest chieftain's residence known from the Viking Age, Borg in Lofoten, with a great hall measuring eighty-one yards in length!

In the unification process of Norway kings confiscated many of the farms and estates of their opponents. These properties, usually referred to as royal farms, afforded the kingdom a relatively stable income, and they became important elements in its economic foundation. There is no information

Figure 17. The great hall on a chieftain's farm. Source: *Snorre Sturlason kongesagaer*, trans. Gustav Storm (Christiania: J. M. Stenersen, 1899).

about the extent of these confiscations, but much points to this being a widespread practice. We know of about twenty royal farms in the period before 1130. In addition to these, there are about thirty-five to forty larger royal, clerical, and/or ecclesiastical properties known from the High and Late Middle Ages. These farms were either run by the king's *ármaðr* (from *árr*, servant) or given to the king's *hirðmenn*.[29] These farms were by all accounts thought of as estates belonging to the kingdom, and they could be granted or rented out only for the duration of the king's reign. However, the king could still give away his private properties as gifts to his friends.

Plunder and Treasure

> Here terrible portents came about in the land of Northumbria, and miserably frightened the people: these were immense flashes of lightening, and fiery dragons were seen flying in the air. A great famine immediately followed these signs; and a little after that in the same year on 8 January the raiding of heathen men miserably devastated God's church in Lindisfarne island by looting and slaughter.[30]

Thus reads the famous inscription from the *Anglo-Saxon Chronicle* about the Viking attack on the monastery of Lindisfarne in northeastern England in the year 793.[31] After this attack, the Vikings set course for Ireland. The attacks on England started anew around 830, and for the next two hundred years, the country remained the Vikings' main target. In 850, a Viking fleet, probably consisting of around 350 ships, wintered there for the first time, on the island of Thanet at the mouth of the river Thames, and used this as a base from which to raid. Up until this time, the Viking voyages to England had been seasonal phenomena. The English attempted to pay off the Vikings to stop the attacks. The first such payment of tribute or protective money, known as the Danegeld, was made in 865. The next year, the largest Viking fleet to have attacked England up to this point arrived. This army had rampaged through the Carolingian Empire on the continent for several years and went to England with a new goal in sight: settlement.

The arrival of the Vikings in 866 is often referred to as the second phase of the attacks on England, when the Vikings went from sporadic attacks to campaigning. With this assault, the Danes began their conquest of eastern

England, the area that later would be known as the Danelaw. Prior to 865, only rarely were the forces attacking England larger than about twenty ships—the fighting force aboard a Viking ship is often thought to have been around thirty to sixty men, in addition to the helpers, children, and women. After 865, the forces are said to have consisted of between eighty and 350 ships. The leaders of the Viking raids were usually kings, pretenders to thrones, and chieftains. For example, in 994 Svein Forkbeard and Olaf Tryggvason led an attack on London with ninety-four ships.[32] By all accounts, these changes in the size of the fleets reflect the fact that kings, and especially the Danish kings, had started to play a greater role in organizing Viking raids. It should be stressed, however, that the *Anglo-Saxon Chronicle* and the Irish *Annals*, which are our main sources for the Viking attacks in England and Ireland, mention only the larger ones. None of the small-scale assaults led by the local chieftains from Scandinavia, bringing only two, three, or four ships, were recorded.[33]

The payment of Danegeld continued throughout the 800s and 900s and secured great riches for the Vikings. According to the *Anglo-Saxon Chronicle*, the English paid around two hundred thousand pounds of silver to the Vikings during the period from around 991 to 1050. We do not know how large a percentage of the riches acquired by the Vikings abroad made its way back to Scandinavia. Everything points to a significant amount having been brought home and used, for example in the local power games. A large portion of the riches acquired by the Vikings on their raids probably ended up in the pockets of the Danish kings. It is no coincidence that during the years 991 to 1014, the golden age of paying Danegeld, two Viking kings, Olaf Tryggvason and Olaf Haraldsson, literally bought their way to power in Norway. We do not know the extent of the riches the two Olafs brought home with them from England, but according to the sagas, they used the English silver to establish friendships with Norwegian chieftains. The wealth could also be used by the kings to maintain their positions of power and their networks. This is made clear by Swedish rune stones, which mention Cnut the Great giving silver to his men.[34] However, it was not only through pillaging and extortion that the Vikings secured riches. They also frequently served as mercenaries to kings in Europe, which brought them great wealth.

The Vikings were not as busy with extortion in other parts of Western Europe. In the Baltics they both traded and plundered, but their main activity was mercantile.[35] In the northern areas, the Sami had to pay taxes to the Vikings, and if we are to believe the written sources, such as the tales of Ohthere, this was a common practice that seems to have been quite lucrative. The difference between paying taxes and giving gifts was often unclear. This is seen in the term *kattgjöf* (tax-gift).[36] This means that the taxes paid were perceived as both a tax and a gift, and that the purpose of paying them was both to signal submission and to establish friendship and, as a consequence, protection. It was not just the chieftains in Northern Norway who demanded taxes from the Sami, but also the kings. Here, the information in *Egil's saga* is interesting. The saga states that chieftain Thorolf Kveldulfsson collected taxes from the Sami on behalf of the Norwegian king. In return, the Sami were provided with protection against other kings and chieftains operating in the northern parts, whether Swedish or Russian. Thorolf's relationship with the Sami was not one-sided, however; he also arranged for trade with them, signaling the importance of the relationship to both parties. We can presume that it was important to the Sami to acquire iron tools, which would make it easier for them to use the natural resources of the north. Through this taxation and trade, the Sami were integrated into the redistributive system of the northern chieftains.[37]

The skins provided by the Sami were a resource with which chieftains and kings could make large profits in the European markets. We can clearly see from Adam of Bremen's description of Sweden and the Swedes that skins were sought after in Europe. Adam writes that Sweden is very fertile, that it is rich in everything, and that the Swedes worship "vainglory; that is, gold, silver, stately chargers, beaver and marten pelts, which make us lose our minds admiring them."[38] These products were costly: three marten pelts equaled the value of a whole cow.[39]

Much suggests that the earls of Lade, up to the beginning of the 1000s, controlled the trade route northward along the coast to Northern Norway and further into the White Sea south of the Barents Sea, and eastward to Härjedalen and Jämtland. This hegemony probably provided the earls of Lade with a great deal of wealth. But when all these goods were shipped further south, into the kingdom of Vestlandet and then into the realm of the Danish kings, the merchants probably had to give gifts or pay tribute to the kings—a form of tax that would provide them with protection. This means that there was great potential for income along the "northern way." This was probably a contributing factor to the Danish kings' strong interest in these regions. However, the trade routes, which stretched from the north down into the realm of the Swedish king, were on land for the most part, and the Danish kings could not take control of the overland routes without conquering the Swedish kingdom.

The relationship between the Sami and the Norwegian chieftains and kings has similarities with the situation in England between the Vikings and the English. The Vikings must have been aware of the foolishness of plundering and taxing the English too heavily. This would reduce their willingness to run their farms, and consequently their surplus. To the Vikings it was therefore a matter of finding the right balance and, in a way, coming to an understanding with the people they were raiding. Danegeld can be considered a tax the natives had to pay to the Vikings, but it also bought them peace. We can even go so far as to claim that Viking control of England benefited most people more than it hurt them, since unlike the English kings, the Vikings could ensure peace. This was a win-win situation: the householders had to pay taxes as they had before, now to the Vikings, but in return they were provided with peace. For their part, the Vikings did not have to bother with raiding, but could concentrate on giving protection and collecting revenue.[40] That the Danish Vikings were considerate to the local population of England is evident in the events of 1005 CE as reported by the *Anglo-Saxon Chronicle*. That year, they came to plunder but returned home without attacking because of a famine in England. The year after, they came again and pillaged. The English king ordered the whole population of Wessex and Mercia to be conscripted to the defense of their country during the harvest, meaning that food production suffered. The king was unsuccessful in stopping the Vikings, and they plundered everywhere. The chronicler then adds that the king's tactics did more harm than any internal or external army could have done.[41]

We cannot presume that the Vikings maintained similar relationships with the other areas they attacked, such as Ireland, Scotland, France, and the Baltics. In Ireland, the Vikings did establish some towns, but they were primarily on the hunt for goods or slaves to sell.[42]

Peter Sawyer has claimed that the incredible development of the English economy in the century before the Norman Conquest of 1066 was based on its "abundant and widely dispersed coinage, which was made possible by a flourishing export trade."[43] Because of the regular Viking attacks during most of this period and the Viking rule of England up to about 1040, it seems quite unthinkable that English merchants or farmers were running this trade by themselves. Either the Vikings ran it, or they protected it. The Vikings were the dominant party in almost all foreign trade during the Viking Age in western, northern, and parts of eastern Europe. They either organized this trade themselves or collected payoffs from merchants who needed their protection. This means that at the same time the Vikings were being paid large sums of Danegeld, they were also collaborating in trade across the North Sea and toward the Rhine. The income from this trade or protection, of which the Danish kings undoubtedly acquired a large share, was possibly even more significant than the Danegeld.

Trade, Marketplaces, and Towns

The saga about St. Olaf Haraldsson describes the close connection between *blót*, *þing*, and trade in Uppsala. After the introduction of Christianity, the Swedes stopped the *blóts* but continued to have *þing* and markets. There are no such records of *þing* locations within the borders of the Danish or the Norwegian kingdoms, but we can safely assume that trade occurred in larger and smaller *þing* across Scandinavia. Therefore, we have every reason to believe that the regional lawthings, such as the *Gulaþing* in Norway, were among the most preeminent marketplaces in Scandinavia during the Viking Age. In addition, it is thought that there were many local *þing*, not always organized regularly, that were also used as seasonal markets.

Trade of course also took place at markets. Most of the few Viking Age trading sites we can locate with any certainty are found in close proximity to the power centers. Among these are, for example, Avaldnes, Giske, Lade, and Bjarkøy in Norway; Åhus and Löddeköpinge, both in Skåne; and Sebbersund by Limfjorden in Denmark. For those who came to trade, it was important that the exchange happen in places where it would be undisturbed, either at a sacred *þing* site or, after the introduction of Christianity, in a church or churchyard—that is, a place under the protection of the chieftain, king or saint. Most of these trading sites were in use for only a short period of time probably because of the instability of the power structures around them.[44]

But what about the towns?[45] We can divide the growth of towns during this time into two phases: the first phase from 800 to 950, and the second from 950 to 1050. From the first phase, only four towns are known: Ribe (c. 710),

Birka (c. 770), Kaupang (c. 800), and Hedeby (c. 810). These are also the places in Scandinavia where there was long-distance trade and where finds of silver and silver coins attest to silver's use as currency. During the second phase, Kaupang permanently disappears from the scene, activity in Ribe diminishes, and the activities in Birka are moved to Sigtuna, further north along Mälaren (map 8). At the same time, a number of new towns are established, nearly all of them in the part of Scandinavia ruled by the Danish kings. Evidently, the royalty was active in this development, later on further supported by the church: many of the most important towns also became episcopal sees.[46]

By all accounts, Birka in Mälaren was founded by the Swedish king in the second half of the 700s. On the neighboring island of Adelsö, there was a royal farm which could offer protection to nearby trading. Around 800, as many as seven hundred to one thousand people might have lived in the town, which served as the point of origin for trade routes spanning large parts of Europe, particularly toward the east. These activities ceased around 1000 CE, probably because upheaval changed the depth of the water, making it impossible for ships to sail in from the Baltic Sea through the route that passes modern-day Södertälje.[47]

Ribe, on the west coast of Jylland, is the oldest town in the north, and was founded around the same time the Kanhave Canal at Samsø was dug (726 CE) and the Danevirke expanded (737 CE). From the end of the 700s, there are traces of permanent settlement at Ribe, so we can assume that life carried on there throughout the year. Trade activity in Ribe appears to have been absent from the second half of the 800s to the mid-1000s. In 948, in the midst of its economic crisis, Ribe became an episcopal see, which probably contributed to the town's continued survival. The episcopal sees benefited from trading and extensive construction-related activity, and every year they had several thousand visitors, all of whom needed a place to spend the night and something to eat.[48]

The border toward the south of the Danish kingdom was not only significant for military reasons, it was also economically important. The Danish kings channeled as much of the trade in the border areas as possible through Hedeby to make the most profit for themselves. In 808, the Danish king Gudfred attacked the Slavic Obotrites and ruined their blooming trading town of Reric on the Baltic coast, possibly near present-day Lübeck in Schleswig-Holstein. Gudfred kidnapped the merchants there and installed

Map 8. Towns in Scandinavia

them in Hedeby. Hedeby grew quickly and became the largest trading town in the north.[49]

Kaupang was founded about the same time as Hedeby. Its most active period was in the 800s, and the excavations that have taken place there reveal that it received goods from the British Isles, the Baltic countries, and the areas around the Rhine. The imported goods were probably exchanged for local raw materials and products. In the beginning of the 900s, the trading site was abandoned. We are uncertain why, but it was probably due to changes in the political situation in the area and/or the establishment of newer trading routes.

All of this means that around the year 800, the Danish kings controlled three of the four important towns in Scandinavia. These three were very strategically placed. Hedeby dominated the trade into the Baltic Sea, Baltic countries, and Germany, Ribe the trading around the North Sea, and Kaupang toward the trading route along the coast of Vestlandet, Trøndelag, and Northern Norway. The Danish kings therefore had control of most of the foreign trade in Scandinavia, and by all accounts it provided them with great profits through taxation.[50]

Over the course of one hundred years beginning in the mid-900s, town development in Scandinavia underwent great changes. Of the old towns, Hedeby was the only one still flourishing at the end of this period. Birka and Kaupang, as mentioned, disappeared from the map, and Ribe was greatly reduced in size and importance. On the other hand, a number of new towns were established, most of them within the jurisdiction of the Danish kings. There is scholarly consensus about the kings being the primary force behind the establishment of towns in Scandinavia, though the church and the chieftains also played their parts. Towns sprang up around trade routes and merchants, but the kings, and to a lesser degree the chieftains, were the ones who, for a price, provided the trade with the necessary security.[51] The second half of the 900s saw the establishment of Visby, Lund, Viborg, Roskilde, and Aarhus, all already or soon to become episcopal sees, and Aalborg, where coins were minted at the beginning of the 1000s. Sigtuna was founded around 980 by Erik the Victorious (c. 970–995). Skara was established around 1020 and Lödöse around 1050. In Norway, according to the sagas, Trondheim was founded by Olaf Tryggvason (c. 1000), Sarpsborg by Olaf Haraldsson (c. 1016), and Oslo by Harald Hardruler (c. 1050). Some scholars have argued that the founding of Oslo must be seen in light of political conditions and their attendant power relations at the end of the 900s. The theory is that either Harald Bluetooth or Svein Forkbeard (d. 1014) was behind the town's establishment, and that Oslo was first and foremost a military and administrative center during the period up to the middle of the 1000s.[52] One can hardly doubt Oslo's strategic significance. As mentioned, Snorri Sturluson writes in *Heimskringla* that Harald Hardruler was based in Oslo because it was easiest to defend the country and attack the Danes from there.

How did the towns function in relation to the land around them? The most common definition of a medieval town has two elements—role and structure. Towns were responsible for certain tasks in relation to the surrounding areas. The most important roles were economic, administrative, cultural, and religious. This resulted in the development of specialist groups in the towns, such as merchants, craftsmen, clergy, and officials. Only the largest towns, however, encompassed all of these roles, and they developed over time. Medieval towns were also distinct from their surroundings in that they had their own sets of laws and government, and a denser population.[53] This definition can be applied to European towns in the 1100s and 1200s, but not to the Viking towns. These did not have their own laws, nor did they have any administrative or religious central functions, apart from the small number of towns that later became episcopal sees. This means that we can define the Viking Age towns only as primarily trading and artisanal sites with year-round settlements, denser populations, and some economic specialization.

How great a percentage of all trading in Scandinavia took place in towns is uncertain, but most of the trade happened at the local markets, where the chieftains were far less dependent on foreign merchants. The chieftains owned their own ships and certainly used these to a large extent to obtain the goods they needed from abroad. We can also assume that there were others besides the chieftains who sailed abroad in order to trade locally. These merchants were probably organized in a *félag*, which means that they came together to cover the expenses of goods and to rent ships if they did not own ships themselves. *Félag* could also be established between parties where one person owned the ship and the other the goods. The number of such partners could sometimes become large, up to several dozen. The merchants enjoyed great social standing, and in addition they were often good warriors, as they needed to be able to protect themselves—not least from other Vikings.[54]

The towns in Scandinavia brought in goods from diverse and distant areas, such as chalices from Francia, Slavic ceramics, and Byzantine glass beads. The Vikings' trade routes and networks stretched across large parts of the known world (map 5). Our understanding of goods production in the towns and the trade that took place there is built on the material discovered through archaeological excavations. But this does not tell the whole story. A large percentage of the trade in the earliest towns was probably in luxury items, such as skins, silks, and wine, which leave almost no archaeological traces. The same applies to the slave trade. How the goods were priced is unknown, but it probably came down to the merchants and the customers agreeing on a price, with the king or the chieftain providing a guarantee of purchase.

The Vikings were skilled craftsmen. Archaeological finds bear witness to the practice of many types of crafts. Wood was carved into tools, leather tanned and made into shoes, wool woven into fabrics that were made into clothes. Iron was necessary to make tools, ships, and weapons. The weaponsmiths had the highest social standing, which reflects the warrior mentality of the society. Other craftsmen worked in gold, silver, and bronze; still others made beads and combs of bone. We have seen that the Vikings gained prestige by showing off their wealth through the use and gifting of costly jewelry and items. *Rígsþula* stresses this: Rig was served food on a plate decorated with silver, and wine from a silver chalice. Craftsmen might have made such items in the hall of the chieftain, and they were possibly part of the chieftain's household.[55] The craftsmen in the towns, on the other hand, were probably more independent.

The use of rare metals and coinage changed over the course of the Viking Age. Apart from in Ribe, archaeologists have found very few coins in Scandinavia from the beginning of the period. All treasure finds from the period circa 900 to 950 include a preponderance of unminted silver: jewelry, silver objects, and hacksilver—that is, silver items chopped up for use in trade. Coins make up only about 15 percent of the silver, and they are primarily Kufic (Arabic), as well as a few of early English and Frankish origin. The regional differences are great when it comes to the supply: of the approximately eighty thousand Kufic coins found in Scandinavia, only about four hundred are found within the present-day Norwegian borders. During the period from 950 to 1000 CE, early English and Frankish coins became increasingly common, a reflection of the fact that the supply of silver from the

Persian caliphate ended in around 970 and silver mining in the Harz Mountains in Germany began around the same time; coins make up around 45 percent of all treasure finds from this period. Minted silver largely dominates the treasure finds from the last fifty years of the Viking Age—up to 85 percent.[56]

The area under the rule of the Danish kings appears to have acted as one collective economic unity, unlike the other parts of Scandinavia. This is seen, for example, in the deposit finds (valuable items that were hidden or buried for religious or political reasons) from Vestlandet and the Oslo area from the 900s. In Vestlandet, silver was used for precious jewelry, whereas it served as currency in eastern Norway and southern Scandinavia.[57] Even though silver became important to trade in Scandinavia and was easy to transport, it was the exchange of goods for natural resources that characterized local trade in Scandinavia.

If we were to describe the economic system in Scandinavia during the Viking Age using two terms, they would have to be *food* and *gifts*. The foundational unit of Scandinavian society was the farm. The starting point of farming was self-sufficiency, but far from every farm managed to be self-sufficient. They therefore needed to specialize in producing certain goods, which were sold to secure the items they needed to survive but could not make themselves. The Danish householders must have been completely dependent on iron imports to run their farms, and it is likely that the kings organized this importation. A large part of the population was occupied with plundering and trade, but for the society to survive, it was vital that the households produced enough food, and it is here in particular that the efforts of the wives and other women enter the picture. Much suggests that it was the women who kept the wheels turning, as it were, and made it possible for many men, and some women, to disappear for large parts of the year. We will never be able to fully establish the actual value of the riches the Vikings brought home with them to Denmark, Sweden, and Norway as a result of plunder, extortion, taxation, customs, mercenary wages, and trade, but we do know that it was enormous. Its magnitude is probably best demonstrated by the fact that in Denmark it seems there were no regular taxes until the 1100s, and in Norway, the *leiðangr* was transformed into a fixed yearly tax around the same time. In Sweden little is known about taxes and fees paid to the kings before the 1200s.[58]

Which, then, was more important—agriculture, or plundering and trading abroad? Scholars disagree on the relative significance of the internal and external resources. Thomas Lindkvist believes that resources in Scandinavia were few and insignificant, and coupled with the fact that taxation of the householders was fairly random, plunder and tribute from other areas were crucial to the local chieftains. At the same time, he stresses that some of the chieftains had large estates, but these were an exception to the rule.[59] Here, Lindkvist is inspired by Sawyer, who claimed that most of the resources the Vikings needed came from plunder and extortion in areas outside of Scandinavia.[60] But what about trade? As opposed to the raids, which did not occur every year, trade was conducted on a more regular schedule. The Vikings controlled the seas in western and northern Europe, the routes that bound the trading networks together, and this provided them with stable income. If we are to consider these three elements—agriculture, foreign trade, and plunder—we need to see them as a whole. It is the combination of these three elements that characterizes the economy of the Vikings.

Further Reading

Ashby, Steven P., and Søren M. Sindbæk, eds. *Crafts and Social Networks in Viking Towns.* Oxford: Oxbow Books, 2020.

Callmer, Johan, Ingrid Gustin, and Mats Roslund, eds. *Identity Formation and Diversity in the Early Medieval Baltic and Beyond: Communicators and Communication.* Leiden: Brill, 2016.

Gruszczynski, Jacek. *Viking Silver, Hoards, and Containers: The Archaeological and Historical Context of Viking-Age Silver Coin Deposits in the Baltic c. 800–1050.* London: Routledge, 2019.

Karras, Ruth Mazo. *Slavery and Society in Medieval Scandinavia.* New Haven, CT: Yale University Press, 1988.

Kurrild-Klitgaard, Peter, and Gert Tinggaard Svendsen. "Rational Bandits: Plunder, Public Goods, and the Vikings." *Public Choice* 117 (2003): 255–72.

Mägi, Marika. *The Viking Eastern Baltic.* Leeds: ARC Humanities Press, 2019.

Poulsen, Bjørn, and Søren M. Sindbæk, eds. *Settlement and Lordship in Viking and Early Medieval Scandinavia.* Turnhout, Belgium: Brepols, 2011.

Raffield, Ben. "The Slave Markets of the Viking World: Comparative Perspectives on an 'Invisible Archaeology.'" *Slavery and Abolition* 40 (2019): 1–24.

Skre, Dagfinn. "The Development of Urbanism in Scandinavia." In *The Viking World*, edited by Stefan Brink and Neil S. Price, 83–93. London: Routledge, 2008.

Wyatt, David. *Slaves and Warriors in Medieval Britain and Ireland, 800–1200.* Leiden: Brill, 2009.

Conclusion

The Viking Age Dynamic

This book began with a question: What characterizes the Viking Age in Scandinavia? To answer it, we have emphasized the following elements:

1. The Danish kings were dominant, and politics consisted of building networks
2. Power bases were built from the bottom up
3. The political situation was unstable but relatively peaceful
4. The Scandinavians were prone to war, but the violence was largely practiced abroad
5. Leaders competed by displaying their wealth and power, and their power centers were important for purposes of conspicuous consumption
6. There were clear ideas about distinct social ranks
7. The social elite controlled the practice of religion, and
8. The farm was the fundamental societal unit

Of course, there are also other elements that can be emphasized, but they are beyond the scope of this book. In explaining the Viking Age dynamic, we must focus on the interplay between political games at home and activities outside of Scandinavia. Resources obtained abroad were transported home in large quantities and used in local political maneuvering.

Chieftains needed to secure the friendship of the householders, who comprised the chieftains' power base. This happened through protection, gifts, and feasts, a costly business. There was aggressive competition between the chieftains over who could bestow the greatest gifts and organize the largest feasts. In addition, the chieftains and the kings competed in building the greatest halls and burial monuments. This also cost a great deal. To participate in the political game, a person needed great riches, which they had to give away generously to remain powerful. To become powerful, one needed to gain as many friends as possible—one had to become *vinsæll*. Because the householders made up this most central element of the chieftains' and kings' power bases, they could not be taxed, or the chieftains and kings risked losing their friendship.

Chieftains and kings were first and foremost concerned with their own power. The chieftains and kings also established friendships among themselves, but the loyalty to such a friendship was often weak, as participants were willing to exchange the friendship of a weak leader for one who was more powerful. These friendships were often established through marriage and the exchange of costly gifts. To the chieftains, entering into a friendship with another chieftain and maintaining it was less costly than establishing friendships with the householders. The same can be said about friendships among kings.

The Vikings were excellent craftsmen. For the chieftains, the kings, and their women, it was necessary to display their wealth, including bracelets, weapons, and jewelry. It was therefore important to the social elite to employ skilled craftsmen in their households. The competition this spurred also led to the development of newer methods of creating ever more elegant objects. The same goes for the Viking ships—their development should be seen in connection with the continuing need of the Vikings for larger and better ships.

We can assume that parts of the workforce on many farms spent significant time abroad—not just during spring and summer, but for several years at a time, and many probably never returned. Some of those who came back had been wounded and could resume their responsibilities only to a limited degree. To compensate for this and to be able to continue their activities abroad, Vikings bought or captured thralls. In a way, this was a self-intensifying process. The more wealth the Vikings acquired abroad, the more thralls they could buy, and the more people could be freed from their traditional tasks on the farms to engage in Viking activities. The number of men available to go on Viking voyages was still limited, however. It therefore became important to the great men, especially the kings, to secure the support of warriors from outside Scandinavia. At home, much points to women running the daily operations of the farms, taking on the very significant role of householder and having to fill both typical female and male roles to a much greater extent than in the High Middle Ages. This situation probably resulted in young women having much more freedom in their everyday lives than in the later period, including when it came to whom they were to marry and take as lovers.

The activities of the chieftains and the kings can be compared to a snowball—as it rolls on, it grows increasingly larger; if it stops, it starts to melt.

Figure 18. Harald Sigurdsson Hardruler is fatally wounded at the Battle of Stamford Bridge in 1066. Source: *Snorre Sturlason kongesagaer,* trans. Gustav Storm (Christiania: J. M. Stenersen, 1899).

To the chieftains and the kings, sitting still in times of peace could prove catastrophic. Without the income provided by raids and related activities, they could fulfill their obligations to their friends and *hirðmenn* only to a limited degree. If this continued, it would eventually decrease their power. Obtaining wealth was therefore an all-consuming goal. Without riches, there would be no feasts, no gifts, no friends, no power, and no honor. Attacking was the best defense.

The Scandinavian political situation was unstable. This was caused mainly by two factors. One was the economic instability of any individual leader, which would result in a loss of power and a changing political scene. The other was the problem of producing fit heirs. If there were no suitable heirs to inherit a family's position of power, that family would disappear from the political stage. This led to the chieftains becoming fewer and fewer in number, and the chiefdoms ever larger. At the same time, the kings' power increased during the Viking Age, at the expense of these same local chieftains. The tension and competition between the chieftains themselves and between the chieftains and the kings thus diminished. Political developments after the 1030s also evened up the balance between the three kingdoms in Scandinavia, as the Danish kings lost their dominant position. The new kings in England were strong enough to become a threat to the Scandinavian kings and could attack if provoked. This is why the Danish kings, like the Swedes, turned toward the Baltic Sea and Baltic countries. The Norwegian kings were cut off from this possibility, and so their focus shifted toward the North Atlantic and the islands to the west. In other words, it was the combination of internal and external factors that brought about the end to this period, which is sometimes referred to as Scandinavia's contribution to world history.

Rulers in Scandinavia
during the Viking Age

Earls of Lade

Hakon Grjotgardsson, d. c. 915
Sigurd Hakonsson, d. c. 962
Hakon Sigurdsson, d. c. 995
Svein Hakonsson, d. c. 1016
Eirik Hakonsson, d. c. 1024
Hakon Eiriksson, d. 1029

Kings of Norway (Viken, Vestlandet, and Trøndelag)

Harald Fairhair, c. 865–931
Erik Haraldsson Bloodaxe, c. 931–933
Hakon Haraldsson Adalsteinfostre, c. 933–960
Harald Eriksson Grafell, c. 960–970
Hakon Sigurdsson, c. 970–995
Olaf Tryggvason, 995–1000
Eirik and Svein Hakonsson, 1000–1015

St. Olaf Haraldsson, 1015–1028
Hakon Eiriksson, 1028–1029
Cnut Sveinsson the Great, 1028–1030
Svein Cnutsson (Alfivason), 1030–1035
Magnus Olafsson the Good, 1035–1047
Harald Sigurdsson Hardruler, 1045–1066
Magnus Haraldsson, 1066–1069
Olaf Haraldsson Kyrre (the Peaceful), 1067–1093

Danish Kings

Gorm the Old, c. 936–958/9
Harald Gormsson Bluetooth, c. 958/9–985/6
Svein Haraldsson Forkbeard, c. 986–1014
Harald Sveinsson, 1014–1018
Cnut Sveinsson the Great, 1018–1035
Harthacnut Cnutsson, 1035–1042
Magnus Olafsson the Good, 1042–1047
Svend Estridsson, 1047–1074

Swedish Kings

Erik the Victorious, c. 970–995
Olof Eriksson Skötkonung, c. 995–1022
Anund Olofsson Jacob, c. 1022–1050
Emund Olofsson the Old, c. 1050–1060
Stenkil Ragnvaldsson, c. 1060–1066

NOTES

Introduction

1. As we will see in our discussions of raiding, Viking expeditions, and the discovery of the islands in the northern Atlantic Ocean, there is no single explanation for the outbreak of the Viking Age. Rather, it is important to stress the interaction between several factors—for example, the need for wealth to secure power, the warrior mentality, and the level of technology. See, for example, Peter H. Sawyer, "The Causes of the Viking Age," in *The Vikings*, ed. R. T. Farrell (London: Phillimore, 1982), 1–7; Else Roesdahl, *The Vikings* (London: Viking Penguin, 1991), 187–94; Bjørn Myhre, "The Beginning of the Viking Age," in *Viking Revaluations*, ed. Anthony Faulkes and Richard Perkins (London: Viking Society for Northern Research, University College London, 1993), 182–204; Paddy Griffith, *The Viking Art of War* (London: Greenhill Books, 1995), 38–72; Peter H. Sawyer, "The Viking Expansion," in *The Cambridge History of Scandinavia*, vol. 1, *Prehistory to 1520*, ed. Knut Helle (Cambridge: Cambridge University Press, 2003), 106–9; Alex Woolf, *From Pictland to Alba: 789–1070* (Edinburgh: Edinburgh University Press, 2007), 52–57; James H. Barrett, "What Caused the Viking Age?," *Antiquity* 82 (2008): 671–85; Steven P. Ashby, "What Really Caused the Viking Age? The Social Content of Raiding and Exploration," *Archaeological Dialogues* 22 (2015): 89–106; Irene Baug et al., "The Beginning of the Viking Age in the West,"

Journal of Maritime Archaeology 13 (2018): 1–38; Aina Margrethe Heen-Pettersen, "The Earliest Wave of Viking Activity? The Norwegian Evidence Revisited," *European Journal of Archaeology* 22 (2019): 523–41; James H. Barrett et al., "Ecological Globalisation, Serial Depletion and the Medieval Trade of Walrus Rostra," *Quaternary Science Reviews* 229 (2020): 106–22; David Griffiths, "Rethinking the Early Viking Age in the West," *Antiquity* 93 (2019): 468–77; Richard Abels, "Paying the Danegeld: Anglo-Saxon Peacemaking with Vikings," in *War and Peace in Ancient and Medieval History*, ed. Philip De Souza and John France (Cambridge: Cambridge University Press, 2008), 173–92.

2. Håkon Melberg, *Origin of the Scandinavian Nations and Languages: An Introduction* (Halden, Norway: H. Melberg, 1951), 759–61, 840–924; *Kulturhistorisk leksikon for nordisk middelalder*, 22 vols., ed. Finn Hødnebø et al., 2nd ed. (Oslo: Gyldendal, 1980–1982), 2:662–64; Einar Haugen, *The Scandinavian Languages: An Introduction to Their History* (London: Faber and Faber, 1976), 135; Stephen Pax Leonard, "Relative Linguistic Homogeneity in a New Society: The Case of Iceland," *Language in Society* 40 (2011): 171; Judith Jesch, *The Viking Diaspora* (London: Routledge, 2015), 75–79. NB The West-Norse (Norwegian and descendants) and East-Norse (Swedish and Danish) languages probably started to separate at the end of the Viking Age. See Michael Barnes, "Languages and Ethnic Groups," in *The Cambridge History of Scandinavia*, ed. Knut Helle (Cambridge: Cambridge University Press, 2003), 100–101.

3. For references, see, for example, William Ian Miller, *Bloodtaking and Peacemaking: Feud, Law, and Society in Saga Iceland* (Chicago: University of Chicago Press, 1990), 43–76; Jón Viðar Sigurðsson, *Chieftains and Power in the Icelandic Commonwealth* (Odense: Odense University Press, 1999), 17–38; Jón Viðar Sigurðsson, "Tendencies in the Historiography on the Medieval Nordic States (to 1350)," in *Public Power in Europe: Studies in Historical Transformation*, ed. James S. Amelang and Sigfried Beer (Pisa: PLUS-Pisa University Press, 2006), 1–15; Sverre Bagge, "Mellom kildekritikk og historisk antropologi: Olav den hellige, aristokratiet og rikssamlingen," *Historisk tidsskrift* 81 (2002): 173–212; Knut Helle, "Den primitivistiske vendingen i norsk historisk middelalderforskning," *Historisk Tidsskrift* 88 (2009): 571–609; Knut Helle, "Hvor står den historiske sagakritikken i dag?," *Collegium Medievale* 24 (2011): 50–86; Shami Ghosh, *Kings' Sagas and Norwegian History: Problems and Perspectives* (Leiden: Brill, 2011).

4. For an overview of the archaeological materials, see the first volume in *The Pre-Christian Religions of the North*, 4 vols., ed. Jens Peter Schjødt, John Lindow, and Anders Andrén (Turnhout, Belgium: Brepols, 2020).

1. The Powerful Danish Kings

1. Thorkild Ramskou, *Normannertiden: 600–1060*, ed. John Danstrup and Hal Koch (Copenhagen: Politikens forlag, 1963), 89–106; Inge Skovgaard-Petersen, Aksel E. Christensen, and Helge Paludan, *Danmarks historie*, vol. 1, *Tiden indtil 1340* (Copenhagen: Gyldendal, 1977), 117–19; Claus Krag, *Norges historie fram til 1319* (Oslo: Universitetsforlaget, 2000), 55; Esben Albrectsen, Gunner Lind, and Karl-Erik Frandsen,

Konger og krige: 700–1648 (Copenhagen: Danmarks Nationalleksikon, 2001), 23–24; Jørgen Markvad, *Danske konger—før Gorm den Gamle* (Gedved, Denmark: Yduns Æbler, 2004), 75–125.

2. When the Danish kings established their rule over Blekinge is unclear. See Thomas Lindkvist and Maria Sjöberg, *Det svenska samhället 800–1720: Klerkernas och adelns tid* (Lund: Studentliteratur, 2003), 33–34.

3. For an overview of the discussion about the political development in Denmark from circa 700 to the mid-1000s, see Peter H. Sawyer, *Da Danmark blev Danmark: Fra ca. år 700 til ca. 1050* (Copenhagen: Gyldendal, 1988), 37–48, 213–88; Niels Lund, *Lið, leding og landeværn: Hær og samfund i Danmark i ældre middelalder* (Roskilde, Denmark: Vikingeskibshallen, 1996), 83–144; Ulf Näsman, "Sydskandinavisk sämhallsstruktur i ljuset av merovingisk och anglosaxisk analogi eller i vad är det som centralplatserna är centrala?," in *Centrala platser, centrala frågor: Samhällsstrukturen under Järnåldern: En vänbok till Berta Stjernquist*, ed. Birgitta Hårdh, Berta Stjernquist, and Lars Larsson (Stockholm: Almqvist & Wiksell, 1998), 1–26; Albrectsen, Lind, and Frandsen, *Konger og krige*, 10–53; Inge Skovgaard-Petersen, "The Making of the Danish Kingdom," in *The Cambridge History of Scandinavia*, vol. 1, *Prehistory to 1520*, ed. Knut Helle (Cambridge: Cambridge University Press, 2003), 168–83; Jørgen Jensen, *Danmarks oldtid*, vol. 1, *Fra stenalder til vikingetid* (Copenhagen: Gyldendal, 2013), 935–45; Andres Siegfried Dobat, "The State and the Strangers: The Role of External Forces in a Process of State Formation in Viking-Age South Scandinavia (c. AD 900–1050)," *Viking and Medieval Scandinavia* 5 (2009): 65–104; Andres Siegfried Dobat, "A Contested Heritage: The Dannevirke as a Mirror and Object of Military and Political History," in *Schleswig Holstein: Contested Region(s) through History*, ed. Michael Bregnsbo and Kurt Villads Jensen (Odense: University Press of Southern Denmark 2016), 193–217; Ole Feldbæk, *Danmarks historie*, 3rd ed. (Copenhagen: Gyldendal, 2010), 17–26; Kasper H. Andersen, "Glimt af Nordens etnografi i de frankiske kilder fra det 9. århundrede," in *Et fælles hav: Skagerrak og Kattegat i vikingetiden*, ed. Anne Pedersen and Søren M. Sindbæk (Copenhagen: Nationalmuseet, 2015), 44; Hermann Kamp, "Der Frieden mit den Heiden: Die Karolinger, die dänischen Könige und die Seeräuber aus dem Norden," in *La productivité d'une crise: Le règne de Louis le Pieux (814–840) et la transformation de l'empire carolingien. Produktivität einer Krise. Die Regierungszeit Ludwigs des Frommen (814–840) und die Transformation des karolingischen Imperiums*, ed. Philippe Depreux et al. (Ostfildern, Germany: Jan Thorbecke Verlag, 2018), 129–55.

4. Ulf Näsman, "Raids, Migrations, and Kingdoms: The Danish Case," *Acta Archaeologica* 71 (2000): 1–7.

5. "Danevirke," *Store norske leksikon*, September 1, 2020, https://snl.no/Danevirke; Roger Pihl, "Kanhave Kanal," *Store norske leksikon*, April 19, 2017, https://snl.no/Kanhave_kanal; Lotte Flugt Kold, "Dannevirke," Danmarks Historien (Aarhus University), August 7, 2018, http://danmarkshistorien.dk/leksikon-og-kilder/vis/materiale/dannevirke/; Else Roesdahl, "Rigsdannelsen 'Danmark' og 'Danern,'" Danmarks Historien (Aarhus University), 2009, http://danmarkshistorien.dk/perioder/vikingetiden-ca-800-1050/rigsdannelsen-danmark-og-danerne/; Ramskou, *Normannertiden*, 89, 91; Skovgaard-Petersen, Christensen, and Paludan, *Danmarks historie*, 1:117–18; Albrectsen, Lind, and Frandsen, *Konger og krige*, 19–32; Aoife Daly, "The Dendrochronological

Dating of Timber Crossings in West Jutland, Denmark," *Journal of Wetland Archaeology* 6 (2006): 40–41; Andres Siegfried Dobat, "Danevirke Revisited: An Investigation into Military and Socio-political Organisation in South Scandinavia (c. AD 700 to 1100)," *Medieval Archaeology* 52 (2008): 27–67; Anne Pedersen, "Monumental Expression and Fortification in Denmark in the Time of King Harald Bluetooth," in *Fortified Settlements in Early Medieval Europe: Defended Communities of the 8th–10th Centuries*, ed. Christie Neil and Herold Hajnalka (Oxford: Oxbow Books, 2016), 75–76. Cf. Richard Hodges, *Dark Age Economics: The Origins of Towns and Trade A.D. 600–1000* (London: Duckworth, 1982), 187; Christopher J. Arnold, "Social Evolution in Post-Roman Western Europe," in *European Social Evolution: Archaeological Perspectives*, ed. John Bintliff and Colin Renfrew (Bradford, UK: University of Bradford, 1984), 277; Steven Bassett, "In Search of the Origins of Anglo-Saxon Kingdoms," in *The Origins of Anglo-Saxon Kingdoms*, ed. Steven Bassett (London: Leicester University Press, 1989), 23–24.

6. *Kulturhistoriskt lexikon för nordisk medeltid*, 22 vols., ed. Ingvar Andersson and John Granlund (Malmö: Allhems Förlag, 1956–1978), 1:264–66 (hereafter cited as *KLNM*).

7. "Qui tamen eo tempore domi non erant, sed ad Westarfoldam cum exercitu profecti, quae regio ultima regni eorum inter septentrionem et occidentem sita, contra aquilonem Brittaniae summitatem respicit, cuius principes ac populus eis subici recusabant." *Annales regni Francorum inde ab a 741 usque ad a 829: Qui dicuntur Annales Laurissenses maiores et Einhardi*, ed. Georg Heinrich Pertz and Friedric Kurze (Hanover: Impensis bibliopolii Hahniani, 1895), 138–39.

"I 843 ble Nantes plyndret af 'Wesfaldingi,' det vil si vikinger fra Vestfold." Andersen, "Glimt af Nordens," 45.

8. P. A. Munch, *Det norske Folks Historie*, 8 vols. (Christiania: Tønsbergs Forlag, 1852–1863) 2:391–92; Erling Albrectsen, "Vikingetidens Odense," *Fynske Minder* (1970): 125; Ove Jørgensen, *Alfred den store, Danmarks geografi: En undersøgelse af fire afsnit i Den gamle engelske Orosius* (Odense: Odense Universitetsforlag, 1985), 84; *Reallexikon der germanischen Altertumskunde*, 37 vols., ed. Heinrich Beck et al. (Berlin: De Gruyter, 1973–2008), 32:304; Claus Krag, *Vikingtid og rikssamling: 800–1130* (Oslo: Aschehoug, 1995), 89; Jørgen Jensen, *Danmarks Oldtid*, vol. 4, *Yngre jernalder og vikingetid, 400–1050 e. Kr* (Copenhagen: Gyldendal, 2004), 427; Dagfinn Skre, "Towns and Markets, Kings and Central Places in South-Western Scandinavia c. AD 800–950," in *Kaupang in Skiringssal: Norske oldfunn*, ed. Dagfinn Skre (Aarhus: Aarhus University Press, Kaupang Excavation Project, University of Oslo, 2007), 460–61; Andersen, "Glimt af Nordens," 45.

9. Ellen Anne Pedersen, Per G. Norseng, and Frans-Arne Stylegar, *Øst for Folden* (Sarpsborg, Norway: Østfold fylkeskommune, 2003), 382–86.

10. *Heimskringla 1*, ed. Bjarni Aðalbjarnarson (Reykjavík: Hið íslenzka fornritafélag, 1941–1951), 1:240.

11. *Two Voyagers at the Court of King Alfred: The Ventures of OHTHERE and WULFSTAN Together with the Description of Northern Europe from the Old English Orosius*, ed. Niels Lund et al. (York: William Sessions, 1984), 22. Cf. Erik Kroman, *Det danske rige i den ældre vikingetid* (Copenhagen: Rosenkilde og Bagger, 1976), 12–14.

12. Kroman, *Det danske rige*, 19. Helge Braathen, *Ryttergraver: Politiske strukturer i eldre rikssamlingstid* (Oslo: Universitetet i Oslo, 1989), 99–101, 130–39; Pål Nymoen,

"Bøleskipet—og brynesteinseksport fra Norge," in *Ressourcer og kulturkontakter: Arkæologi rundt om Skagerrak og Kattegat*, ed. Liv Appel and Kjartan Langsted (Helsingør, Denmark: Gilleleje Museum, 2011), 84–93; Anne Pedersen, "Ryttergrave: Hvorfor netop her?," in Pedersen and Sindbæk, *Et fælles hav*, 136–51.

13. Ole Tveitan and Kjetil Loftsgarden, "The Extensive Iron Production in Norway in the Tenth to Thirteenth Century: A Regional Perspective," in *Viking-Age Transformations: Trade, Craft and Resources in Western Scandinavia*, ed. Ann Zanette Tsigaridas Glørstad and Kjetil Loftsgarden (London: Routledge, 2017), 114; Bernt Rundberget, "Late Iron Age (ca. AD 6/700–1000): A White Spot in the Iron Extraction History?," in *Exploitation of Outfield Resources: Joint Research at the University Museums of Norway*, ed. Svein Indrelid, Kari Loe Hjelle, and Kathrine Stene (Bergen: University Museum of Bergen, 2015), 107–16.

14. Arnvid Lillehammer, *Fra jeger til bonde: Inntil 800 e.Kr.* (Oslo: Aschehoug, 1994), 219; Irmelin Martens, "Recent Investigations of Iron Production in Viking Age Norway," *Norwegian Archaeological Review* 15 (1982): 29–44; Bergljot Solberg, *Jernalderen i Norge: 500 før Kristus til 1030 etter Kristus* (Oslo: Cappelen Akademisk Forlag, 2000), 113, 122; Lise Bender Jørgensen, "Rural Economy: Ecology, Hunting, Pastoralism, Agricultural and Nutritional Aspects," in *The Scandinavians from the Vendel Period to the Tenth Century: An Ethnographic Perspective*, ed. Judith Jesch (Woodbridge, UK: Boydell & Brewer, 2002), 139; Lindkvist and Sjöberg, *Det svenska samhället*, 130–31; Vagn Fabritius Buchwald, *Iron and Steel in Ancient Times* (Copenhagen: Det Kongelige Danske Videnskabernes Selskab, 2005), 294; Bernt Rundberget, "Sørskandinavisk jernutvinning i vikingtiden—lokal produksjon eller handelsprodukt?," in Pedersen and Sindbæk, *Et fælles hav*, 168–87; Bernt Rundberget, *Tales of the Iron Bloomery: Ironmaking in Southeastern Norway—Foundation of Statehood, c. AD 700–1300* (Leiden: Brill, 2017); Tveitan and Loftsgarden, "Extensive Iron Production in Norway," 111–23; Kjetil Loftsgarden, "The Prime Movers of Iron Production in the Norwegian Viking and Middle Ages," *Fornvännen* 114 (2019): 75–87.

15. Ian Peirce and Ewart Oakeshott, eds., *Swords of the Viking Age* (Woodbridge, UK: Boydell & Brewer, 2002); Fedir Androshchuk, *Viking Swords: Swords and Social Aspects of Weaponry in Viking Age Societies* (Stockholm: Statens Historiska Museum, 2014).

16. Björn Ambrosiani, "Background to the Boat-Graves of the Mälaren Valley," in *Vendel Period Studies: Transactions of the Boat-Grave Symposium in Stockholm, February 2–3, 1981*, ed. Jan Peder Lamm and Hans-Åke Nordström (Stockholm: Statens Historiska Museum, 1983), 22; Katarina Eriksson and Olof Sundqvist, "Järn, makt och kult i Gästrikland under yngre järnåldern," *Arkeologi i norr* 13 (2012): 133–61; *Eddukvæði*, 2 vols., ed. Jónas Kristjánsson and Vésteinn Ólason (Reykjavík: Hið íslenzka fornritafélag, 2014), 1:455. Cf. Hanna Dahlström, "Networks of Iron: The Role of Blacksmithing in Medieval Copenhagen," *Acta Archaeologica* 90 (2019): 127–52.

17. Irene Baug, "Lokalsamfunn, regionar og nettverk i mellomalderen: Ulike arkeologiske tilnærmingar," *Viking* 79 (2016): 155–74; Irene Baug et al., "The Beginning of the Viking Age in the West," *Journal of Maritime Archaeology* 13 (2018): 1–38.

18. Per Sveaas Andersen, *Samlingen av Norge og kristningen av landet 800–1130* (Bergen: Universitetsforlaget, 1977), 295–99; Klavs Randsborg, *The Viking Age in Denmark:*

The Formation of a State (London: Duckworth, 1980), 32; Tina L. Thurston, *Landscapes of Power, Landscapes of Conflict: State Formation in the South Scandinavian Iron Age* (New York: Kluwer Academic/Plenum, 2001), 74; Jensen, *Danmarks oldtid*, 1:952; Andersen, "Glimt af Nordens," 43–44. Cf. John W. Bernhardt, *Itinerant Kingship and Royal Monasteries in Early Medieval Germany, c. 936–1075* (Cambridge: Cambridge University Press, 1993); J. B. L. D. Strömberg, "The Swedish Kings in Progress—and the Centre of Power," *Scandia* 70 (2004): 167–217; J. B. L. D. Strömberg, *De svenska resande kungarna: Och maktens centrum* (Uppsala: Svenska fornskriftsällskapet, 2013).

19. Mads Kähler Holst et al., "The Late Viking-Age Royal Constructions at Jelling, Central Jutland, Denmark," *Praehistorische Zeitschrift* 87, no. 2 (2012): 501; Mads Dengsø Jessen et al., "A Palisade Fit for a King: Ideal Architecture in King Harald Bluetooth's Jelling," *Norwegian Archaeological Review* 47 (2014): 61–62; Mads Blom, ed., *Vinkler på vikingetiden* (Copenhagen: Nationalmuseet, Skoletjenesten, 2013), 66.

20. For an overview of the Old Norse religion, see Jens Peter Schjødt, John Lindow, and Anders Andrén, eds., *The Pre-Christian Religions of the North*, 4 vols. (Turnhout, Belgium: Brepols, 2020). Cf. H. Munro Chadwick, *The Cult of Othin: An Essay in the Ancient Religion of the North* (London: Clay, 1899), 49; Terry Gunnell, "From One High-One to Another: The Acceptance of Óðinn as Preparation for the Acceptance of God," in *Conversions: Looking for Ideological Change in the Early Middle Ages*, ed. Rudolf Simek and Leszek Slupecki (Vienna: Fassbaender, 2013), 163–64.

21. Holst et al., "Late Viking-Age Royal Constructions," 475, 488, 498; Andres Siegfried Dobat, "Viking Stranger-Kings: The Foreign as a Source of Power in Viking Age Scandinavia or, Why There Was a Peacock in the Gokstad Ship Burial?," *Early Medieval Europe* 23 (2015): 161–201.

22. *Two Voyagers*, 21–22; *Adam av Bremen: Beretningen om Hamburg stift, erkebiskopenes bedrifter og øyrikene i Norden*, ed. Bjørg Tosterud Danielsen and Anne-Katrine Frihagen (Oslo: Aschehoug, 1993), bk. 4:11, 33. Cf. Anton Englert, "Resjehastighed over Kattegat og Skagerrak i vikingtiden," in Appel and Langsted, *Ressourcer og kulturkontakter*, 113; Anton Englert, "Forbundet af havet: Vilkår for sejlads og kommunikation over Skagerrak og Kattegat," in Pedersen and Sindbæk, *Et fælles hav*, 58–67; *Alfræði íslenzk: Islandsk encyklopædisk litteratur*, 3 vols., ed. Kristian Kålund (Copenhagen: S.L. Møllers Bogtrykkeri, 1908–1918), 1:13; *Sturlunga saga: Árna saga biskups, Hrafns saga Sveinbjarnarsonar hin sérstaka*, 3 vols., ed. Örnólfur Thorsson et al. (Reykjavík: Svart á hvítu, 1988), 3:55.

In England, by comparison, you could travel twenty to thirty miles in a day. F. M. Stenton, "The Road System of Medieval England," *Economic History Review* 7 (1936): 1–12.

23. "Haraldr konungr bað gera kuml þessi ept Gorm, fǫður sinn, ok ept Þyrvé, móður sína, sá Haraldr er sér vann Danmǫrk alla ok Norveg ok dani gerði kristna." "DR 42 (DR42)—Jelling 2," *The Skaldic Project*, accessed February 13, 2021, https://skaldic.abdn.ac.uk/m.php?p=ms&i=18867.

For an overview of the discussion about the inscription on the larger Jelling stone, see Else Roesdahl, ". . . vandt sig Danmark al . . . - hvad mente Harald?," in *Enogtredivte tværfaglige vikingesymposium: Aarhus Universitet 2012*, ed. Peder Gammeltoft (Højbjerg, Denmark: Forlaget Wormianum, 2013), 33–46.

24. As Jan Bill and Aoife Daly have pointed out, a sign of this Christianization could be the grave robbings of Oseberg and Gokstad c. 950–990. Jan Bill and Aoife Daly, "The Plundering of the Ship Graves from Oseberg and Gokstad: An Example of Power Politics?," *Antiquity* 86 (2012):808–24.

25. For an overview of the power games during this period, see Andersen, *Samlingen av Norge*, 91–101; Krag, *Vikingtid og rikssamling*, 92–103; Ole Steinar Tøtlandsmo, *Før Norge ble Norge: Politiske forhold på Sørvestlandet i vikingtid* (Sola, Norway: Sola kommune, 1996).

26. *Heimskringla 3*, ed. Bjarni Aðalbjarnarson (Reykjavík: Hið íslenzka fornritafélag, 1951), 139.

27. James Graham-Campbell, ed., *Vikingenes verden* (Oslo: Tiden, 1981), 56; Per G. Norseng and Arnved Nedkvitne, *Byen under Eikaberg: Fra Byens oppkomst til 1536* (Oslo: J. W. Cappelens Forlag, 1991), 37–38; Erik Schia, "Den første urbaniseringen i Oslofjord-regionen," in *Våre første byer*, ed. Ingvild Øye (Bergen: Bryggens Museum, 1992), 50–51; Solberg, *Jernalderen i Norge*, 306; Albrectsen, Lind, and Frandsen, *Konger og krige*, 33; Else Roesdahl and Søren Michael Sindbæk, "The Dating of Aggersborg," in *Aggersborg: The Viking-Age Settlement and Fortress*, ed. Else Roesdahl et al. (Højberg, Denmark: National Museum of Denmark, Jutland Archaeological Society, 2014), 205–8.

28. *KLNM*, 13:384–95; Niels Lund and Kai Hørby, *Samfundet i vikingetid og middelalder 800–1500*, vol. 2 (Copenhagen: Gyldendal, 1980), 107; Ole Jørgen Benedictow, *The Medieval Demographic System of the Nordic Countries* (Oslo: Middelalderforlaget, 1993), 179–86; Bjørn Myhre and Ingvild Øye, *Jorda blir levevei: 4000 f.Kr.–1350 e.Kr* (Oslo: Samlaget, 2002), 252–53; Nils Hybel and Bjørn Poulsen, *The Danish Resources c. 1000–1550: Growth and Recession* (Leiden: Brill, 2007), 128; Jensen, *Danmarks oldtid*, 1:965.

The population of Denmark at the "end of the old ages" was probably seven to eight hundred thousand. Peder Gammeltoft, Johnny G. G. Jakobsen, and Søren M. Sindbæk, "Vikingtidens bebyggelse omkring Kattegat og Skagerak," in Pedersen and Sindbæk, *Et fælles hav*, 19.

29. Josiah Cox Russell, "Population in Europe 500–1500," in *The Fontana Economic History of Europe*, vol. 1, ed. by Carlo M. Cipolla (London: Collins/Fontana, 1972), 36; Carlo M. Cipolla, *Before the Industrial Revolution: European Society and Economy, 1000–1700*, 3rd ed. (London: Routledge, 1993), 3.

2. Kings and Chieftains in the Shadow of the Danish Kings

1. The following discussion draws on Carl Fredrik Hallencreutz, "Rimbert, Sverige och religionsmötet," in *Boken om Ansgar: Rimbert: Ansgars liv*, ed. Eva Odelman et al. (Stockholm: Proprius Förlag, 1986), 163–80; Thomas Lindkvist and Maria Sjöberg, *Det svenska samhället 800–1720: Klerkernas och adelns tid* (Lund: Studentliteratur, 2003), 33–36; Thomas Lindkvist, "Early Political Organisation: Introductory Survey," in *The Cambridge History of Scandinavia*, vol. 1, *Prehistory to 1520*, ed. Knut Helle (Cambridge: Cambridge University Press, 2003), 221–24; Henrik Janson, *Till frågan om*

Sveariḳets vagga (Vara, Sweden: Västergötlands, hembygdsförbund, 1999), 71–143; Philip Line, *Kingship and State Formation in Sweden, 1130–1290* (Leiden: Brill, 2007), 34–68; Dick Harrison, *Sveriges historia 600–1350* (Stockholm: Norstedt, 2009), 13–130.

2. *Two Voyagers at the Court of King Alfred: The Ventures of OHTHERE and WULF-STAN Together with the Description of Northern Europe from the Old English Orosius*, ed. Niels Lund et al. (York: William Sessions, 1984), 21.

3. *Two Voyagers*, 23; Lindkvist and Sjöberg, *Det svensḳa samhället*, 33–34.

4. Lindkvist and Sjöberg, *Det svensḳa samhället*, 33–34; Bengt Staffan Söderberg, *Aristoḳratisḳt rum och gransoversḳridande: Jarrestad och sydostra sḳaane mellan region och riḳe 600–1100* (Stockholm: Riksantikvarieambetets forlag, 2005), 63–184, 403–42; Dick Harrison, *Sveriges historia 600–1350*, 68–70.

5. Line, *Kingship and State Formation*, 54–68.

6. Lindkvist, "Early Political Organisation," 223.

7. Lindkvist, 223–24.

8. Odelman et al., *Boḳen om Ansgar*, 55–56; Harrison, *Sveriges historia 600–1350*, 120.

9. *Adam av Bremen: Beretningen om Hamburg stift, erḳebisḳopenes bedrifter og øyriḳene i Norden*, ed. Bjørg Tosterud Danielsen and Anne-Katrine Frihagen (Oslo: Aschehoug, 1993), 206–7; Henrik Janson, *Templum nobilissimum: Adam av Bremen, Uppsalatemplet och ḳonfliḳtlinjerna i Europa ḳring år 1075* (Gothenburg: Institutionen, 1998); Olof Sundqvist, *Freyr's Offspring: Rulers and Religion in Ancient Svea Society* (Uppsala: Uppsala Universitet, 2002); Olof Sundqvist, *Kultledare i fornsḳandinavisḳ religion* (Uppsala: Department of Archaeology and Ancient History, Uppsala University, 2007), 113–34; John Ljungkvist and Per Frölund, "Gamla Uppsala—the Emergence of a Centre and a Magnate Complex," *Journal of Archaeology and Ancient History* 16 (2015): 3–29; Jens Peter Schjødt, John Lindow, and Anders Andrén, eds., *The Pre-Christian Religions of the North*, 4 vols. (Turnhout, Belgium: Brepols, 2020).

10. Ann-Marie Pettersson, ed., *Spillingssḳatten: Gotland i viḳingatidens världshandel* (Visby, Sweden: Länsmuseet på Gotland, 2008); Harrison, *Sveriges historia 600–1350*, 94; Ny Björn Gustafsson, *Casting Identities in Central Seclusion: Aspects of Non-ferrous Metalworking and Society on Gotland in the Early Medieval Period* (Stockholm: Stockholm University, 2013), 29–48; Emily M. Peschel et al., "Who Resided in Ridanäs? A Study of Mobility on a Viking Age Trading Port in Gotland, Sweden," *Journal of Archaeological Science: Reports* 13 (2017): 175–84; Christoph Kilger, "Silver, Land, Towns, and the Elites: Social and Legal Aspects of Silver in Scandinavia c. 850–1150," in *Nordic Elites in Transformation, c. 1050–1250*, vol. 1, *Material Resources*, ed. Bjørn Poulsen, Helle Vogt, and Jón Viðar Sigurðsson (New York: Routledge, 2019), 130–60.

11. Christoph Anz, *Gilden im mittelalterlichen Skandinavien* (Göttingen: Vandenhoeck & Ruprecht, 1998), 159–61; Judith Jesch, *Ships and Men in the Late Viking Age: The Vocabulary of Runic Inscriptions and Sḳaldic Verse* (Woodbridge, UK: Boydell Press, 2001), 65, 239–41; Gun Westholm, "Gotland och omvärlden," in Pettersson, *Spillingssḳatten*, 121.

12. For an overview of the power games in this period and the earls of Lade's position, see Per Sveaas Andersen, *Samlingen av Norge og ḳristningen av landet 800–1130* (Bergen: Universitetsforlaget, 1977), 75–101; Claus Krag, *Viḳingtid og rissamling: 800–1130* (Oslo: Aschehoug, 1995), 72–119; Claus Krag, *Norges historie fram til 1319* (Oslo:

Universitetsforlaget, 2000), 213–17; Bruce Lincoln, *Between History and Myth: Stories of Harald Fairhair and the Founding of the State* (Chicago: University of Chicago Press, 2014); Eirin Holberg and Merete Røskaft, *Håløygriket: Nordland historie 1—før 1600* (Bergen: Fagbokforlaget, 2015), 145–88, 219–66.

13. Bergljot Solberg, *Jernalderen i Norge: 500 før Kristus til 1030 etter Kristus* (Oslo: Cappelen Akademisk Forlag, 2000), 286.

14. *Skaldic Poetry of the Scandinavian Middle Ages*, vol. 1, *Poetry from the Kings' Sagas 1*, ed. Diana Whaley (Turnhout, Belgium: Brepols, 2012), 103.

15. Krag, *Vikingtid og rikssamling*, 86; Krag, *Norges historie*, 44–46, 215–17; *Heimskringla 1*, ed. Bjarni Aðalbjarnarson (Reykjavík: Hið íslenzka fornritafélag, 1941–1951), 1:240, 307, 370–71, 434, 438; *Heimskringla 2*, edited by Bjarni Aðalbjarnarson (Reykjavík: Hið íslenzka fornritafélag, 1945), 192; *Ágrip af Nóregskonunga sǫgum: Fagrskinna—Nóregs konunga tal*, ed. Bjarni Einarsson (Reykjavík: Hið íslenzka fornritafélag, 1985), 110, 121, 163; *Danakonunga sǫgur; Skjǫldunga saga; Knýtlinga saga; Ágrip af sǫgu danakonunga*, ed. Bjarni Guðnason (Reykjavík: Hið íslenzka fornritafélag, 1982), 95; Jón Viðar Sigurðsson, *Norsk historie 800–1300. Frå høvdingmakt til konge- og kyrkjemakt* (Oslo: Det Norske Samlaget, 1999), 68, 70–71, 84. For the discussion about the dating of the battle see Krag, *Norges historie*, 215–16.

16. Ole Steinar Tøtlandsmo, *Før Norge ble Norge: Politiske forhold på Sørvestlandet i vikingtid* (Sola, Norway: Sola Kommune, 1996), 43.

17. Jón Viðar Sigurðsson and Synnøve Veinan Hellerud, *Håkon den gode* (Oslo: Saga Bok & Spartacus, 2012).

18. *Heimskringla 1*, 136–38; Claus Krag, "Gunnhild-2," *Norsk biografisk leksikon*, February 13, 2009, https://nbl.snl.no/Gunnhild_-_2. Whether the Norwegian Eric is the same Eric who ruled in York is the subject of debate. Tøtlandsmo, *Før Norge ble Norge*, 41–42; Clare Downham, "The Chronology of the Last Scandinavian Kings of York, AD 937–954," *Northern History* 40, no. 1 (2003): 25–51; Clare Downham, "Eric Bloodaxe—Axed? The Mystery of the Last Viking King of York," *Mediaeval Scandinavia* 14 (2004): 51–77; Clare Downham, *Viking Kings of Britain and Ireland: The Dynasty of Ívarr to A.D. 1014* (Edinburgh: Dunedin Academic Press, 2007), 116–19.

19. *Kulturhistoriskt lexikon för nordisk medeltid*, 22 vols., ed. Ingvar Andersson and John Granlund (Malmö: Allhems Förlag, 1956–1978), 10:432–59 (hereafter cited as *KLNM*); Geir Atle Ersland and Terje H. Holm, *Krigsmakt og kongemakt 900–1814* (Oslo: Eide, 2000), 42–53; Sigurðsson and Hellerud, *Håkon den gode*, 90–116.

20. The following discussion about the hirð draws on *KLNM*, 6:568–77; *KLNM*, 10:498–99; Andersen, *Samlingen av Norge*, 284–94; Paddy Griffith, *The Viking Art of War* (London: Greenhill Books, 1995), 127–60; Niels Lund, *Lið, leding og landeværn: Hær og samfund i Danmark i ældre middelalder* (Roskilde, Denmark: Vikingeskibshallen, 1996); Ersland and Holm, *Krigsmakt og kongemakt*, 14–96; Esben Albrectsen, Gunner Lind, and Karl-Erik Frandsen, *Konger og krige: 700–1648* (Copenhagen: Danmarks Nationalleksikon, 2001), 23; Claus Krag, "The Early Unification of Norway," in Helle, *Prehistory to 1520*, 198–200; Lauren Goetting, "Þegn and drengr in the Viking Age," *Scandinavian Studies* 78 (2006): 375–404; Stefan Brink, *Vikingarnas slavar den nordiska träldomen under yngre järnålder och äldsta medeltid* (Stockholm: Atlantis, 2012), 114–16, 139–49.

21. *Egils saga Skalla-Grímssonar*, ed. Sigurður Nordal (Reykjavík: Hið íslenzka fornritafélag, 1933), 50.

22. Rudolf Simek, *Dictionary of Northern Mythology* (Cambridge: D. S. Brewer, 1993).

23. Sven B. F. Jansson, *Swedish Vikings in England: The Evidence of the Rune Stones* (London: H. K. Lewis, 1966), 1–18; Aksel E. Christensen, *Vikingetidens Danmark*, 2nd ed. (Copenhagen: Det Historiske Institut ved Københavns Universitet, 1977), 218; Andres Siegfried Dobat, "The State and the Strangers: The Role of External Forces in a Process of State Formation in Viking-Age South Scandinavia (c. AD 900–1050)," *Viking and Medieval Scandinavia* 5 (2009): 72–76, 93–94; T. Douglas Price et al., "Who Was in Harold Bluetooth's Army? Strontium Isotope Investigation of the Cemetery at the Viking Age Fortress at Trelleborg, Denmark," *Antiquity* 85 (2011): 476–89. Cf. Andrzej Buko, ed., *Bodzia: A Late Viking-Age Elite Cemetery in Central Poland* (Leiden: Brill, 2014).

24. Andersen, *Samlingen av Norge*, 255–58.

25. *KLNM*, 10:32–56; *The Blackwell Encyclopaedia of Anglo-Saxon England*, ed. Michael Lapidge et al. (Oxford: Blackwell, 1999), 44–48; Lund, *Lið, leding og landeværn*, 27–144, 286–90; Ersland and Holm, *Krigsmakt og kongemakt*, 45–48; Rikke Malmros, *Vikingernes syn på militær og samfund: Belyst gennem skjaldenes fyrstedigtning* (Aarhus: Aarhus Universitetsforlaget, 2010), 15–158

26. Fridtjov Birkeli, *Tolv vintrer hadde kristendommen vært i Norge* (Oslo: Verbum, 1995), 65–101; Solberg, *Jernalderen i Norge*, 315.

27. *The Anglo-Saxon Chronicle*, ed. Michael Swanton (London: Dent, 1996), 126–29; Andersen, *Samlingen av Norge*, 104–105; Per Sveaas Andersen, "Enkelte trekk ved forholdet mellom Danmark og Norge i 2. halvdel av 900–tallet," in *Kongsmenn og krossmenn: Festskrift til Grethe Authén Blom*, ed. Steinar Supphellen (Trondheim: Universitetsforlaget, 1992), 17; Narve Bjørgo, "800–1536: Makt og avmakt," in *Selvstendighet og union: Fra middelalderen til 1905*, ed. Narve Bjørgo, Øystein Rian, and Alf Kaartvedt (Oslo: Universitetsforlaget, 1995), 35–37.

28. Bjørgo, "800–1536," 37; Krag, *Vikingtid og rikssamling*, 137–41; Sverre Bagge, "Mellom kildekritikk og historisk antropologi: Olav den hellige, aristokratiet og rikssamlingen," *Historisk tidsskrift* 81 (2002): 173–212.

29. Timothy Bolton, *The Empire of Cnut the Great: Conquest and the Consolidation of Power in Northern Europe in the Early Eleventh Century* (Leiden: Brill, 2009), 303.

30. *Monumenta historica Norvegiæ: Latinske kildeskrifter til Norges Historie i middelalderen*, ed. Gustav Storm (Christiania: A. W. Brøgger, 1880), 46.

31. *Ágrip af Nóregskonunga sǫgum*, 34.

32. *Ágrip af Nóregskonunga sǫgum*, 211–12.

33. *Morkinskinna 1*, ed. Ármann Jakobsson and Þórður Ingi Guðjónsson (Reykjavík: Hið íslenska fornritafélag, 2011), 27–28.

34. *Gesta Danorum*, 2 vols., ed. Peter Zeeberg and Karsten Friis-Jensen (Copenhagen: Det Danske Sprog- og Litteraturselskab & Gads Forlag, 2005), 10, 21,2.

35. *Heimskringla 3*, ed. Bjarni Aðalbjarnarson (Reykjavík: Hið íslenzka fornritafélag, 1951), 12–13 (my translation).

36. Bjørgo, "800–1536," 43.

37. Claus Krag, "Vestfold som utgangspunkt for den norske rikssamlingen," *Collegium Medievale* 3 (1990/2): 187–90; Peter H. Sawyer, *När Sverige blev Sverige* (Alingsås, Sweden: Viktoria, 1991), 44–63; Henrik Janson, "Bakgrunden till kungamötet—riken och gränser," in *Nordiska möten: Antologi utgiven av Föreningen Kungälvs Musei Vänner till 900-årsjubileet av trekungamötet i Kungälv 1101*, ed. Lars Linge (Kungälv, Sweden: Föreningen, 2001), 78; Line, *Kingship and State Formation*, 54–68.

3. Networks of Power

1. The following discussion is to a large extent based on Jón Viðar Sigurðsson, *Viking Friendship: The Social Bond in Iceland and Norway, c. 900–1300* (Ithaca, NY: Cornell University Press, 2017). Cf. Martin Kilduff and Wenpin Tsai, *Social Networks and Organizations* (London: Sage, 2003); Einar Hreinsson and Tomas Nilson, eds., *Nätverk som social resurs: Historiska exempel* (Lund: Studentlitteratur, 2003); Live Fyrand, *Sosialt nettverk: Teori og praksis*, 2nd ed. (Oslo: Universitetsforlaget, 2005); Peter J. Carrington, John Scott, and Stanley Wasserman, eds., *Models and Methods in Social Network Analysis* (Cambridge: Cambridge University Press, 2005); Bruno Latour, *Reassembling the Social: An Introduction to Actor-Network-Theory* (Oxford: Oxford University Press, 2005); Manuel Castells, "A Network Theory of Power," *International Journal of Communication* 5 (2011): 773–87; Charles Kadushin, *Understanding Social Networks: Theories, Concepts, and Findings* (Oxford: Oxford University Press, 2012); Pádraig Mac Carron and Ralph Kenna, "Viking Sagas: Six Degrees of Icelandic Separation—Social Networks from the Viking Era," *Significance* 10 (2013): 12–17; Pádraig Mac Carron and Ralph Kenna, "Network Analysis of the Íslendinga Sögur—the Sagas of Icelanders," *European Physical Journal B* 86 (2013): 1–9; Ralph Kenna and Pádraig Mac Carron, "Character Networks of the Íslendinga Sögur and Þættir," in *Nordic Elites in Transformation, c. 1050–1250*, vol. 2, *Social Networks*, ed. Kim Esmark, Lars Hermanson, and Hans Jacob Orning (New York: Routledge, 2020), 144–68; Judith Jesch, *The Viking Diaspora* (London: Routledge, 2015), 163–82.

Archaeologists have used both trading-network analyses and archaeological materials to identify important trade networks and routines. See, for example, Søren M. Sindbæk, "Networks and Nodal Points: The Emergence of Towns in Early Viking Age Scandinavia," *Antiquity* 81 (2007): 119–32; Søren M. Sindbæk, "The Small World of the Vikings: Networks in Early Medieval Communication and Exchange," *Norwegian Archaeological Review* 40 (2007): 59–74; Per Östborn and Henrik Gerding, "Network Analysis of Archaeological Data: A Systematic Approach," *Journal of Archaeological Science* 46 (2014): 75–88; Steven P. Ashby and Søren M. Sindbæk, eds., *Crafts and Social Networks in Viking Towns* (Oxford: Oxbow Books, 2020).

2. *Eddukvæði*, 2 vols., ed. Jónas Kristjánsson and Vésteinn Ólason (Reykjavík: Hið íslenzka fornritafélag, 2014), 1:145–63. Scholars are also not in agreement about this division. *Eddukvæði*, 1:144–50; *Eddadigte 1*, ed. Jón Helgason (Oslo: Dreyer, 1971), xvi–xvii; Phillip Pulsiano and Kirsten Wolf, eds., *Medieval Scandinavian: An Encyclopedia* (New York: Garland, 1993), 272.

3. *Eddukvæði*, 1:328–31, 352. All translations of *Hávamál* are from *The Poetic Edda*, ed. Carolyne Larrington (Oxford: Oxford University Press, 2008), 17–19, with two changes: in stanza 39, Larrington translates *fé* as "possessions," while I translate it as "wealth," and in stanza 41, she translates *váðom* as "gift," and I translate as "clothes." For a more detailed discussion about friendship in *Hávamál*, see Sigurðsson, *Viking Friendship*, 12–14.

4. *Eddukvæði*, 1:328, 330–32, 346, 354.

5. *Eddukvæði*, 1:330.

6. *Heimskringla 3*, ed. Bjarni Aðalbjarnarson (Reykjavík: Hið íslenzka fornritafélag, 1951), 125.

7. *Heimskringla 2*, ed. Bjarni Aðalbjarnarson (Reykjavík: Hið íslenzka fornritafélag, 1945), 294.

8. *Heimskringla 3*, 184.

9. *Hákonar saga Hákonarsonar*, vol. 2, *Magnúss saga Lagabœtis*, ed. Þorleifur Hauksson, Sverrir Jakobsson, and Tor Ulset (Reykjavík: Hið íslenzka fornritafélag, 2013), 118, 158–59.

10. Sigurðsson, *Viking Friendship*, 11–36; *The Laws of the Earliest English Kings*, ed. and trans. F. L. Attenborough (New York: Russell & Russell, 1963), 144, 145, 148, 149, 152, 153.

11. Cf. Arnold van Gennep, *Overgangsriter* (Oslo: Pax, 1999), 113.

12. *Heimskringla 1*, ed. Bjarni Aðalbjarnarson (Reykjavík: Hið íslenzka fornritafélag, 1941), 274.

13. Sigurðsson, *Viking Friendship*, 128.

14. David Gaunt, *Familjeliv i Norden* (Malmö: Gidlund, 1983), 186–88, 196–210; Torben Anders Vestergaard, "The System of Kinship in Early Norwegian Law," *Mediaeval Scandinavia* 12 (1988): 160–93; Else Mundal, "Kvinnesynet og forståinga av biologisk arv i den norrøne kulturen," in *Atlantisk dåd og drøm: 17 essays om Island/Norge*, ed. Asbjørn Aarnes (Oslo: Aschehoug, 1998), 153–70; Lars Ivar Hansen, "'Ætten' i de eldste landskapslovene—realitet, konstruksjon og strategi," in *Norm og praksis i middelaldersamfunnet*, ed. Else Mundal and Ingvild Øye (Bergen: Senter for europeiske kulturstudier, 1999), 23–55; Lars Ivar Hansen, "Slektskap," in *Holmgang: Om førmoderne samfunn: Festskrift til Kåre Lunden*, ed. Anne Eidsfelt et al. (Oslo: Historisk institutt, Universitetet i Oslo, 2000), 104–32; Helle Vogt, "Slægtens funktion i nordisk højmiddelalderret: Kanonisk retsideologi og fredsskabende lovgivning" (Copenhagen: Københavns Universitet, 2005), 33–37; Sigurðsson, *Viking Friendship*, 104.

15. Andrzej Buko, ed., *Bodzia: A Late Viking-Age Elite Cemetery in Central Poland* (Leiden: Brill, 2014); Marika Mägi, *In Austrvegr: The Role of the Eastern Baltic in Viking Age Communication across the Baltic Sea* (Leiden: Brill, 2018); Sarah Croix and Nelleke Ijssennagger-Van Der Pluijm, "Cultures without Borders? Approaching the Cultural Continuum in the Danish–Frisian Coastal Areas in the Aarly Viking Age," *Scandinavian Journal of History* (2019): 1–24; John H. Lind, "Nordic and Eastern Elites: Contacts across the Baltic Sea: An Exiled Clan," in Esmark, Hermanson, and Orning, *Social Networks*, 104–24; Marie Bønløkke Missuno, "Contact and Continuity: England and the Scandinavian Elites in the Early Middle Ages," in Esmark, Hermanson, and Orning, *Social Networks*, 125–43; Ashot Margaryan et al., "Population Genomics of the Viking World," *Nature* 585 (2020): 390–96.

4. Peace and Conflict Resolution

1. *Eddukvæði*, 2 vols., ed. Jónas Kristjánsson and Vésteinn Ólason (Reykjavík: Hið Íslenzka fornritafélag, 2014), 1:329.

2. *Heimskringla 3*, ed. Bjarni Aðalbjarnarson (Reykjavík: Hið íslenzka fornritafélag, 1951), 12–13 (my translation).

3. *Heimskringla 3*, 201–2, 208.

4. Merete Røskaft, "Tora Torbergsdatter," *Store norske leksikon*, February 13, 2009, https://nbl.snl.no/Tora_Torbergsdatter.

5. Jeroen Duindam, "Dynasties," *Medieval Worlds* 2 (2015): 61.

6. Duindam, 63. Roger of Howden (d. 1201), in his annals, finds it strange that all kings' sons in Norway, even those born out of wedlock with women of low social status, could become kings themselves. *Chronica magistri Rogeri de Houedene*, vol. 3, ed. William Stubbs (London: Longman, 1870), 271.

7. *Morkinskinna 1*, ed. Ármann Jakobsson and Þórður Ingi Guðjónsson (Reykjavík: Hið íslenska fornritafélag, 2011), 166 (my translation).

8. Seán Duffy, Ailbhe MacShamhráin, and James Moynes, eds., *Medieval Ireland: An Encyclopedia* (New York: Routledge, 2005), 79.

9. Stephen Pollington, "The Mead-Hall Community," *Journal of Medieval History* 37 (2011): 21–22.

10. *Heimskringla 1*, ed. Bjarni Aðalbjarnarson (Reykjavík: Hið íslenzka fornritafélag, 1941), 12. See, for example, *Heimskringla 1*, 293, 316, 318, 347; *Heimskringla 2*, ed. Bjarni Aðalbjarnarson (Reykjavík: Hið íslenzka fornritafélag, 1945), 107, 160; *Heimskringla 3*, 326, 406. In the settlements of conflicts between the Danish kings and the German emperors, direct negotiations seem to have been the norm. See for example, *Vikingerne i Franken: Skriftlige kilder fra det 9. århundrede*, ed. Erling Albrectsen (Odense: Odense Universitetsforlag, 1976), 16–17, 18, 20; *Annales regni Francorum inde ab a 741 usque ad a 829: Qui dicuntur Annales Laurissenses maiores et Einhardi*, ed. Georg Heinrich Pertz and Friedric Kurze (Hanover: Impensis bibliopolii Hahniani, 1895), 128–29, 134–35, 138.

11. Wendy Davies and Paul Fouracre, eds., *The Settlement of Disputes in Early Medieval Europe* (Cambridge: Cambridge University Press, 1986), 207–40. Other central contributions include Patrick Wormald, "Lex Scripta and Verbum Regis: Legislation and Germanic Kingship, from Euric to Cnut," in *Early Medieval Kingship*, ed. Peter H. Sawyer and Ian N. Wood (Leeds: School of History, University of Leeds, 1977), 105–38; Hermann Nehlsen, "Zur Aktualität und Effektivität germanischer Rechtsaufzeichnungen," in *Recht und Schrift im Mittelalter*, ed. Peter Classen (Sigmaringen, Germany: 1977), 449–502; Stephen D. White, "'Pactum . . . Legem Vincit et Amor Judicium': The Settlement of Disputes by Compromise in Eleventh-Century Western France," *American Journal of Legal History* 22 (1978): 281–308; Stephen D. White, *Feuding and Peace-Making in Eleventh-Century France* (Aldershot, UK: Ashgate, 2005); Edward Powell, "Settlement of Disputes by Arbitration in Fifteenth-Century England," *Law and History Review* 2 (1984): 21–43; Llinos Beverley Smith, "Disputes and Settlements in Medieval Wales: The Role of Arbitration," *English Historical Review* 106 (1991): 835–60; Marios Costambeys, "Disputes and Courts in Lombard and Carolingian Central Italy," *Early Medieval Europe* 15 (2007): 265–89; Rob Meens, "Sanctuary, Penance, and

Dispute Settlement under Charlemagne: The Conflict between Alcuin and Theodulf of Orléans over a Sinful Cleric," *Speculum* 82 (2007): 277–300; Richard Keyser, "'Agreement Supersedes Law, and Love Judgment': Legal Flexibility and Amicable Settlement in Anglo-Norman England," *Law and History Review* 30 (2010): 37–88; Jón Viðar Sigurðsson, "The Role of Arbitration in the Settlement of Disputes in Iceland c. 1000–1300," in *Law and Disputing in the Middle Ages: Proceedings of the Ninth Carlsberg Academy Conference on Medieval Legal History 2012*, edited by Per Andersen et al. (Copenhagen: DJØF Publishing, 2013), 123–35; Levi Roach, "Penance, Submission, and *Deditio*: Religious Influences on Dispute Settlement in Later Anglo-Saxon England (871–1066)," *Anglo-Saxon England* 41 (2012): 343–71; Levi Roach, *Kingship and Consent in Anglo-Saxon England, 871–978: Assemblies and the State in the Early Middle Ages* (Cambridge: Cambridge University Press, 2013), 1–121; Anne Irene Riisøy, "Vǫlundr: A Gateway into the Legal World of the Vikings," in *Narrating Law and Laws of Narration in Medieval Scandinavia*, ed. Roland Scheel (Berlin: Walter de Gruyter, 2020), 255–74.

12. Knut Helle, "dóm," *Store norske leksikon*, November 10, 2017, https://snl.no/dóm; *Kulturhistoriskt lexikon för nordisk medeltid*, 22 vols., ed. Ingvar Andersson and John Granlund (Malmö: Allhems Förlag, 1956–1978), 3:214–18, 18:346–47 (hereafter cited as *KLNM*); Per Sveaas Andersen, *Samlingen av Norge og kristningen av landet 800–1130* (Bergen: Universitetsforlaget, 1977), 248.

13. Sigurðsson, "Role of Arbitration," 123–35.

14. Jón Viðar Sigurðsson, "Narrating Law and Laws of Narration in Medieval Scandinavia," in Scheel, *Narrating Law and Laws of Narration*, 39–55.

15. When it comes to the discussion about *þing* in Scandinavia, see, for example, *KLNM*, 18:334–71; Andersen, *Samlingen av Norge*, 58–59, 247–61; Knut Helle, *Gulatinget og gulatingslova* (Leikanger, Norway: Skald, 2001); *Frostatingslova*, ed. Jørn Sandnes and Jan Ragnar Hagland (Oslo: Samlaget i samarbeid med Frosta historielag, 1994), xvii–xxiii; Michael Irlenbusch-Reynard, "Thingstätten als Erzählelemente in den Íslendingasögur und Íslendingaþættir" (master's thesis, Universitetet i Bergen, 2005), 6–13; Inger Storli, "Court Sites of Arctic Norway: Remains of Thing Sites and Representations of Political Consolidation Processes in the Northern Germanic World during the First Millennium A.D.?," *Norwegian Archaeological Review* 43 (2010): 128–44; Stefan Brink et al., "Comments on Inger Storli: Court Sites of Arctic Norway: Remains of Thing Sites and Representations of Political Consolidation Processes in the Northern Germanic World during the First Millennium AD?," *Norwegian Archaeological Review* 44 (2011): 89–117; Sarah Semple and Alexandra Sanmark, "Assembly in North West Europe: Collective Concerns for Early Societies?," *European Journal of Archaeology* 16 (2013): 518–42; Frode Iversen, "Concilium and Pagus: Revisiting the Early Germanic Thing System of Northern Europe," *Journal of the North Atlantic* 5 (2013): 5–17; Anne Irene Riisøy, "Sacred Legal Places in Eddic Poetry: Reflected in Real Life?," *Journal of the North Atlantic* 5 (2013): 28–41; Anne Irene Riisøy, "Eddic Poetry: A Gateway to Late Iron Age Ladies of Law," *Journal of the North Atlantic* 8 (2015): 157–71; Anne Irene Riisøy, "Performing Oaths in Eddic Poetry: Viking Age Fact or Medieval Fiction?," *Journal of the North Atlantic* 8 (2016): 141–56; Alexandra Sanmark, "Women at the Thing," in *Kvinner i vikingtid*, ed. Nanna Løkka and Nancy L. Coleman (Oslo: Scandinavian Academic Press, 2014), 89–105; Alexandra Sanmark, Frode Iversen, and Natascha

Mehler, eds., "Debating the *Thing* in the North I: Selected Papers from Workshops Organized by The Assembly Project," special issue, *Journal of the North Atlantic* 5 (2013).

For Europa, see Timothy Reuter, "Assembly Politics in Western Europe from the Eighth Century to the Twelfth," in *The Medieval World*, ed. Janet L. Nelson and Peter Linehan (London: Routledge, 2001), 432–44; Paul S. Barnwell and Marco Mostert eds., *Political Assemblies in the Earlier Middle Ages* (Turnhout, Belgium: Brepols, 2003), 3.

16. *KLNM*, 10:228–33; Thomas Lindkvist and Maria Sjöberg, *Det svenska samhället 800–1720: Klerkernas och adelns tid* (Lund: Studentliteratur, 2003), 136–38.

17. *Heimskringla 2*, 109. Cf. Olof Sundqvist and Per Vikstrand, "Disevid och Distingen—spår av östnordisk diskult?," in *Den heliga platsen: Handlingar från symposiet Den heliga platsen. Härnösand 15–18 september 2011*, ed. Eva Nyman, Jörgen Magnusson, and Elżbieta Strzelecka (Sundsvall, Sweden: Avdelningen för Humaniora vid Mittuniversitetet, 2014), 153–78.

18. *Den eldre Gulatingslova*, ed. Tor Ulset, Bjørn Eithun, and Magnus Rindal (Oslo: Riksarkivet, 1994), 131; *KLNM*, 18:350, 352–53.

19. *Heimskringla 1*, 169 (my translation).

20. *Vita Anskarii auctore Rimberto: Accedit Vita Rimberti*, ed. G. Waitz (Hanover: Hanhsche Buchhandlung, 1884), 55–59; Eva Odelman et al., eds., *Boken om Ansgar: Rimbert: Ansgars liv* (Stockholm: Proprius Förlag, 1986), 52–55. Cf. Bernd Schneidmüller, "Konsensuale Herrschaft: Ein Essay über Formen und Konzepte politischer Ordnung im Mittelalter," in *Reich, Regionen und Europa in Mittelalter und Neuzeit: Festschrift für Peter Moraw*, ed. Paul-Joachim Heinig et al. (Berlin: Duncker & Humblot, 2000), 53–87; Steffen Patzold, "Konsens und Konkurrenz: Überlegungen zu einem aktuellen Forschungskonzept der Mediävistik," *Frühmittelalterliche Studien* 41 (2007): 75–104; Gerd Althoff, *Kontrolle der Macht Formen und Regeln politischer Beratung im Mittelalter* (Darmstadt: Wissenschaftliche Buchgesellschaft, 2016).

5. Honor and Posthumous Reputation

1. The following is based on Henri J. M. Claessen and Jarich G. Oosten, "Discussion and Considerations," in *Ideology and the Formation of Early States*, ed. Henri J. M. Claessen and Jarich G. Oosten (Leiden: E. J. Brill, 1996), 389–92; Timothy K. Earle, *How Chiefs Come to Power: The Political Economy in Prehistory* (Stanford, CA: Stanford University Press, 1997), 8, 143–57; John Gerring, "Ideology: A Definitional Analysis," *Political Research Quarterly* 50 (1997): 974–83; L. L. Junker, "Archaeology of Chiefdoms," in *International Encyclopedia of the Social and Behavioral Sciences*, vol. 3, ed. Neil J. Smelser and Paul B. Baltes (Amsterdam: Elsevier, 2001), 1670.

2. Merete Røskaft, *Maktens landskap: Sentralgårder i Trøndelag ved overgangen fra vikingtid til kristen middelalder ca. 800–1200* (Trondheim: Historisk Institutt, Norges Teknisk-naturvitenskapelige Universitet, 2003), 14–16, 149–65; Lotte Hedeager, "Scandinavian 'Central Places' in a Cosmological Setting," in *Central Places in the Migration and Merovingian Periods: Papers from the 52nd Sachsensymposium, Lund, August 2001*, ed. Birgitta Hårdh and Lars Larsson (Stockholm: Almqvist & Wiksell, 2002), 3–7; Knut Helle et al., *Norsk byhistorie urbanisering gjennom 1300 år* (Oslo: Pax, 2006), 13; Dagfinn

Skre, "Centrality, Landholding, and Trade in Scandinavia c. AD 700–900," in *Settlement and Lordship in Viking and Early Medieval Scandinavia*, ed. Søren M. Sindbæk and Bjørn Poulsen (Turnhout, Belgium: Brepols, 2011), 197–212; Lydia Carstens, "Powerful Space: The Iron-Age Hall and Its Development during the Viking Age," in *Viking Worlds: Things, Spaces, and Movement*, ed. Marianne Hem Eriksen et al. (Oxford: Oxbow Books, 2014), 12–27. Cf. Frands Herschend, *Livet i hallen: Tre fallstudier i den yngre järnålderns aristokrati* (Uppsala: Institutionen för arkeologi och antik historia, Uppsala Universitet, 1997).

Borg was abandoned at the end of the tenth century for unknown reasons.

3. David Arnold, *Famine: Social Crisis and Historical Change* (Oxford: Basil Blackwell, 1988), 3; Carole M. Counihan, "Introducton—Food and Gender: Identity and Power," in *Food and Gender: Identity and Power*, ed. Carole M. Counihan and Steven L. Kaplan (Amsterdam: Harwood Academic Publishers, 1998), 2–7.

4. *Eddukvæði*, 2 vols., ed. Jónas Kristjánsson and Vésteinn Ólason (Reykjavík: Hið íslenzka fornritafélag, 2014), 1:322.

5. Materials such as silk were imported from the East. Only a small percentage of the population was able to purchase clothes and products made from silk, as we read in *Rígsþula*, and they would therefore stand out. See Marianne Vedeler, *Silk for the Vikings* (Oxford: Oxbow Books, 2014), and Eva Andersson, *Kläderna och människan i medeltidens Sverige och Norge*, 2nd ed. (Gothenburg: Historiska Institutionen, Göteborgs Universitet, 2006), 223–305.

6. Michael J. Enright, *Lady with a Mead Cup: Ritual, Prophecy and Lordship in the European Warband from La Tène to the Viking Age* (Dublin: Four Courts Press, 1996), 1–37.

7. *The Word Exchange: Anglo-Saxon Poems in Translation*, ed. Greg Delanty and Michael Matto (New York: W. W. Norton, 2011), 176–79.

8. *Eddukvæði*, 1:323.

9. *Edda Snorra Sturlusonar*, ed. Heimir Pálsson (Reykjavík: Mál og menning, 1996), 59, 60–61, 63 (my translation).

10. *Heimskringla 1*, ed. Bjarni Aðalbjarnarson (Reykjavík: Hið íslenzka fornritafélag, 1941), 67–68 (my translation).

11. *Kulturhistoriskt lexikon för nordisk medeltid*, 22 vols., ed. Ingvar Andersson and John Granlund (Malmö: Allhems Förlag, 1956–1978), 3:324–25 (hereafter cited as *KLNM*).

12. Michael Dietler, "Feasts and Commensal Politics in the Politicial Economy," in *Food and the Status Quest: An Interdisciplinary Perspective*, ed. Polly Wiessner and Wulf Schiefenhövel (Providence, RI: Berghahn Books, 1996), 92, 96, 98. Cf. Michael Dietler, "Feasting and Fasting," in *The Oxford Handbook on the Archaeology of Ritual and Religion*, ed. Timothy Ingersoll (Oxford: Oxford University Press, 2011), 184–86.

13. Bjørn Qviller, *Rusens historie* (Oslo: Samlaget, 1996), 43–44, 54–56, 84–89; Peter Scholliers, "Meals, Food Narratives, and Sentiments of Belonging in Past and Present," in *Food, Drink and Identity. Cooking, Eating and Drinking in Europe since the Middle Ages*, ed. Peter Scholliers and Inger Johanne Lyngø (Oxford: Berg, 2001), 7–9; Katrinka Reinhart, "Ritual Feasting and Empowerment at Yanshi Shangcheng," *Journal of Anthropological Archaeology* 39 (2015): 77; Lars Kjær and A. J. Watson, "Feasts and Gifts:

Sharing Food in the Middle Ages," *Journal of Medieval History* 37 (2011): 1–5; Dietler, "Feasting and Fasting," 181–86.

14. Peter Burke, *History and Social Theory*, 2nd ed. (Cambridge: Polity, 2005), 67.

15. *Heimskringla 1*, 145 (my translation). The original text switches back and forth between the present and past tenses.

16. *Eddukvæði*, 1:337.

17. See, for example, Sverre Bagge, *Society and Politics in Snorri Sturluson's Heimskringla* (Berkeley: University of California Press, 1991), 160–63, 171–73; Preben Meulengracht Sørensen, *Fortælling og ære: Studier i islændingesagaerne* (Aarhus: Aarhus Universitetsforlag, 1993), 187–248.

18. Helgi Þorláksson, "Virtir menn og vel metnir," in *Sæmdarmenn: Um heiður á þjóðveldisöld*, ed. Preben Meulengracht Sørensen, Helgi Þorláksson, Sverrir Jakobsson, et al. (Reykjavík: Hugvísindastofnun Háskóla Íslands, 2001), 20–21.

19. *KLNM*, 3:351–52, 4:425–26.

20. *Skaldic Poetry of the Scandinavian Middle Ages*, vol. 3, *Poetry from Treatises on Poetics*, ed. Kari Ellen Gade and Edith Marold (Turnhout, Belgium: Brepols, 2017), 28–31; *Edda Snorra Sturlusonar: Nafnaþulur og Skáldatal*, ed. Guðni Jónsson (Reykjavík: Íslendingasagnaútgáfan, 1954), 338; Gabriel Turville-Petre, *Scaldic Poetry* (Oxford: Clarendon Press, 1976), xxi–xxiii; "Ragnarsdrápa—Bragi Rdr," The Skaldic Project, accessed February 13, 2021, https://skaldic.abdn.ac.uk/m.php?p=text&i=1130.

21. *Edda Snorra Sturlusonar: Nafnaþulur og Skáldatal*, 343, 351, 353; *Egils saga Skalla-Grímssonar*, ed. Sigurður Nordal (Reykjavík: Hið íslenzka fornritafélag, 1933), 19; Sandra Ballif Straubhaar, ed., *Old Norse Women's Poetry: The Voices of Female Skalds* (Cambridge: D. S. Brewer, 2011), 12–20, 23–37; Erin Michelle Goeres, *The Poetics of Commemoration: Skaldic Verse and Social Memory, c. 890–1070* (Oxford: Oxford University Press, 2015), 85–110.

22. *Beowulf*, ed. Michael Swanton (Manchester: Manchester University Press, 1997), 168. Cf. Katherine O'Brien O'Keeffe, "Heroic Values and Christian Ethics," in *The Cambridge Companion to Old English Literature*, ed. Michael Lapidge and Malcolm Godden (Cambridge: Cambridge University Press, 1991), 10; Peter Bratt, *Makt uttryckt i jord och sten: Stora högar och maktstrukturer i Mälardalen under järnåldern* (Stockholm: Institutionen för Arkeologi och Antikens Kultur, Stockholms Universitet, 2008); Jan Bill, "Vikingetidens monumentale skibsgrave," in *Et fælles hav—Skagerrak og Kattegat i vikingetiden*, ed. Anne Pedersen and Søren M. Sindbæk (Copenhagen: Nationalmuseet, 2015), 156–57.

23. Terje Gansum, "Jernaldermonumenter og maktstrukturer—Vestfold som konfliktarena," in *Konflikt i forhistorien*, ed. Ingrid Fuglestvedt and Bjørn Myhre (Stavanger, Norway: Arkeologisk museum i Stavanger, 1997), 28; Johannes Brøndsted, *Danmarks Oldtid*, vol. 3, *Jernalderen* (Copenhagen: Gyldendal, 1940), 20.

24. Bergljot Solberg, *Jernalderen i Norge: 500 før Kristus til 1030 etter Kristus* (Oslo: Cappelen Akademisk Forlag, 2000), 223; Bill, "Vikingetidens monumentale skibsgrave," 152–56, 162; Mads Kähler Holst et al., "The Late Viking-Age Royal Constructions at Jelling, Central Jutland, Denmark," *Praehistorische Zeitschrif* 87 (2012): 474–504; Mads Dengsø Jessen et al., "A Palisade Fit for a King: Ideal Architecture in King Harald Bluetooth's Jelling," *Norwegian Archaeological Review* 47 (2014): 42–64.

25. *Heimskringla 3*, ed. Bjarni Aðalbjarnarson (Reykjavík: Hið íslenzka fornritafélag, 1951), 141 (my translation).

The largest warship known from the 1000s is a vessel with a gilded beak, equipped for eighty warriors, which Earl Godwin is supposed to have bestowed on Harthacnut. Rikke Malmros, *Vikingernes syn på militær og samfund: Belyst gennem skjaldenes fyrstedigtning* (Aarhus: Aarhus Universitetsforlaget, 2010), 100.

26. Gansum, "Jernaldermonumenter og maktstrukturer," 28–30; Arnfrid Opedal, *De glemte skipsgravene: Makt og myter på Avaldsnes* (Stavanger, Norway: Arkeologisk museum i Stavanger, 1998), 13, 40–64; Solberg, *Jernalderen i Norge*, 203, 207–8; Lars F. Stenvik, "Nytt lys på en gammel historie. Stiklestad sett i et arkeologisk perspektiv," *Verdal historielags årbok* (1989): 14.

27. Marilyn Dunn, *The Christianization of the Anglo-Saxons c. 597–c. 700: Discourses of Life, Death and Afterlife* (London: Continuum, 2010), 9.

28. Terje Gansum, "Fra Jord til handling," in *Plats och praxis: Studier av nordisk förkristen ritual*, ed. Kristina Jennbert, Anders Andrén, and Catharina Raudvere (Lund: Nordic Academic Press, 2002), 249–52, 272–82; Brit Solli, "Norrøn sed og skikk," in *Norges religionshistorie*, ed. Arne Bugge Amundsen (Oslo: Universitetsforlaget, 2005), 44.

29. Arnold van Gennep, *Overgangsriter* (Oslo: Pax, 1999), 103–13. Cf. Catherine Bell, *Ritual Theory, Ritual Practice* (Oxford: Oxford University Press, 1992), 98–101.

30. Jan Brendalsmo and Gunnhild Røthe, "Haugbrot: Eller de levendes forhold til de døde—en komparativ analyse," *META* 1–2 (1992): 82–111; Gro Steinsland, "Herskermaktens ritualer: Kan mytologien sette oss på spor av gjenstander og kult knyttet til herskerens intronisasjon," in Jennbert, Andrén, and Raudvere, *Plats och praxis*, 94–96; Gro Steinsland, *Norrøn religion: Myter, riter, samfunn* (Oslo: Pax, 2005), 414–15; Bill, "Vikingetidens monumentale skibsgrave," 163–64.

6. Class and Gender in Viking Society

1. *Eddukvæði*, 2 vols., ed. Jónas Kristjánsson and Vésteinn Ólason (Reykjavík: Hið íslenzka fornritafélag, 2014), 1:329.

2. Frederic Amory, "The Historical Worth of *Rígsþula*," *Alvíssmál* 10 (2001): 3–20. Cf. Karl G. Johansson, "Rígsþula och Codex Wormianus: Textens funktion ur ett kompilationsperspektiv," *Alvíssmál* 8 (1998): 67–84.

3. *Eddukvæði*, 1:449–51. All translations of *Rígsþula* are from *The Poetic Edda*, ed. Carolyne Larrington (Oxford: Oxford University Press, 2014), 238–44.

4. *Eddukvæði*, 1:452–53. The part of the poem depicting the householders' meal is lost. In Holm-Olsen's version, he believes Rígr was given cooked veal by the householders. *Edda-dikt*, ed. Ludvig Holm-Olsen (Oslo: Den norske lyrikklubben, 1993), 150.

5. *Eddukvæði*, 1:453–57; Jere Fleck, "Konr—Óttarr—Geirroðr: A Knowledge Criterion for Succession to Germanic Sacred Kingship." *Scandinavian Studies* 42, (1970): 39–49.

6. *Eddukvæði*, 1:455–56.

7. *Heimskringla 2*, ed. Bjarni Aðalbjarnarson (Reykjavík: Hið íslenzka fornritafélag, 1945), 28–29 (my translation). Translation of the stanza is from *Skaldic Poetry of the Scandinavian Middle Ages*, vol. 1, *Poetry from the Kings' Sagas 1*, ed. Diana Whaley (Turnhout, Belgium: Brepols, 2012), 642.

8. *Heimskringla 1*, ed. Bjarni Aðalbjarnarson (Reykjavík: Hið íslenzka fornritafélag, 1941), 333; Olof Sundqvist, "Asarnas idrotter och religion," in *Zlatan frälsaren och andra texter om religion och idrott: En festskrift till David Westerlund*, ed. David Susanne Olsson, Olof Sundqvist, and David Thurfjell (Farsta, Sweden: Molin & Sorgenfrei, 2014), 122–38.

9. *Morkinskinna 1*, ed. Ármann Jakobsson and Þórður Ingi Guðjónsson (Reykjavík: Hið íslenska fornritafélag, 2011), 116; *Orkneyinga saga: Legenda de sancto Magno, Magnúss saga skemmri, Magnúss saga lengri, Helga þáttr ok Úlfs*, ed. Finnbogi Guðmundsson (Reykjavík: Hið íslenzka fornritafélag, 1965), 130.

10. Elise Naumann et al., "Slaves as Burial Gifts in Viking Age Norway? Evidence from Stable Isotope and Ancient DNA Analyses," *Journal of Archaeological Science* 41 (2014): 534–39.

11. *Edda Snorra Sturlusonar*, ed. Heimir Pálsson (Reykjavík: Mál og menning, 1996), 36–37 (my translation).

12. *Edda Snorra Sturlusonar*, 11; *Danakonunga sǫgur; Skjǫldunga saga; Knýtlinga saga; Ágrip af sǫgu danakonunga*, ed. Bjarni Guðnason (Reykjavík: Hið íslenzka fornritafélag, 1982), 39.

13. *Íslensk hómilíubók fornar stólræður*, ed. Guðrún Kvaran, Sigurbjörn Einarsson, and Gunnlaugur Ingólfsson (Reykjavík: Hið íslenska bókmenntafélag, 1993), 66 (my translation).

14. *Heimskringla 3*, ed. Bjarni Aðalbjarnarson (Reykjavík: Hið íslenzka fornritafélag, 1951), 198–99 (my translation).

15. *Danakonunga sǫgur*, 87.

16. *Danakonunga sǫgur*, 127.

17. *Heimskringla 2*, 4.

18. *Heimskringla 2*, 378, 387, 392, 405.

19. *Heimskringla 1*, 143 (my translation).

20. *Den norsk-islandske skjaldedigtning*, 2 vols., ed. Finnur Jónsson (Copenhagen: Rosenkilde and Bagger 1908–1915), A 1:648.

21. *Fornaldar sögur Norðurlanda*, 4 vols., ed. Guðni Jónsson (Reykjavík: Íslendingasagnaútgáfan, 1954), 1:232–33. Cf. Else Mundal, "Kvinnesynet og forståinga av biologisk arv i den norrøne kulturen," in *Atlantisk dåd og drøm: 17 essays om Island/Norge*, ed. Asbjørn Aarnes (Oslo: Aschehoug, 1998), 153–70.

22. *Heimskringla 1*, 213.

23. *Orkneyinga saga*, 41, 54.

24. *Sturlunga saga*, 2 vols., ed. Jón Jóhannesson, Magnús Finnbogason, and Kristján Eldjárn (Reykjavík: Sturlunguútgáfan, 1946), 1:242, 243, 364, 2:98; *Eyrbyggja saga; Brands þáttr Qrva; Eiríks saga rauða; Grænlendinga saga; Grænlendinga þáttr*, ed. Matthías Þórðarson and Einar Ólafur Sveinsson (Reykjavík: Hið íslenzka fornritafélag, 1935), 6, 21, 26.

25. See, for example, *Brennu-Njáls saga*, ed. Einar Ólafur Sveinsson (Reykjavík: Hið íslenzka fornritafélag, 1954), 70, 237.

26. Gen. 33:19; Ps. 104:1, 31; Saul: 1 Sam. 9:2; Sam. 16:12, 17:42, Ps. 45:3; Esther 1:11. Cf. Daniel A. Binchy, *Celtic and Anglo-Saxon Kingship: The O'Donnell Lectures for 1967–8, Delivered in the University of Oxford on 23 and 24 May 1968* (London: Oxford University Press, 1970), 10; Jarich Oosten, "Ideology and the Development of European Kingdoms," in *Ideology and the Formation of Early States*, ed. Henri J. M. Claessen and Jarich G. Oosten (Leiden: E. J. Brill, 1996), 234; Bart Jaski, *Early Irish Kingship and Succession* (Dublin: Four Courts Press, 2000), 86–88; Máire Ni Mhaonaigh, "The Literature of Medieval Ireland, 800–1200: From the Vikings to the Normans," in *The Cambridge History of Irish Literature*, ed. Margaret Kelleher and Philip O'Leary (Cambridge: Cambridge University Press, 2006), 49; Amy C. Eichhorn-Mulligan, "The Anatomy of Power and the Miracle of Kingship: The Female Body of Sovereignty in a Medieval Irish Kingship Tale," *Speculum* 81 (2006): 1021.

27. Arne Emil Christensen, Bjørn Myhre, and Anne Stine Ingstad, eds., *Osebergdronningens grav: Vår arkeologiske nasjonalskatt i nytt lys* (Oslo: Schibsted, 1992); Bergljot Solberg, *Jernalderen i Norge: 500 før Kristus til 1030 etter Kristus* (Oslo: Cappelen Akademisk Forlag, 2000), 264–66, 284.

28. For example, in the saga about St. Olaf (*Heimskringla 2*, 415).

29. *Den eldre Gulatingslova*, ed. Tor Ulset, Bjørn Eithun, and Magnus Rindal (Oslo: Riksarkivet, 1994), 186.

30. Edward James, "Royal Burials among the Franks," in *The Age of Sutton Hoo: The Seventh Century in North-Western Europe*, ed. M. O. H. Carver (Suffolk: Boydell Press, 1992), 245.

31. *Eddukvæði*, 1:455–56.

32. Percy Ernst Schramm, *Herrschaftszeichen und Staatssymbolik: Beiträge zu ihrer Geschichte vom dritten bis zum sechzehnten Jahrhundert*, 3 vols. (Stuttgart: Hiersemann, 1954–1956), 3:792–802. Cf. Catherine Bell, *Ritual Theory, Ritual Practice* (Oxford: Oxford University Press, 1992), 193–94.

33. Bell, *Ritual Theory, Ritual Practice*, 128.

34. Gro Steinsland, *Det hellige bryllup og norrøn kongeideologi: En analyse av hierogami-myten i Skírnismál, Ynglingatal, Háleygjatal og Hyndluljóð* ([Oslo]: Solum, 1991), 85; Solberg, *Jernalderen i Norge*, 223.

35. Thralls were killed and placed in graves alongside their masters. Naumann et al., "Slaves as Burial Gifts," 533–40.

36. *Íslendingabók: Landnámabók*, ed. Jakob Benediktsson (Reykjavík: Hið íslenzka fornritafélag, 1968), 136–38, 140–44; *Laxdæla saga: Halldórs þættir Snorrasonar, Stúfs þáttr*, ed. Einar Ólafur Sveinsson (Reykjavík: Hið íslenzka fornritafélag, 1934), 6–9, 14, 19, 48–49, 143; Jón Viðar Sigurðsson, Berit Gjerland, and Gaute Losnegård, *Ingólfr: Norsk-islandsk hopehav 870–1536* (Førde, Norway: Selja Forlag, 2005), 145–47.

37. *Orkneyinga saga*, 114–19, 142–44, 146, 167, 171, 176–78.

38. Birgit Sawyer, *The Viking-Age Rune-Stones: Custom and Commemoration in Early Medieval Scandinavia* (Oxford: Oxford University Press, 2000), 7–70.

39. Gro Steinsland, *Mytene som skapte Norge: Myter og makt fra vikingtid til middelalder* (Oslo: Pax, 2012), 131–43.

40. Ben Raffield et al., "Ingroup Identification, Identity Fusion, and the Formation of Viking War Bands," *World Archaeology* 48 (2015): 40.

41. *Gesta Danorum*, 2 vols., ed. Peter Zeeberg and Karsten Friis-Jensen. (Copenhagen: Det Danske Sprog- og Litteraturselskab & Gads Forlag, 2005), 7,6,1–7,6,3; 8,4,3–8,4,5; 8,4,3; 8,5,2–8,5,3; 9,4,2–9,4,11; Judith Jesch, *Women in the Viking Age* (Woodbridge, UK: Boydell Press, 1991), 176–80; Lise Præstgaard Andersen, "On Valkyries, Shield-Maidens and Other Armed Women in Old Norse Sources and Saxo Grammaticus," in *Mythological Women: Studies in Memory of Lotte Motz, 1922–1997*, ed. Rudolf Simek and Wilhelm Heizmann (Vienna: Fassbaender, 2002), 291–318.

42. Leszek Gardela, "'Warrior-Women' in Viking Age Scandinavia? A Preliminary Archaeological Study," *Analecta Archaeologica Ressoviensia: Rzeszow* 8 (2013): 290–92, 298–99.

43. Charlotte Hedenstierna-Jonson et al., "A Female Viking Warrior Confirmed by Genomics," *American Journal of Physical Anthropology* 164 (2017): 853–60; Neil Price et al., "Viking Warrior Women? Reassessing Birka Chamber Grave Bj.581," *Antiquity* 93 (2019): 181–98. Cf. Anna Kjellström, "People in Transition: Life in the Mälaren Valley from an Osteological Perspective," in *Shetland and the Viking World: Papers from the Proceedings of the 17th Viking Congress 2013*, ed. Val Turner (Lerwick, UK: Shetland Amenity Trust, 2017), 197–202. Cf. Jóhanna Katrín Friðriksdóttir, *Valkyrie: The Women of the Viking World* (London: Bloomsbury Academic, 2020). For a critical view on the Birka warrior, see Fedir Androshchuk, "Female Viking Revisited," *Viking and Medieval Scandinavia* 14 (2018): 47–60.

44. Raffield et al., "Ingroup Identification," 40.

45. See, for example, Marie Louise Stig Sørensen, "Gender, Material Culture, and Identity in the Viking Diaspora," *Viking and Medieval Scandinavia* 5 (2009): 253–69; Friðriksdóttir, *Valkyrie*.

46. Ann Swidler, "Culture in Action: Symbols and Strategies," *American Sociological Review* 51 (1986): 273. Cf. Friðriksdóttir, *Valkyrie*.

47. *Grágás: Konungsbók*, ed. Vilhjálmur Finsen (Odense: Odense Universitetsforlag, 1974), Ib:203–4.

48. Frans-Arne Stylegar, "Hvorfor er det færre kvinne- enn mannsgraver fra vikingtiden i Norge?," *Primitive tider* 12 (2012): 71–72. Cf. Solberg, *Jernalderen i Norge*, 268–69; Sørensen, "Gender, Material Culture," 253–69.

49. *Eddukvæði*, 1:340.

50. For example, Ingvild Øye, "Kvinner, kjønn og samfunn," in *Med kjønnsperspektiv på norsk historie: Fra vikingtid til 2000-årsskiftet*, ed. Ida Blom and Sølvi Sogner (Oslo: Cappelen akademisk forlag, 2006), 64–67; Jón Viðar Sigurðsson, *Det norrøne samfunnet: Vikingen, kongen, erkebiskopen og bonden* (Oslo: Pax, 2008), 21, 201.

51. *Eddukvæði*, 1:338.

52. *Eddukvæði*, 1:338, 352.

53. See, for example, Jenny Jochens, "The Medieval Icelandic Heroine: Fact or Fiction?," *Viator* 17 (1986): 35–50; Jenny Jochens, *Old Norse Images of Women* (Philadelphia: University of Pennsylvania Press, 1996), 162–203; Zoe Borovsky, "Never in Public: Women and Performance in Old Norse Literature," *Journal of American Folklore* 112 (1999): 6–39.

54. *Heimskringla 2*, 46 (my translation).

7. Religion and Power

1. For an overview of the Norse religion and the Norse gods, see Jens Peter Schjødt, John Lindow, and Anders Andrén, eds., *The Pre-Christian Religions of the North*, 4 vols. (Turnhout, Belgium: Brepols, 2020); Britt-Mari Näsström, *Fornskandinavisk religion: En grundbok* (Lund: Studentlitteratur, 2001); Britt-Mari Näsström, *Blot: Tro og offer i det førkristne Norden* (Oslo: Pax, 2001); Gro Steinsland, *Norrøn religion: Myter, riter, samfunn* (Oslo: Pax, 2005); Olof Sundqvist, *Kultledare i fornskandinavisk religion* (Uppsala: Institutionen för arkeologi och antik historia, Uppsala Universitet, 2007); Jens Peter Schjødt, *Initiation between Two Worlds: Structure and Symbolism in Pre-Christian Scandinavian Religion* ([Odense]: University Press of Southern Denmark, 2008); Terry Gunnell, "Pantheon? What Pantheon? Concepts of a Family of Gods in Pre-Christian Scandinavian Religions," *Scripta Islandica* 66 (2015): 55–76; Olof Sundqvist, *An Arena for Higher Powers: Ceremonial Buildings and Religious Strategies for Rulership in Late Iron Age Scandinavia* (Leiden: Brill, 2016); Schjødt, Lindow, and Andrén, *Pre-Christian Religions of the North*.

2. *Edda Snorra Sturlusonar*, ed. Heimir Pálsson (Reykjavík: Mál og menning, 1996), 34.

3. The following discussion is based on *Danakonunga sǫgur; Skjǫldunga saga; Knýtlinga saga; Ágrip af sǫgu danakonunga*, ed. Bjarni Guðnason (Reykjavík: Hið íslenzka fornritafélag, 1982), lii–lxxii; Sundqvist, *Kultledare i fornskandinavisk religion*, 81–140; Sundqvist, *Arena for Higher Powers*; Bergsveinn Birgisson, *Inn i skaldens sinn: Kognitive, estetiske og historiske skatter i den norrøne skaldediktningen* (Bergen: Universitetet i Bergen, 2008), 181–250; Jan Bill, "Vikingetidens monumentale skibsgrave," in *Et fælles hav: Skagerrak og Kattegat i vikingetiden*, ed. Anne Pedersen and Søren M. Sindbæk (Copenhagen: Nationalmuseet, 2015), 162–63; Cf. H. Munro Chadwick, *The Cult of Othin: An Essay in the Ancient Religion of the North* (London: Clay, 1899), 49; David N. Dumville, "Kingship, Genealogies and Regnal Lists," in *Early Medieval Kingship*, ed. Peter H. Sawyer and Ian N. Wood (Leeds: School of History, University of Leeds, 1977), 72–104; Terry Gunnell, "From One High-One to Another: The Acceptance of Óðinn as Preparation for the Acceptance of God," in *Conversions: Looking for Ideological Change in the Early Middle Ages*, ed. Rudolf Simek and Leszek Slupecki (Vienna: Fassbaender, 2013), 163–64.

4. Gabriel Turville-Petre, *Myth and Religion of the North: The Religion of Ancient Scandinavia* (Westport, CT: Greenwood Press, 1964), 61–63; Rudolf Simek, *Hugtök og heiti í norræni goðafræði* (Reykjavík: Heimskringla, 1993), 193; Rikard Hornby, "Fornavne i Danmark i middelalderen," in *Nordisk kultur 7*, ed. Johs. Bröndum-Nielsen, Sigurd Erixon, and Magnus Olsen (Stockholm: Bonnier, 1948), 190; Stefan Brink, "How Uniform Was the Old Norse Religion?," in *Learning and Understanding in the Old Norse World: Essays in Honour of Margaret Clunies Ross*, ed. Judy Quinn, Kate Heslop, and Tarrin Wills (Turnhout, Belgium: Brepols, 2007), 111–12.

5. Brink, "How Uniform Was the Old Norse Religion?," 109–10.

6. For an overview of the scholarly debate, see Rory W. McTurk, "Sacral Kingship in Ancient Scandinavia: A Review of Some Recent Writings," *Saga-Book* 19 (1975–1976): 139–69; Rory W. McTurk, "Scandinavian Sacral Kingship Revisited," *Saga-Book* 24 (1994): 19–32; Jens Peter Schjødt, "Det sakrale kongedømme i det førkristne Skandinavien," *Chaos: Dansk-Norsk tidsskrift for Religionshistoriske Studier* 13 (1990): 48–67; Jens Peter Schjødt, "Fyrsteideologi og religion i vikingetiden," in *Mammen: Grav, kunst og samfund i*

vikingetid, ed. Mette Iversen (Aarhus: Jysk Arkæologisk Selskab, 1991), 305–10; Gro Stein-sland, *Det hellige bryllup og norrøn kongeideologi: En analyse av hierogami-myten i Skírn-ismál, Ynglingatal, Háleygjatal og Hyndluljóð* (Oslo: Solum, 1991), 307–13; Anders Hultgård, "Altskandinavische Opferrituale und das Problem der Quellen," in *The Problem of Ritual,* ed. Tore Ahlbäck (Åbo, Finland: Donner Institute, Åbo Akademi, 1993), 221–59; Olof Sundqvist, *Freyr's Offspring: Rulers and Religion in Ancient Svea Society* (Uppsala: Uppsala Universitet, 2002), 18–38; Olof Sundqvist, "Aspects of Rulership Ideology in Early Scandi-navia, with Particular References to the Skaldic Poem Ynglingatal," in *Das frühmittelal-terliche Königtum: Ideelle und religiöse Grundlagen,* ed. Franz-Reiner Erkens (Berlin: De Gruyter, 2005), 87–124; Philip Line, *Kingship and State Formation in Sweden, 1130–1290* (Leiden: Brill, 2007), 350–61; Franz-Reiner Erkens, *Herrschersakralität im Mittelalter: Von den Anfeangen bis zum Investiturstreit* (Stuttgart: W. Kohlhammer, 2006); *Danakonunga sǫgur,* lii–lxxii; Birgisson, *Inn i skaldens sinn,* 181–250; Patrick Vinton Kirch, *How Chiefs Became Kings: Divine Kingship and the Rise of Archaic States in Ancient Hawai'i* (Berkeley: University of California Press, 2010), 4–5; Erin Michelle Goeres, *The Poetics of Commemo-ration: Skaldic Verse and Social Memory, c. 890–1070* (Oxford: Oxford University Press, 2015), 19–53; Andres Siegfried Dobat, "Viking Stranger-Kings: The Foreign as a Source of Power in Viking Age Scandinavia or, Why There Was a Peacock in the Gokstad Ship Burial?," *Early Medieval Europe* 23 (2015): 161–202.

    7. William A. Chaney, *The Cult of Kingship in Anglo-Saxon England: The Transition from Paganism to Christianity* (Manchester: Manchester University Press, 1970), 7, 29–38; Jarich Oosten, "Ideology and the Development of European Kingdoms," in *Ideology and the Formation of Early States,* ed. Henri J. M. Claessen and Jarich G. Oosten (Leiden: E. J. Brill, 1996), 226–27; Dumville, "Kingship, Genealogies and Regnal Lists," 72–104. Cf. Henri J. M. Claessen and Jarich G. Oosten, "Discussion and Consid-erations," in Claessen and Oosten, *Ideology and the Formation of Early States,* 385; Nata-lia B. Kochakova, "The Sacred Ruler as the Ideological Centre of an Early State: The Precolonial States of the Bright of Benin Coast," in Claessen and Oosten, *Ideology and the Formation of Early States,* 18, 54; Gábor Klaniczay, *Holy Rulers and Blessed Princesses: Dynastic Cults in Medieval Central Europe* (Cambridge: Cambridge University Press, 2002), 66; Helena Hamerow, "The Earliest Anglo-Saxon Kingdoms," in *The New Cam-bridge Medieval History,* vol. 1, *c. 500–c. 700,* ed. Paul Fouracre (Cambridge: Cambridge University Press, 2005), 283; Kirch, *How Chiefs Became Kings,* 4–5.

    8. Walter Baetke, *Yngvi und die Ynglinger: Eine quellenkritische Untersuchung über das nordische "Sakralkönigtum"* (Berlin: Akademie-Verlag, 1964); Claus Krag, *Ynglin-gatal og Ynglingesaga en studie i historiske kilder* (Oslo: Universitetsforlaget, 1991).

    9. Knut Helle, "Hovedlinjer i utviklingen av den historiske sagakritikken," in *Leiv Eriksson, Helge Ingstad og Vinland: Kjelder og tradisjonar,* ed. Jan Ragnar Hagland and Steinar Suphellen (Trondheim: Tapir Akademisk Forlag, 2001), 31; Olof Sundqvist, "Frö—mer än en fruktbarhetsgud?," *Saga och Sed* (2014): 50.

    10. Schjødt, "Fyrsteideologi og religion," 308. Cf. Ted C. Lewellen, *Political Anthro-pology: An Introduction,* 3rd ed. (Westport, CT: Praeger, 2003), 66.

    11. *Eyrbyggja saga; Brands þáttr Qrva; Eiríks saga rauða; Grænlendinga saga, Græn-lendinga þáttr,* ed. Matthías Þórðarson and Einar Ólafur Sveinsson (Reykjavík: Hið íslenzka fornritafélag, 1935), 12–13, 19–20.

12. Lúðvík Ingvarsson, *Goðorð og goðorðsmenn*, 3 vols. (Egilsstaðir, Iceland: Höfundur, 1986–1987).

13. Elias Wessén, *Nordiska namnstudier* (Uppsala: Lundequist, 1927), 72–73; Hornby, "Fornavne i Danmark i middelalderen," 190; Assar Janzén, "De fornvästnordiska personnamnen," in Bröndum-Nielsen, Erixon, and Olsen, *Nordisk kultur 7*, 28, 93–94, 258; Kristian Hald, *Personnavne i Danmark*, vol. 1, *Oldtiden* (Copenhagen: Dansk historisk fællesforening, 1971), 42, 48; Jón Viðar Sigurðsson, *Den vennlige vikingen: Vennskapets makt i Norge og på Island ca. 900–1300* (Oslo: Pax, 2010), 122–24; Lasse C. A. Sonne, "Kings, Chieftains and Public Cult in Pre-Christian Scandinavia," *Early Medieval Europe* 22 (2014): 53–68.

14. The following discussion draws on Richard Perkins, *Thor the Wind-Raiser and the Eyrarland Image* (London: Viking Society for Northern Research, University College London, 2001); Steinsland, *Norrøn religion*, 274–303; Jens Peter Schjødt, "Ideology of the Ruler in Pre-Christian Scandinavia: Mythical and Ritual Relations," *Viking and Medieval Scandinavia* 6 (2010): 161–94; Martin Arnold, *Thor: Myth to Marvel* (London: Continuum, 2011); Christopher Abram, *Myths of the Pagan North: The Gods of the Norsemen* (London: Continuum, 2011); Olof Sundqvist, "'Religious Ruler Ideology' in Pre-Christian Scandinavia: A Contextual Approach," in *More than Mythology: Narratives, Ritual Practices and Regional Distribution in Pre-Christian Scandinavian Religions*, ed. Catharina Raudvere and Jens Peter Schjødt (Lund: Nordic Academic Press, 2012), 225–62; Sundqvist, *Arena for Higher Powers*; Lasse C. A. Sonne, *Thor-kult i vikingetiden: Historiske studier i vikingetidens religion* (Copenhagen: Museum Tusculanums forlag, 2013).

15. *Íslensk hómilíubók fornar stólræður*, ed. Guðrún Kvaran, Sigurbjörn Einarsson, and Gunnlaugur Ingólfsson (Reykjavík: Hið íslenska bókmenntafélag, 1993), 39.

16. *Nordens historie i middelalderen etter arabiske kilder*, ed. Harris Birkeland (Oslo: I kommisjon hos Jacob Dybwad, 1954), 103–4; Bjørn Qviller, *Rusens historie* (Oslo: Samlaget, 1996), 43–44, 54–56, 84–89.

17. *Eddukvæði*, 2 vols., ed. Jónas Kristjánsson and Vésteinn Ólason (Reykjavík: Hið íslenzka fornritafélag, 2014), 1:330.

18. Steinsland, *Norrøn religion*, 345; Jón Viðar Sigurðsson, *Viking Friendship: The Social Bond in Iceland and Norway, c. 900–1300* (Ithaca, NY: Cornell University Press, 2017), 87–90.

19. *Eyrbyggja saga*, 8–9.

20. Olaf Olsen, *Hørg, hov og kirke: Historiske og arkæologiske vikingetidsstudier* (Copenhagen: Det Kongelige nordiske Oldskriftselskab, 1966), 94.

21. Bjarni F. Einarsson presents a good overview of this discussion in *Landnám og landnámsfólk: Saga af bæ og blóti* (Reykjavík: Skrudda, 2015), 329–39.

22. Dagfinn Skre, "Herredømmet: Bosetning og besittelse på Romerike 200–1350 e. Kr" (PhD diss., Universitetet i Oslo, 1996), 300–309; Steinsland, *Norrøn religion*, 344–46.

23. Olof Sundqvist, "The Pre-Christian Cult of Dead Royalty in Old Norse Sources: Medieval Speculations or Ancient Traditions?," *Scripta Islandica* 66 (2015): 177–212.

24. For an overview of the Christianisation of the Nordic realms, see Jörn Staecker, "Gotlands kyrkogårdar: Genus, mission och sosial hierarki," *Hikuin* 24 (1997): 73–88; Jón Viðar Sigurðsson, *Kristninga i Norden 750–1200* (Oslo: Samlaget, 2003); Jón Viðar

Sigurðsson, "Conversion and Identity in the Viking-Age North: Some Afterthoughts," in *Conversion and Identity in the Viking Age*, ed. Ildar Garipzanov (Turnhout, Belgium: Brepols, 2014), 225–43; Stefan Brink, ed., *New Perspectives on the Christianization of Scandinavia and the Organization of the Early Church* (Leiden: Brepols, 2004); Anders Andrén, "The Significance of Places: The Christianizaton of Scandinavia from a Spatial Point of View," *World Archaeology* 45 (2013): 27–45; Ildar H. Garipzanov and Rosalind Bonté, eds., *Conversion and Identity in the Viking Age* (Turnhout, Belgium: Brepols, 2014); Janet Fairweather, *Bishop Osmund: A Missionary to Sweden in the Late Viking Age* (Skara, Sweden: Skara Stiftshistoriska Sallskap, 2014), 64–217; Egil Mikkelsen, *Looting or Missioning: Insular and Continental Sacred Objects in Viking Age Contexts in Norway* (Oxford: Oxbow Books, 2019).

25. Thomas Lindkvist and Kurt Ågren, *Sveriges medeltid* ([Solna, Sweden]: Esselte Studium, 1985), 61–62. Cf. Per Sveaas Andersen, *Samlingen av Norge og kristningen av landet 800–1130* (Bergen: Universitetsforlaget, 1977), 190.

26. Jane Stevenson, "Christianising the Northern Barbarians," in *Karmøyseminaret (Nordsjøen: Handel, religion og politikk)*, ed. Helge-Rolf Naley and Jens Flemming Krøger (Stavanger, Norway: Dreyer, 1996): 162–84.

27. Rodney Stark, *The Rise of Christianity: A Sociologist Reconsiders History* (Princeton, NJ: Princeton University Press, 1996), 20, 68. Cf. Tarald Rasmussen and Einar Thomassen, *Kristendommen: En historisk innføring*, 2nd ed. (Oslo: Universitetsforlaget, 2002), 61.

28. John Lindow, "Akkerisfrakki: Traditions concerning Olafr Tryggvason and Hallfredr Ottarsson Vandraedaskald and the Problem of the Conversion," *Journal of English and Germanic Philology* 106 (2007): 64–80; Erin Goeres, "The Many Conversions of Hallfreðr Vandræðaskáld," *Viking and Medieval Scandinavia* 7 (2011): 45–62; Haki Antonsson, "The Conversion and Christianization of Scandinavia: A Critical Review of Recent Scholarly Writings," in Garipzanov and Bonté, *Conversion and Identity*, 49–73.

29. Peter Brown, *The Rise of Western Christendom: Triumph and Diversity, AD 200–1000* (Oxford: Blackwell, 2003), 15.

30. Bruce Dickens, "Cult of S. Olave in the British Isles," *Saga-Book of the Viking Society* 12 (1937–1945): 53–80; Sigurðsson, *Kristninga i Norden*, 84–92.

31. Sigurðsson, *Viking Friendship*, 86–102; Jan Brendalsmo and Jón Viðar Sigurðsson, "The Social Elites and Incomes from Churches c. 1050–1250," in *Nordic Elites in Transformation, c. 1050–1250*, vol. 1, *Material Resources*, ed. Bjørn Poulsen, Helle Vogt, and Jón Viðar Sigurðsson (New York: Routledge, 2019), 248–74.

32. Lewellen, *Political Anthropology*, 66. Cf. Aziz Al-Azmeh, "Monotheistic Kingship," in *Monotheistic Kingship: The Medieval Variants*, ed. Aziz Al-Azmeh and János M. Bak (Budapest: Central European University Press, 2004), 9–29.

8. Livelihoods

1. For an overview of this discussion, see Bjørn Poulsen and Søren M. Sindbæk, eds., *Settlement and Lordship in Viking and Early Medieval Scandinavia* (Turnhout, Belgium: Brepols, 2011), 4–18.

2. Linzi Simpson, "Viking Warrior Burials in Dublin: Is This the Longphort?," in *Medieval Dublin 4: Proceedings of the Friends of Medieval Dublin Symposium 2004*, ed. Seán Duffy (Dublin: Four Courts Press, 2005), 15.

3. David Herlihy, *Medieval Households* (Cambridge, MA: Harvard University Press, 1985), 74–78; Hans-Werner Goetz, *Leben im Mitelalter* (Munich: C. H. Beck, 1986), 41; Ole Jørgen Benedictow, "The Demography of the Viking Age and the High Middle Ages in the Nordic Countries," *Scandinavian Journal of History* 21 (1996): 181–82; Ole Jørgen Benedictow, "Demographic Conditions," in *The Cambridge History of Scandinavia*, vol. 1, *Prehistory to 1520*, ed. Knut Helle (Cambridge: Cambridge University Press, 2003), 2237–49.

4. Lotte Hedeager, "Jernalderen," in *Det Danske landbrugs historie*, vol. 1, *Oldtid og middelalder*, ed. Claus Bjørn and Troels Dahlerup (Odense: Landbohistorisk Selskab, 1988), 111–13; Bergljot Solberg, *Jernalderen i Norge: 500 før Kristus til 1030 etter Kristus* (Oslo: Cappelen Akademisk Forlag, 2000), 144–48; Bjørn Myhre, "The Early Viking Age in Norway," *Acta Archaeologica* 71 (2000): 35; Tina L. Thurston, *Landscapes of Power, Landscapes of Conflict: State Formation in the South Scandinavian Iron Age* (New York: Kluwer Academic/Plenum, 2001), 100; Bjørn Myhre and Ingvild Øye, *Norges landbrukshistorie*, vol. 1, *4000 f.Kr.–1350 e.Kr.: Jorda blir levevei* (Oslo: Samlaget, 2002), 237–53; Anne Birgitte Nielsen et al., "Quantitative Reconstructions of Changes in Regional Openness in North-Central Europe Reveal New Insights into Old Questions," *Quaternary Science Reviews* 47 (2012): 144; Ellen Anne Pedersen and Mats Widgren, "Agriculture in Sweden, 800 BC–AD 1000," in *The Agrarian History of Sweden: 4000 BC to AD 2000*, ed. Janken Myrdal and Mats Morell (Lund: Nordic Academic Press, 2011), 65–66; Peder Gammeltoft, Johnny G. G. Jakobsen, and Søren M. Sindbæk, "Vikingtidens bebyggelse omkring Kattegat og Skagerak," in *Et fælles hav: Skagerrak og Kattegat i vikingetiden*, ed. Anne Pedersen and Søren M. Sindbæk (Copenhagen: Nationalmuseet, 2015), 12–15.

5. *Ottar og Wulfstan: To rejsebeskrivelser fra vikingtiden*, ed. Niels Lund (Roskilde, Denmark: Vikingeskibshallen i Roskilde, 1983), 22.

6. Per Ethelberg et al., *Det sønderjyske landbrugs historie: Jernalder, vikingetid og middelalder* (Haderslev, Denmark: Haderslev Museum, 2003), 28; M. Stenak et al., "Landskabsforandringer gennem 2000 år," in *Danske landbrugslandskaber gennem 2000 år: Fra digevoldinger til støtteordninger*, ed. Bent Odgaard and Jørgen Rydén Rømer (Aarhus: Aarhus Universitetsforlag, 2009), 288–89; Pedersen and Widgren, "Agriculture in Sweden," 65–68; Lars Agersnap Larsen, "Muldfjælsplovens tidlige historie: Fra yngre romersk jernalder til middelalder," *KUML* 2015 (2015): 185–86; Lars Agersnap Larsen, "The Early Introduction of the Moldboard Plow in Denmark: Agrarian Technology and the Medieval Elites," in *Nordic Elites in Transformation, c. 1050–1250*, vol. 1, *Material Resources*, ed. Bjørn Poulsen, Helle Vogt, and Jón Viðar Sigurðsson (New York: Routledge, 2019), 80–106.

7. *Kulturhistoriskt lexikon för nordisk medeltid*, 22 vols., ed. Ingvar Andersson and John Granlund (Malmö: Allhems Förlag, 1956–1978), 11:656, 20:689–98; John Moberg, *Graut* (Oslo: Samlaget, 1989), 11–21; Lynn A. Martin, "Old People, Alcohol and Identity in Europe, 1300–1700," in *Food, Drink and Identity: Cooking, Eating and Drinking in Europe since the Middle Ages*, ed. Peter Scholliers and Inger Johanne Lyngø (Oxford: Berg, 2001), 120–21.

8. Arnvid Lillehammer, *Fra jeger til bonde: Inntil 800 e.Kr.* (Oslo: Aschehoug, 1994), 202–4; Solberg, *Jernalderen i Norge*, 204.

9. Jørgen Jensen, *Danmarks oldtid: Fra stendalder til vikingetid* (Copenhagen: Gyldendal, 2013), 947–48 (my translation).

10. Jensen, *Danmarks oldtid*, 948. Cf. Jensen, *Danmarks oldtid*, 959; Hedeager, "Jernalderen," 159–63, 180–83. Other Viking Age settlements that have been examined are, for example, Kirke Hyllinge in Hornherred and Bøgelund by Varpelev at Stevns (Jensen, *Danmarks oldtid*, 949).

11. Alexander Bugge, "Tingsteder, gilder og andre gamle mittpunkter i de norske bygder," *Historisk Tidsskrift* 25 (1920): 195–252; Christoph Anz, *Gilden im mittelalterlichen Skandinavien* (Göttingen: Vandenhoeck & Ruprecht, 1998), 83–292; Christoph Anz, "Gildernes form og funksjon i middelalderens Skandinavia," in *Gilder, lav og broderskaber i middelalderens Danmark*, ed. Lars Bisgaard and Leif Søndergaard (Odense: Syddansk Universitetsforlag, 2002), 21–40; Lars Bisgaard and Leif Søndergaard, "Indledning," in Bisgaard and Søndergaard, *Gilder, lav og broderskaber*, 9–19.

12. There is extensive discussion about how the term "household" is to be defined: see, for example, J. Krause, "The Medieval Household: Large or Small?," *Economic History Review* 9 (1957): 420–32; Herlihy, *Medieval Households*; William Ian Miller, "Some Aspects of Householding in the Medieval Icelandic Commonwealth," *Continuity and Change* 3 (1988): 321–56; Michel Verdon, *Rethinking Households: An Atomistic Perspective on European Living Arrangements* (London: Routledge, 1998); Roberta Gilchrist, *Medieval Life: Archaeology and the Life Course* (Woodbridge, UK: Boydell Press, 2012), 114–68; Marco Madella et al., *The Archaeology of Household* (Oxford: Oxbow Books, 2013).

13. *Eddukvæði*, 2 vols., ed. Jónas Kristjánsson and Vésteinn Ólason (Reykjavík: Hið íslenzka fornritafélag, 2014), 1:336.

14. *Edda Snorra Sturlusonar*, ed. Heimir Pálsson (Reykjavík: Mál og menning, 1996), 141.

15. Jón Viðar Sigurðsson, "Becoming 'Old': Ageism and Taking Care of the Elderly in Iceland c. 900–1300," in *Youth and Age in the Medieval North*, ed. Shannon Lewis-Simpson (Leiden: Brill, 2008), 227–42.

16. Sigurðsson, 227–42.

17. *Norges gamle Love*, 4 vols., ed. Rudolf Keyser et al. (Christiania: Grøndahl og søn, 1846–1895), 1:171.

18. Jørn Sandnes, "Bondesamfunnet," in *Norges kulturhistorie 1*, ed. Ingrid Semmingsen et al. (Oslo: Aschehoug, 1979), 50; Jørn Sandnes, "'Tolv kyr, to hester og tre trælar': Litt om omfanget av træleholdet i Norge i vikingtid og tidlig kristen tid," *Historisk Tidsskrift* 62 (1983): 81; Jørn Sandnes, "Bønder, herrer og treller: Hvordan var egentlig det gammelnorske samfunnet?," *Heimen* 37 (2000): 202; Tore Iversen, "Slavery and Unfreedom from the Middle Ages to the Beginning of the Early Modern Period," in *Peasants, Lords, and State: Comparing Peasant Conditions in Scandinavia and the Eastern Alpine Region, 1000–1750*, ed. Tore Iversen, Jon Ragnar Myking, and Stefan Sonderegger (Leiden: Brill, 2020), 41–87.

19. On Sweden, see Mats Widgren and Ellen Anne Pedersen, "Järnålder 500 f.Kr.–1000 e.Kr," in *Jordbrukets första femtusen år 4000 f.Kr.–1000 e.Kr.: Det Svenska*

jordbrukets historia Stockholm, ed. Stig Welinder et al. (Stockholm: Natur och kultur, 1998), 437. On Denmark, see Janken Myrdal, "Milking and Grinding, Digging and Herding: Slaves and Farmwork 1000–1300," in Poulsen and Sindbæk, *Settlement and Lordship*, 293–94.

20. David Pelteret, "Slavery in the Danelaw," in *Social Approaches to Viking Studies*, ed. Ross Samson (Glasgow: Cruithne Press, 1991), 182.

21. John S. Moore, "Domesday Slavery," *Anglo-Norman Studies* 11 (1988): 192–94; David A. E. Pelteret, *Slavery in Early Mediaeval England: From the Reign of Alfred until the Twelfth Century* (Woodbridge, UK: Boydell Press, 1995), 232–40; Pelteret, "Slavery in the Danelaw," 179–88; David Wyatt, *Slaves and Warriors in Medieval Britain and Ireland, 800–1200* (Leiden: Brill, 2009), 35; Ben Raffield, "The Slave Markets of the Viking World: Comparative Perspectives on an 'Invisible Archaeology,'" *Slavery and Abolition* 40 (2019): 1–24.

22. Myrdal, "Milking and Grinding," 293–94. Stefan Brink has come to the exact opposite conclusion and has launched the theory that thralls were "quite uncommon during Viking Age Nordic agrarian society" and that they were items of prestige for local chieftains. Brink, *Vikingarnas slavar den nordiska träldomen under yngre järnålder och äldsta medeltid* (Stockholm: Atlantis, 2012), 260. If we accept such a thesis, we also need to explain how the increase in food production occured without imported work forces, which can prove problematic. See, also, Tore Iversen, "Thralls' Manumission, Land Clearing, and State Building in Medieval Norway," in Poulsen and Sindbæk, *Settlement and Lordship*, 263–91.

23. *The Annals of Ulster (to A.D. 1131)*, ed. Seán Mac Airt and Gearóid Mac Niocaill (Dublin: Dublin Institute for Advanced Studies, 1983), 469.

24. Ruth Mazo Karras, *Slavery and Society in Medieval Scandinavia* (New Haven, CT: Yale University Press, 1988), 75; Ruth Mazo Karras, "Concubinage and Slavery in the Viking Age," *Scandinavian Studies* 62 (1990): 141; Tore Iversen, *Trelldommen: Norsk slaveri i middelalderen* (Bergen: Historisk institutt, Universitetet i Bergen, 1997), 82–112; Alex Woolf, *From Pictland to Alba: 789–1070* (Edinburgh: Edinburgh University Press, 2007), 19, 55, 72; Wyatt, *Slaves and Warriors*, 61–172; Raffield, "Slave Markets of the Viking World," 5–10, 15.

25. Halvard Bjørkvik, "Kva slags samfunn var det som tok mot kristendommen? Den vestnorske samfunnsstrukturen omkring år 1000," in *Møtet mellom hedendom og kristendom i Norge*, ed. Hans-Emil Lidén (Oslo: Universitetsforlaget, 1995), 71–76; Tore Iversen, "Fremveksten av det norske leilendingsvesenet i middelalderen—en forklaringsskisse," *Heimen* 32 (1995): 169–80; Knut Helle, *Norge blir en stat 1130–1319*, 2nd ed. (Bergen: Universitetsforlaget, 1974), 155–61; Myhre and Øye, *Norges landbrukshistorie*, 1:264–76; Bjørn Poulsen and Søren Michael Sindbæk, "Settlement and Lordship in Viking and Early Medieval Scandinavia," in Poulsen and Sindbæk, *Settlement and Lordship*, 2–15.

26. *Heimskringla 2*, ed. Bjarni Aðalbjarnason (Reykjavík: Hið íslenzka fornritafélag, 1945), 30.

27. Iversen, *Trelldommen*, 210–74; Iversen, "Thralls' Manumission," 263–91; Iversen, "Slavery and Unfreedom," 41–87, 427–30; Ethelberg et al., *Det sønderjyske landbrugs historie*; Poulsen and Sindbæk, "Settlement and Lordship," 10–11.

28. Birgitta Berglund, *Tjøtta-riket: En arkeologisk undersøkelse av maktforhold og sentrumsdannelser på Helgelandskysten fra Kr. f. til 1700 e. Kr* (Trondheim: UNIT, Vitenskapsmuseet, Fakultet for arkeologi og kulturhistorie, Arkeologisk avdeling, 1995), 134–94.

29. Per Sveaas Andersen, *Samlingen av Norge og kristningen av landet 800–1130* (Bergen: Universitetsforlaget, 1977), 294–96. Cf. Brink, *Vikingarnas slavar*, 114–16, 139–49.

30. Tony Jebson, "Manuscript E: Bodleian MS Laud 636," The Anglo-Saxon Chronicle: An Electronic Edition, August 17, 2007, http://asc.jebbo.co.uk/e/e-L.html; *The Anglo-Saxon Chronicle*, ed. Michael Swanton (London: Dent, 1996), 54. Translation from "The Peterborough Manuscript (E)," in *The Anglo-Saxon Chronicle*, trans. and ed. Michael Swanton (New York: Routledge, 1998), 54–57.

31. The first Viking attack probably took place in Wessex in 789.

32. *Anglo-Saxon Chronicle*, 126–29; Andersen, *Samlingen av Norge*, 117; M. K. Lawson, "The Collection of Danegeld and Heregeld in the Reigns of Aethelred and Cnut," *English Historical Review* 99 (1984): 721–38; John Gillingham, "'The Most Precious Jewel in the English Crown': Levels of Danegeld and Heregeld in the Early Eleventh Century," *English Historical Review* 104 (1989): 373–406; Rune Edberg, Mattias Ek, and Mats Vänehem, *Runriket Täby-Vallentuna—en handledning* (Nacka, Sweden: Stockholms läns museum, 2007), 11.

33. Paddy Griffith, *The Viking Art of War* (London: Greenhill Books, 1995), 122–26.

34. Peter H. Sawyer, *Kings and Vikings: Scandinavia and Europe, AD 700–1100* (London: Routledge, 1982), 144; Peter H. Sawyer, "The Age of the Vikings, and Before," in *The Oxford Illustrated History of the Vikings*, ed. Peter H. Sawyer (Oxford: Oxford University Press, 1997), 17; Sven B. F. Jansson, *Swedish Vikings in England: The Evidence of the Rune Stones* (London: Lewis, 1966), 1–18; Aksel E. Christensen, *Vikingetidens Danmark*, 2nd ed. (Copenhagen: Det Historiske Institut ved Københavns Universitet, 1977), 218.

35. Thomas Lindkvist, *Plundring, skatter och den feodala statens framväxt: Organisatoriska tendenser i Sverige under övergången från vikingatid till tidig medeltid*, new ed. (Uppsala: Historiska institutionen vid Uppsala Universitet, 1988), 38–41; Johan Callmer, Ingrid Gustin, and Mats Roslund, eds., *Identity Formation and Diversity in the Early Medieval Baltic and Beyond: Communicators and Communication* (Leiden: Brill, 2016); Marika Mägi, *In Austrvegr: The Role of the Eastern Baltic in Viking Age Communication across the Baltic Sea* (Leiden: Brill, 2018); Marika Mägi, *The Viking Eastern Baltic* (Leeds: ARC Humanities Press, 2019).

36. See, for example, *Heimskringla 1*, ed. Bjarni Aðalbjarnarson (Reykjavík: Hið íslenzka fornritafélag, 1941), 23, 81, 165, 254.

37. *Egils saga Skalla-Grímsonar*, ed. Sigurður Nordal (Reykjavík: Hið íslenzka fornritafélag, 1933), 27; Lars Ivar Hansen and Bjørnar Olsen, *Samenes historie* (Oslo: Cappelen Akademisk Forlag, 2004), 61–69.

38. *History of the Archbishops of Hamburg-Bremen*, ed. Francis J. Tschan and Timothy Reuter (New York: Columbia University Press, 2005), 202 (my translation).

39. Andreas Holmsen, *Nye studier i gammel historie* (Oslo: Universitetsforl, 1976), 59.

40. Peter Kurrild-Klitgaard and Gert Tinggaard Svendsen, "Rational Bandits: Plunder, Public Goods, and the Vikings," *Public Choice* 117 (2003): 256–69; Matthew J.

Baker and Erwin H. Bulte, "Kings and Vikings: On the Dynamics of Competitive Agglomeration," *Economics of Governance* 11 (2010): 212–23. Cf. Peter T. Leeson, "Anarrgh-chy: The Law and Economics of Pirate Organization," *Journal of Political Economy* 115 (2007): 1049–94.

41. *Anglo-Saxon Chronicle*, 136.

42. Woolf, *From Pictland to Alba*, 19, 55.

43. Peter H. Sawyer, *The Wealth of Anglo-Saxon England* (Oxford: Oxford University Press, 2013), 111.

44. See, for example, Andersen, *Samlingen av Norge*, 226–27; Keld Møller Hansen and Henrik Høyer, "Næs—en vikingetidsbebyggelse med hørproduktion," *KUML: Årbog for Jysk Arkæologisk Selskab* (2000): 59–89; Dagfinn Skre, "Kaupang—et handelssted? Om handel og annen vareutveksling i vikingtid," *Collegium Medievale* 13 (2000): 169; Knut Helle et al., *Norsk byhistorie: Urbanisering gjennom 1300 år* (Oslo: Pax, 2006), 31; Jan Bill and Christian Løchsen Rødsrud, "Heimdalsjordet—Trade, Production and Communication," in *Viking-Age Transformations: Trade, Craft and Resources in Western Scandinavia*, ed. Ann Zanette Tsigaridas Glørstad and Kjetil Loftsgarden (London: Routledge, 2017), 212–31.

45. See, for example, Gunnar Lind Haase Svendsen and Gert Tinggaard Svendsen, "How Did Trade Norms Evolve in Scandinavia? Long-Distance Trade and Social Trust in the Viking Age," *Economic Systems* 40 (2016): 198–215; Dagfinn Skre, "Viking-Age Economic Transformations: The West-Scandinavian Case," in *Viking-Age Transformations: Trade, Craft, and Resources in Western Scandinavia*, ed. Ann Zanette Tsigaridas Glørstad and Kjetil Loftsgarden (London: Routledge, 2017), 1–27; Jacek Gruszczynski, *Viking Silver, Hoards and Containers: The Archaeological and Historical Context of Viking-Age Silver Coin Deposits in the Baltic, c. 800–1050* (London: Routledge, 2019); Steven P. Ashby and Søren M. Sindbæk, eds., *Crafts and Social Networks in Viking Towns* (Oxford: Oxbow Books, 2020).

46. Dagfinn Skre, "Centrality, Landholding, and Trade in Scandinavia *c.* AD 700–900," in Sindbæk and Bjørn, eds., *Settlement and Lordship in Viking and Early Medieval Scandinavia*, 207–8; Mogens Bo Henriksen, "Odenses forgængere—eller: én af mange?," in *Beretning fra det toogtredivte tværfaglige vikingesymposium*, ed. Lars Bisgaard, Mette Bruus, and Peder Gammeltoft (Højbjerg, Denmark: Forlaget Wormianum, 2013), 68–83; Hans Krongaard Kristensen and Bjørn Poulsen, *Danmarks byer i middelalderen* (Aarhus: Aarhus Universitetsforlag, 2016), 59.

47. *Medieval Scandinavian: An Encyclopedia*, ed. Phillip Pulsiano and Kirsten Wolf (New York: Garland, 1993), 43; Dagfinn Skre, "The Development of Urbanism in Scandinavia," in *The Viking World*, ed. Stefan Brink and Neil S. Price (London: Routledge, 2008), 84.

For an overview of urbanization during the Viking Age, see Hans Andersson, "Urbanisation," in Helle, *Prehistory to 1520*, 317–29, and Skre, "Development of Urbanism," 83–93.

48. Claus Feveile, "Ribe opstår 700–865," in *Ribe bys historie 1: 710–1520*, ed. Søren Bitsch Christensen (Aarhus: Dansk Center for Byhistorie, 2010), 27, 29; Claus Feveile and Morten Sovso, "Ribe genopstar," in Christensen, *Ribe bys historie 1*, 39. In 825, the Danish kings started minting coins in the town.

49. Thorkild Ramskou, *Normannertiden: 600–1060*, ed. John Danstrup and Hal Koch (Copenhagen: Politikens forlag, 1963), 90; Esben Albrectsen, Gunner Lind, and Karl-Erik Frandsen, *Konger og krige: 700–1648* (Copenhagen: Danmarks Nationalleksikon, 2001), 24–25. This decline fits well with changes in the Viking attacks in England. In 865, the Great Army attacked England and created a permanent settlement there. Their power and trading centers were then moved from Denmark to England, only to return to Denmark at the fall of Cnut the Great's empire in 1035.

50. Dagfinn Skre, ed., *Kaupang in Skiringssal* (Aarhus: Aarhus University Press, 2007), 445–69; Skre, "Development of Urbanism in Scandinavia," 84–85; Skre, "Centrality, Landholding, and Trade in Scandinavia," 207.

51. Anders Andrén, *Den urbana scenen: Städer och samhälle i det medeltida Danmark* (Malmö: LiberFörlag, 1985), 188. Cf. Helle et al., *Norsk byhistorie*, 9–19, 35–63; Erika Harlitz Kern, "The Norwegian Origins of the Swedish Town of Lödöse, c. 1050–1300," *Scandinavian Journal of History* 37 (2012): 9–10.

52. Erik Schia, "Den første urbaniseringen i Oslofjord-regionen," in *Våre første byer*, ed. Ingvild Øye (Bergen: Bryggens Museum, 1992), 50–51; Solberg, *Jernalderen i Norge*, 306; Helle et al., *Norsk byhistorie*, 35–63; Dick Harrison, *Sveriges historia 600–1350* (Stockholm: Norstedt, 2009), 130–35; Erik Ulsig, *Danmark 900–1300: Kongemagt og samfund* (Aarhus: Aarhus Universitetsforlag, 2011), 48; Kern, "Norwegian Origins," 8; Kristensen and Poulsen, *Danmarks byer i middelalderen*, 35–59; Else Roesdahl, "Vikingetidens bebyggelser," Danmarks Historien (Aarhus University), 2009, http://danmarkshistorien.dk /historiske-perioder/vikingetiden-ca-800–1050/vikingetidens-bebyggelser/.

53. Helle et al., *Norsk byhistorie*, 9–19; Kristensen and Poulsen, *Danmarks byer i middelalderen*, 13–15.

54. Judith Jesch, *Ships and Men in the Late Viking Age: The Vocabulary of Runic Inscriptions and Skaldic Verse* (Woodbridge, UK: Boydell Press, 2001), 45, 56–58, 96, 109, 180–84, 225–27, 232–36.

55. Lydia Carstens, "Powerful Space: The Iron-Age Hall and Its Development during the Viking Age," in *Viking Worlds: Things, Spaces and Movement*, ed. Marianne Hem Eriksen et al. (Oxford: Oxbow Books, 2014), 22; Unn Pedersen, "Kaupangs kvinner," in *Kvinner i vikingtid: Vikingatidens kvinnor*, ed. Nancy L. Coleman and Nanna Løkka (Oslo: Scandinavian Academic Press, 2014), 167–85.

56. Birgitta Hårdh, *Wikingerzeitliche Depotfunde aus Südschweden: Probleme und Analysen* (Lund: Liber-Läromedel/Gleerup, 1976), 130, 142; Birgitta Hårdh, "Silverekonomier kring Kattegatt," in Pedersen and Sindbæk, *Et fælles hav*, 102–19; Solberg, *Jernalderen i Norge*, 255; Svein H. Gullbekk, *Pengevesenets fremvekst og fall i Norge i middelalderen* (Copenhagen: Museum Tusculanums Forlag, 2009), 31–35; Jens Christian Moesgaard, "Mønter i Skandinavien cirka 780–850: Ligheder og forskelle set i Kattegat/Skagerrak-perspektiv," in Pedersen and Sindbæk, *Et fælles hav*, 86–101.

57. Hårdh, "Silverekonomier kring Kattegatt," 115–17.

58. Helle, *Norge blir en stat*, 196; Lindkvist, *Plundring, skatter*, 14. Albrectsen, Lind, and Frandsen, *Konger og krige*, 24.

59. Lindkvist, *Plundring, skatter*, 11, 32, 42–43.

60. Sawyer, *Kings and Vikings*, 144; Sawyer, "Age of the Vikings," 1–18.

Bibliography of Primary Sources

Adam av Bremen: Beretningen om Hamburg stift, erkebiskopenes bedrifter og øyrikene i Norden. Edited by Bjørg Tosterud Danielsen and Anne-Katrine Frihagen. Oslo: Aschehoug, 1993.

Ágrip af Nóregskonunga sǫgum: Fagrskinna—Nóregs konunga tal. Edited by Bjarni Einarsson. Reykjavík: Hið íslenzka fornritafélag, 1985.

Alfræði íslenzk: Islandsk encyklopædisk litteratur. 3 vols. Edited by Kristian Kålund. Copenhagen: S. L. Møllers Bogtrykkeri, 1908–1918.

The Anglo-Saxon Chronicle. Edited by Michael Swanton. London: Dent, 1996.

Annales regni Francorum inde ab a 741 usque ad a 829: Qui dicuntur Annales Laurissenses maiores et Einhardi. Edited by Georg Heinrich Pertz and Friedric Kurze. Hanover: Impensis bibliopolii Hahniani, 1895.

The Annals of Ulster (to A.D. 1131). Edited by Seán Mac Airt and Gearóid Mac Niocaill, Dublin: Dublin Institute for Advanced Studies, 1983.

Beowulf. Edited by Michael Swanton. Manchester: Manchester University Press, 1997.

Brennu-Njáls saga. Edited by Einar Ólafur Sveinsson. Reykjavík: Hið íslenzka fornritafélag, 1954.

Chronica magistri Rogeri de Houedene. Vol. 3. Edited by William Stubbs. London: Longman & Company, 1870.

Danakonunga sǫgur; Skjǫldunga saga; Knýtlinga saga; Ágrip af sǫgu danakonunga. Edited by Bjarni Guðnason. Reykjavík: Hið íslenzka fornritafélag, 1982.

Den eldre Gulatingslova. Edited by Tor Ulset, Bjørn Eithun, and Magnus Rindal. Oslo: Riksarkivet, 1994.

Den norsk-islandske skjaldediktning. 2 vols. Edited by Finnur Jónsson. Copenhagen: Rosenkilde and Bagger, 1908–1915.

Edda Snorra Sturlusonar. Edited by Heimir Pálsson. Reykjavík: Mál og menning, 1996.

Edda Snorra Sturlusonar: Nafnaþulur og Skáldatal. Edited by Guðni Jónsson. Reykjavík: Íslendingasagnaútgáfan, 1954.

Edda-dikt. Edited by Ludvig Holm-Olsen (Oslo: Den norske lyrikklubben, 1993).

Eddadigte 1. Edited by Jón Helgason. Oslo: Dreyer, 1971.

Eddukvæði. 2 vols. Edited by Jónas Kristjánsson and Vésteinn Ólason. (keep the name of the series) Reykjavík: Hið íslenzka fornritafélag, 2014.

Egils saga Skalla-Grímssonar. Edited by Sigurður Nordal. Reykjavík: Hið íslenzka fornritafélag, 1933.

Eyrbyggja saga; Brands þáttr Qrva; Eiríks saga rauða; Grænlendinga saga; Grænlendinga þáttr. Edited by Matthías Þórðarson and Einar Ólafur Sveinsson. Reykjavík: Hið íslenzka fornritafélag, 1935.

Fornaldar sögur Norðurlanda. 4 vols. Edited by Guðni Jónsson. Reykjavík: Íslendingasagnaútgáfan, 1954.

Frostatingslova. Edited by Jørn Sandnes and Jan Ragnar Hagland. Oslo: Samlaget i samarbeid med Frosta historielag, 1994.

Gesta Danorum. 2 vols. Edited by Peter Zeeberg and Karsten Friis-Jensen. Copenhagen: Det Danske Sprog- og Litteraturselskab & Gads Forlag, 2005.

Grágás: Konungsbók. Edited by Vilhjálmur Finsen. Odense: Odense Universitetsforlag, 1974.

Hákonar saga Hákonarsonar. Vol. 2, *Magnúss saga Lagabœtis.* Edited by Þorleifur Hauksson, Sverrir Jakobsson, and Tor Ulset. Reykjavík: Hið íslenzka fornritafélag, 2013.

Heimskringla 1. Edited by Bjarni Aðalbjarnarson. Reykjavík: Hið íslenzka fornritafélag, 1941.

Heimskringla 2. Edited by Bjarni Aðalbjarnarson. Reykjavík: Hið íslenzka fornritafélag, 1945.

Heimskringla 3. Edited by Bjarni Aðalbjarnarson. Reykjavík: Hið íslenzka fornritafélag, 1951.

History of the Archbishops of Hamburg-Bremen, edited by Francis J. Tschan and Timothy Reuter. New York: Columbia University Press, 2005.

Íslendingabók; Landnámabók. Edited by Jakob Benediktsson. Reykjavík: Hið íslenzka fornritafélag, 1968.

Íslensk hómilíubók fornar stólræður. Edited by Guðrún Kvaran, Sigurbjörn Einarsson, and Gunnlaugur Ingólfsson. Reykjavík: Hið íslenska bókmenntafélag, 1993.

The Laws of the Earliest English Kings. Edited and translated by F. L. Attenborough. New York: Russell & Russell, 1963.

Laxdæla saga: Halldórs þættir Snorrasonar, Stúfs þáttr. Edited by Einar Ólafur Sveinsson. Reykjavík: Hið íslenzka fornritafélag, 1934.

Monumenta historica Norvegiæ: Latinske kildeskrifter til Norges Historie i middelalderen. Edited by Gustav Storm. Christiania: A. W. Brøgger, 1880.

Morkinskinna 1. Edited by Ármann Jakobsson and Þórður Ingi Guðjónsson. Reykjavík: Hið íslenska fornritafélag, 2011.

Nordens historie i middelalderen etter arabiske kilder. Edited by Harris Birkeland. Oslo: I kommisjon hos Jacob Dybwad, 1954.

Norges gamle Love. 4 vols. Edited by Rudolf Keyser et al. Christiania: Grøndahl og søn, 1846–1895.

Old Norse Women's Poetry: The Voices of Female Skalds, Translated from the Old Norse. Edited by Sandra Ballif Straubhaar. Cambridge: D. S. Brewer, 2011.

Orkneyinga saga: Legenda de sancto Magno, Magnúss saga skemmri, Magnúss saga lengri, Helga þáttr ok Úlfs. Edited by Finnbogi Guðmundsson. Reykjavík: Hið íslenzka fornritafélag, 1965.

Ottar og Wulfstan: To rejsebeskrivelser fra vikingetiden. Edited by Niels Lund. Roskilde, Denmark: Vikingeskibshallen, 1983.

Skaldic Poetry of the Scandinavian Middle Ages. Vol. 1, *Poetry from the Kings' Sagas 1.* Edited by Diana Whaley. Turnhout, Belgium: Brepols, 2012.

Skaldic Poetry of the Scandinavian Middle Ages. Vol. 3, *Poetry from Treatises on Poetics.* Edited by Kari Ellen Gade and Edith Marold. Turnhout, Belgium: Brepols, 2017.

Sturlunga saga. 2 vols. Edited by Jón Jóhannesson, Magnús Finnbogason, and Kristján Eldjárn. Reykjavík: Sturlunguútgáfan, 1946.

Sturlunga saga: Árna saga biskups, Hrafns saga Sveinbjarnarsonar hin sérstaka. 3 vols. Edited by Örnólfur Thorsson et al. Reykjavík: Svart á hvítu, 1988.

Two Voyagers at the Court of King Alfred: The Ventures of OHTHERE and WULFSTAN Together with the Description of Northern Europe from the Old English Orosius. Edited by Niels Lund, Christine E. Fell, Peter H. Sawyer, and Ole Crumlin-Pedersen. York: William Sessions, 1984.

Vikingerne i Franken: Skriftlige kilder fra det 9. århundrede. Edited by Erling Albrectsen. Odense: Odense Universitetsforlag, 1976.

Vita Anskarii auctore Rimberto: Accedit Vita Rimberti. Edited by G. Waitz. Hanover: Hanhsche Buchhandlung, 1884.

The Word Exchange: Anglo-Saxon Poems in Translation. Edited by Greg Delanty and Michael Matto. New York: W. W. Norton, 2011.

INDEX